Cruising with Kate

A PARVENU IN XANADU

Also by Bernard F. Conners

DANCEHALL

TAILSPIN

THE HAMPTON SISTERS

DON'T EMBARRASS THE BUREAU

Cruising with Kate

A PARVENU IN XANADU

Bernard F. Conners

British American Publishing

British American Publishing, Latham, New York

Published by British American Publishing, Ltd.
19 British American Boulevard
Latham, New York 12110

Author's Note: Although the following is a work of nonfiction, some names have been changed to protect the privacy of individuals.

Library of Congress Cataloging-in-Publication Data
Conners, Bernard F.
Cruising with Kate : a parvenu in Xanadu / Bernard F. Conners.
pages cm
Includes index.
ISBN 978-0-945167-57-0 (hardcover : alkaline paper) 1. Conners, Bernard F.
2. Conners, Bernard F.--Friends and associates. 3. Conners, Bernard F.--Marriage.
4. Novelists, American--Biography. 5. Football players--United States--Biography.
6. Publishers and publishing--United States--Biography. 7. United States. Federal Bureau of Investigation--Biography. 8. United States. Army--Officers--Biography.
9. Paris review. 10. Businessmen--United States--
Biography. I. Title.
CT275.C76383A3 2014
920.00973--dc23

2014037722

Printed in the United States of America

First Edition

Book design by Toelke Associates

For CCC

Contents

Photographs follow pages 118 and 230

Part I

1

Meeting God

AN AUDIENCE with J. Edgar Hoover, director of the FBI, could be unnerving under the best of circumstances. It had been on reckless impulse that Bernard, an agent from the New York office, had requested a meeting. Now he was having misgivings. His only previous encounter with the Director had consisted of a fleeting glacial exchange several years before at his graduation from the FBI Academy in Washington, D.C.

Meeting with "The Man" was at best a calculated risk because virtually anything could result. Prior to seeing an agent, the Director reviewed a statement about his background. Following the interview, he dictated a memorandum containing his impressions of the individual and other information he deemed pertinent. If it were favorable, the agent's future in the organization might be bright indeed, but if it were unfavorable. . . . His memo was treated as the will of a sovereign, and there was little delay in its implementation.

Bernard glanced at his watch as he was being escorted into the Director's office and again when he left, two hours and eleven minutes later. Why a man of Mr. Hoover's stature would spend that much time with an ordinary agent was beyond Bernard's understanding. He did conclude, however, that if Mr. Hoover had the clairvoyance often attributed to him, he most certainly had been thinking, "How in blazes did this recreant end up in my organization?" First off, Bernard slipped on the hard wooden floor as he entered the man's office, barely avoiding taking him out with a full body block. Recovering, he approached the square, ominous figure and, in a voice husky with trepidation and bravado, said, "How do you do, sir. I'm Agent Conners of the New York office."

Bernard's eyes remained riveted on the figure clad in a gray sharkskin suit standing near a furled flag. It was a heavy, block-like form of medium height, firmly planted as though it had grown in that spot with roots extending clear down through the Justice Building into the soil beneath Pennsylvania Avenue. Although there had been attempts to uproot the icon through the years, all had been aborted. As one former assistant director said, "How do you fire God?"

J. Edgar Hoover was an intense-looking man with wiry black hair and a square, belligerent jaw that jutted from a tanned face. The eyes showed little cordiality from beneath the heavy brows, and the face, although flat and expressionless, indicated a man who expected trouble and rather relished the prospect. Although he had anticipated a formidable figure, Bernard was still taken aback.

Following a brief assessment of his young visitor, and a look that suggested far more important matters awaited him elsewhere, the Director offered his hand with a clipped "Pleased to meet you." Racing through Bernard's mind were all manner of things including his mother's comment during his early years that "pleased to meet you" was a socially inappropriate bit of vernacular. Bernard was motioned to a chair in front of the man's desk, where he exchanged brief pleasantries in a voice that was becoming increasingly hoarse. He had anticipated meeting for no more than a few minutes, but it was not to be. The Director inquired about his activities in New York, and, as time passed, settled back in his chair and appeared to be relaxing. He seemed to mellow and became exceedingly gracious, asking about Bernard's family, his work, his future aspirations. Although his countenance softened, his jaw appeared rather stiff or rigid—even when he smiled or laughed. Bernard thought perhaps there might be some sort of physical problem there. Much to Bernard's surprise, the Director spoke about many personal problems that confronted him through the years while running the FBI.

"When I took over the Bureau, dishonesty was rampant," he stated gruffly. "If an agent asked to see the Director, it was expected he'd bring in a bottle of liquor for him. Agents were using their credentials to acquire gifts, all manner of things. Why, I'd fire an agent for using his badge to get into a ball game!"

Bernard's eyes dropped. He couldn't imagine there were many agents in the New York office who'd "tinned" their way into more athletic events than he.

"Those agents up in New Haven," Mr. Hoover continued. "Having coffee every morning in that shop near the office. The owner of the place was wondering when they ever worked. Everyone thought I was a no-good bastard for transferring them. A bachelor who didn't understand the problems of family men."

But it was on the subject of Eleanor Roosevelt that the Director's ire really began to show. The Director referred to her in uncomplimentary terms, and let loose with a puzzling string of reproachful non sequiturs, even referring to her as a "bitch." Bernard had only limited knowledge about the former First Lady and was relieved when the man moved on to more congenial topics. When Mr. Hoover addressed the subject of the Bureau as a career, Bernard felt obliged to comment. How he had the temerity to do it he wasn't sure, but when the Director alluded to opportunities within the organization, Bernard thought about a poem he once memorized, "Opportunity," by Edward Rowland Sill. During a pause in the Director's remarks, he impetuously jumped in. Had Mr. Hoover heard of Mr. Sill's poem "Opportunity"? No, he had not. Bernard proceeded to recite the following lines:

> THIS I beheld, or dreamed it in a dream:—
> There spread a cloud of dust along a plain;
> And underneath the cloud, or in it, raged
> A furious battle, and men yelled, and swords
> Shocked upon swords and shields. A prince's banner
> Wavered, then staggered backward, hemmed by foes.
> A craven hung along the battle's edge,
> And thought, "Had I a sword of keener steel—
> That blue blade that the king's son bears,—but this
> Blunt thing—!" he snapped and flung it from his hand,
> And lowering crept away and left the field.
> Then came the king's son, wounded, sore bestead,
> And weaponless, and saw the broken sword,
> Hilt-buried in the dry and trodden sand,
> And ran and snatched it, and with battle shout
> Lifted afresh he hewed his enemy down,
> And saved a great cause that heroic day.

After what may have been one of the longer periods he had ever remained silent listening to an agent, Mr. Hoover presumably decided he had heard enough from Bernard Conners. Rising from his chair, he extended his hand and wished Bernard well. A few days later Bernard heard the results of the meeting from a friend he had worked with in New York, who was now an executive at the Bureau's headquarters. The man saw the Director's memo regarding the meeting, which he had sent to his close associate and number one man, Clyde Tolson.

The following memo was obtained by the Freedom of Information Act (FOIA).

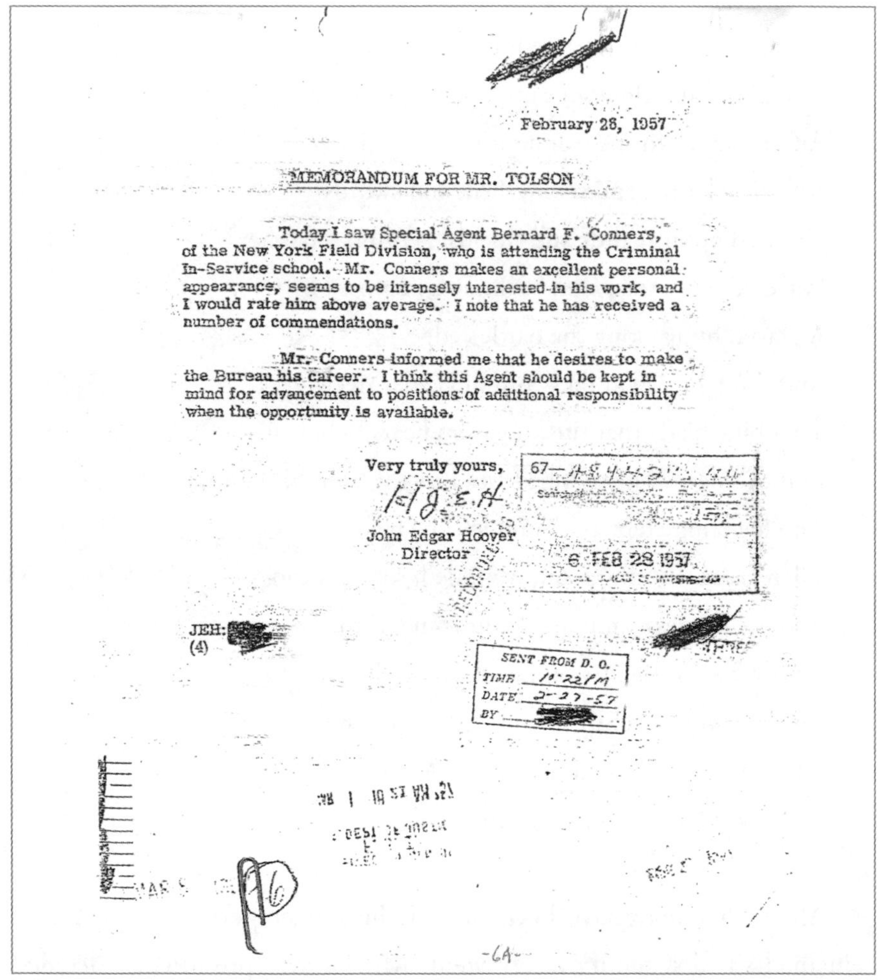

February 28, 1957

MEMORANDUM FOR MR. TOLSON

Today I saw Special Agent Bernard F. Conners, of the New York Field Division, who is attending the Criminal In-Service school. Mr. Conners makes an excellent personal appearance, seems to be intensely interested in his work, and I would rate him above average. I note that he has received a number of commendations.

Mr. Conners informed me that he desires to make the Bureau his career. I think this Agent should be kept in mind for advancement to positions of additional responsibility when the opportunity is available.

Very truly yours,

/s/ J. E. H.

John Edgar Hoover
Director

6 FEB 28 1957

JEH:
(4)

SENT FROM D. O.
TIME 10:22 PM
DATE 2-27-57
BY

J. Edgar Hoover memo 2/28/57. Black marks on the memo are excisions made by government censors.

"None better," said Bernard's friend. "It's the best Hoover would ever say after meeting with an agent. You say you recited that entire poem?" Then he added, incredulous, "And he listened to the whole thing?"

Bolstered by the report, Bernard requested a meeting with Assistant Director Johnny Mohr for the purpose of expressing his interest in a foreign assignment—either in Paris or Rome. He had studied French in college for four years, and had a working knowledge of Italian from having lived there. In fact, agents in the New York office occasionally sought his assistance when interviewing Italian subjects.

"You did what?" said Bernard's friend, alarm in his voice upon learning of the impending meeting with Mohr. "Johnny Mohr! Why in the world would you ask to see Mohr? He can't possibly do you any good." Mohr was regarded by some in the agent corps as a harsh disciplinarian.

The following week Bernard arrived for his meeting with the assistant director, where he was greeted by Mohr's cheerless, no-nonsense countenance, the look of someone who had been disturbed while napping. Bernard realized it was not going to be a good interview from the start. In an effort to conceal his nervousness, he shook Mohr's hand quite firmly.

"God Almighty!" Mohr exclaimed, pulling his hand away, shaking it as though he'd gripped a hot wire.

"Sorry," Bernard murmured apologetically, bewildered as to what he had done.

"All right," muttered the man, holding his wounded fingers. "Sit down!"

But Bernard knew it wasn't "all right." Bernard never recovered from the handshake, nor, would it appear, did Mohr. (Bernard later heard from his Bureau friend that Mohr had injured his fingers playing handball a few days before.) Bernard's overture for an assignment in Paris or Rome was met with little enthusiasm.

"How are your language skills?" Mohr asked skeptically.

"Not that good," Bernard replied, honestly. "But I took four years of French in college and with some accelerated—"

"No, no," Mohr interrupted, shaking his head in disapproval while flipping through papers on his desk. No more than a few minutes into the interview it was apparent that language ability wasn't the only thing about Bernard that Mohr found inadequate. After being brusquely dismissed, Bernard found himself with plunging emotions headed down, down, down, in a Justice Department elevator. Later he would wonder what Mohr might have thought of his poem "Opportunity." . . .

Following is the memorandum reflecting Mohr's impression of Bernard and his aspirations for a foreign assignment.

Office Memo[illegible]ndum • UNITED ST[illegible]ES GOVERNMENT

TO : [redacted] DATE: March 12, 1957

FROM : J. P. MOHR

SUBJECT: BERNARD F. CONNERS
Special Agent
New York Office

Mr. Connors, who was attending In-Service Training School, dropped in to see me on March 8, 1957. He said he just wanted to drop by and say hello since he had heard about "Johnny Mohr" in the field and wanted to come by and see "what Johnny Mohr looked like and say hello." He also said he would like to be kept in mind for a foreign assignment in the event any vacancies occurred in London, Rome or Paris. He stated his conversational French and Italian were poor. I told him that being so his chances of getting to Rome and Paris were practically nil. He was informed, however, that his desires would be listed for possible future consideration. In addition to Mr. Connor's breezy approach, he also needed a haircut, and he did not make a particularly favorable impression on me during the interview.

It is noted that the impression that Mr. Connors made on me is just the opposite of the one he made on the Director when the Director saw him February 26, 1957. As I have indicated, at the time I saw Connors he did need a haircut and I wasn't particularly impressed with the breezy way in which he commenced the conversation.

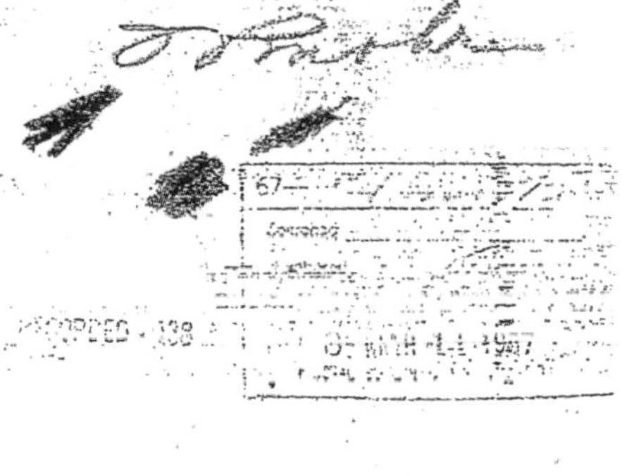

JPM:

John Mohr memo 3/12/57.

It was the only time Bernard ever met with Johnny Mohr, and he was not inclined to repeat the experience. The session with Mr. Hoover, however, was one that he would always value. Later, he would have more contact with the Director, some after he resigned from the Bureau, all of it cordial. Bernard had a high regard for the Director and thought the man treated him exceedingly well. But troubling times lay ahead.

2

Sex with Amelia

OCCASIONALLY, during introspective moments or unusually candid bursts of self-denigration, Bernard might describe himself to a close friend as "rather cowardly." This description seems at odds with his accomplishments in life: Golden Gloves boxing champion, college hall of fame football star, recipient of citations for valor and performance from J. Edgar Hoover and from generals under whom he had served in the military—a life of apparent derring-do.

But beneath this courageous veneer lay a second self, a puzzling personality lacking confidence, a shy alter ego who at times found it difficult to cope with everyday vicissitudes. Perhaps one of the more telling indications of Bernard's latent character was a description of him by classmates that appeared in his eighth-grade yearbook. Under Bernard's photo, rather than a complimentary designation such as "most likely to succeed," appeared a blunt assessment by a jury of his peers: "BERNIE WORRY WART CONNERS."

The third youngest of eight children, all but two of whom were girls, Bernard started life being called "Boy-Boy"—or more frequently just

"Boy"—by his elder sisters. He shared the name with their saddle horse, a docile animal named "Big-Boy." The horse was quartered on the Connerses' property in a combination barn and playhouse where a constant concern was that Big-Boy did not step on Boy-Boy. Although of moderate means, his parents presided over a dignified household where occasional confrontations and arguments quickly dissolved into pouts and sulking of short duration. With the death of his father at an early age and the enlistment of his elder brother as an army officer, Boy-Boy found himself the only male in a household dominated by seven women.

One of Boy-Boy's earliest memories dealing with the opposite sex involved a friend of his elder sisters, a rather daring flighty adventuress whom we shall call "Amelia." Although nine or ten years older than Bernard, who was about three or four, Amelia had already acquired a significant interest in sexual activity, which she proceeded to share with Boy-Boy. She referred to it as her "ticklish game." Although actual copulation could hardly be achieved between a prepubescent girl and a four-year-old, Amelia did her best to consummate the act. Of course such adventures were attended by many warnings from Amelia regarding the secret nature of the ritual: retribution from parents and even police could be swift and dire following any disclosure. These were admonitions that ensured Boy-Boy's confidentiality.

What Freudian consequences resulted from such encounters is difficult to say, but psychologists often attribute residual implications from early sexual experiences. In Bernard's case, suffice it to say, impending visits from Amelia invariably produced his first *Butterflies*—a feeling defined by Webster's Dictionary as a "hollowness or queasiness caused by emotional or nervous tension or anxious anticipation." Although Bernard never attributed any psychological significance to these precocious sexual episodes, they remain the most vivid recollections of his early Butterflies, which were a pronounced characteristic of his other, more subdued personality.

His first romantic experience, however, was far more platonic. It came in the form of a pretty girl named Grace Askew, who sat three desks in front of him in the fourth grade of Public School 16 in Albany, New York. By leaning slightly in his chair he could see her pretty delicate features, her blonde hair curling down over her pristine white collar, and shiver when he heard her tingling childish laugh. From this vantage point he could follow her every movement with besotted puppy love. For Bernard she was a focus of adoration as well as a major distraction during one of the few periods in his life when grades were important to him.

His ability to add and multiply numbers quickly impressed his teacher, who was second in his love life. Praise from Miss Thomas—she had recommended to his parents that he skip a grade had inspired him to be the best in his class. He was first to hand in assignments, and he regarded new students with apprehension lest they impress Miss Thomas more.

But Grace Askew remained the focus of his attention. It was unrequited love. If Grace were aware of his presence, it never showed. He lacked the confidence to say merely "hello," much less initiate a conversation. This strong emotional attraction was confined to occasional glimpses of his beloved from three rows back. Once when she was away, he was close enough to read a paper on her desk, following the arcs and curves of her Palmer Method script attentively, captivated by the thought that it was *her* handwriting.

Such infatuation was not without trauma. One day Miss Thomas asked Grace to recite something at the front of the class. Bernard watched with fascination as Grace moved to the front and turned to face her classmates. Then to his horror she fainted, slipping to the floor. Miss Thomas, terrified, virtually collapsed herself.

"Get the nurse!" she shouted. Bernard was shocked. What happened? The object of his adoration was lying on the floor. Was she dead?

It was all over quickly. Grace was back on her feet, Miss Thomas providing a chair, the nurse pronouncing her fine. Apparently a case of nerves. But for Bernard it was an unforgettable experience. For a moment, Grace Askew was gone! True love lost in the fourth grade. There would be other girls; one, years later, who would become the mainstay of his life. But Grace Askew would remain a riveting memory from the fourth grade.

Competitiveness was another emotion that surfaced in the early years that was to play an important part in Bernard's life. It was a trait that would always be of concern to the Butterflies. "Boy-Boy is going to be a terrific athlete!" was a refrain often heard from his sisters, all of whom were good athletes. At five feet seven to five feet eight they were of Amazonian stature, attractive with lovely figures. Once while sunning on a dock at Lake George in the Adirondack Mountains, his sister Alice—described by many as the most beautiful girl they had ever seen—was the center of attention from a group of young men. One of them, a somewhat scrawny chap, emboldened by her beauty and serene manner, said, "Watch, I'm going to toss Alice in the lake," to which Bernard, who had occasionally skirmished with Alice, replied dubiously, "Good luck." The individual was no match for the tanned athletic figure he had forced into action. A brief struggle ensued, the aggressor found himself in the lake, and Alice coolly returned to a book she'd been reading. Unlike others who witnessed the event, Bernard was not surprised. He thought his sisters were feminine, yet powerful, sometimes commenting with a note of bewilderment, "They'd make great guerrilla fighters!"

3

Confessional Jitters

IN THE fourth grade, Bernard's athletic skills became noticeable. He impressed his gymnastics coach with his ability to perform aerials. While his diminutive stature at this stage was a source of concern to his mother and towering sisters, it proved an asset in acrobatics. But it was another sport in which he truly excelled, much to the consternation of his sisters: boxing! He determined quite young that he could defeat boys in his age bracket. And these skills were not always confined to the ring. Because of his size he was sometimes underestimated by playground bullies, leading to encounters that contributed to a "little man" complex and sometimes to pugnacious overreactions. Although his underlying self was timorous, if Bernard were sufficiently provoked, an assertive machismo might surface, which quickly blew away the Butterflies. The result could lead to consequences for his adversary as well as for Bernard. Consequently, although Bernard was often voted the most popular in his class, some thought he had a rather "short fuse."

An encounter along these lines during junior high school advanced Bernard's boxing career. He was twelve years old, engaged in a confrontation outside a movie theater, when his boxing skills came to the attention of Sammy Bruce, a former world-class boxing champion. After witnessing the skirmish, Bruce reportedly commented to bystanders on Bernard's ability, and expressed a desire to train him. Bruce had boxing facilities in the basement of a local church in Albany's inner city.

With such encouragement, Bernard would later become an impressive force in the ring, winning both novice and open championships of the Golden Gloves, as well as other contests, including US Army titles. His record of numerous victories with only one defeat augured well for a career as a professional. As a youngster, however, Bernard had little notion of what awaited him later in the ring, and confined his elfin physique to occasional confrontations with schoolyard bullies.

In seventh grade, Bernard was transferred from Public School 16 to Vincentian Institute in Albany, New York. "VI" was a Catholic school, the faculty of which was composed of highly conservative nuns enshrouded in stark black habits with high white head cloths and capuche-like bonnets. The effect, whether intentional or not, was to conceal even a scintilla of flesh, save for a frosty visage that peered menacingly from behind rimless glasses. These grim countenances added to the nuns' capacity to rule with uncompromising authority, instilling a no-nonsense discipline for learning, particularly when it involved religious matters and prayers such as the Confiteor and Ave Maria that were part of the daily curriculum. Sister Mary Clement was probably the most severe. She favored group punishment for any transgressions. "With your homework each of you write, 'I will not talk in class' five hundred times." And this meant *everyone* in the class no matter who had been the source of provocation.

Such group punishment was not popular with the parents, who were obliged to help out since no student could handle such prodigious assignments by himself. And the numbers Sister Mary Clement threw around were what one might hear on the floor of the Chicago Commodity Exchange. But it worked: there were few infractions.

If the nuns could inspire anxiety in a twelve-year-old, it was nothing compared to confessions, where one had to disclose sins to a priest. It seemed that the biggest sins of all were those having to do with sex. There were two classes of sins: venial and mortal. Venial amounted to forgetting one's morning prayers or the like. No big deal. But the real heavy stuff had to do with sex—particularly "abusing your body" or "fooling with your body." That could end with hell's fire—that is, unless one could somehow get out "My Jesus, mercy" before expiring. Then, it was nothing more than a stretch in Purgatory.

It was burdensome for a youngster carrying such weighty matters into confession. For the worst sin of all, even worse than "fooling with your body," was *lying* to a priest. And then there was always the question of the priest himself. Did he ask lots of questions? Did he give a heavy penance? (A penance was the punishment, usually consisting of prayers that a priest would mete out at the end of the confession.) One priest was notorious with his penance. Students called him a "hanging judge." His favorite penance was the Stations of the Cross, a process that could take an hour or more. This could be downright embarrassing. One had to come out of the confessional, face those waiting, and then pray to each of the Stations arranged on the walls around the church. It was not an ordeal one wanted to perform before a waiting mother and sisters. Bernard suspected others did the same as he: a few short prayers at the altar implying a mild sentence, and the Stations at a later date when no one was around.

Bernard recalled one occasion sitting in the confessional relating his sins to a priest who sat behind a black veil. The exchange went something like this: "Yes, my child," followed by "Bless me father for I have sinned. My last confession was two weeks ago. Since then I forgot my morning prayers three times. I disobeyed my mother ten times. . . ." One always started off with the easy things, saving the heavy stuff for a quick synopsis at the end. "I uh . . . I may have peeked at my sisters three times." (pause) "I uh . . . I could have had some impure thoughts along the way. . . ." And then the real blockbuster. "Also father . . . uh . . . I might have, you know, maybe, you know, abused my body!" . . . "Yes, my child," from the priest. And then the kicker. "How many times?" Wow!

"Well, father . . . I'm not, you know, *really* sure . . . uh . . . maybe . . . uh . . . maybe impure thoughts thirty times?"

"Thirty?" exclaimed the priest. And then his voice rising with a note of awe, "Did you say you abused your body *thirty* times in the last two weeks?"

"No, no," Bernard said, hurriedly with alarm. "Impure *thoughts*! Impure *thoughts* thirty times!"

There was a pause and then from the priest, "Would you mind if I lift the veil?" He started to move the black cloth that shielded the confessor. Gosh! Talk about Butterflies! There was always a chance that the priest might recognize a student from his voice—a possibility that could affect one's delivery when entering the confessional—but a face-to-face? A confrontation? Over the most *mortal* of sins? "Ah . . . just a second, father. Ah . . . is it okay if I go now? I think my sister's waiting for me outside." There was no time for a penance.

The very worst thing that could happen was to have a priest who couldn't hear well. "Speak up, my child!" Good Lord! Churches are like crypts anyway. With people waiting right outside the confessional, the last thing one wanted to do was "speak up!" To make things worse, confessionals were usually constructed in a way that two penitents were inside the unit at the same time with the priest sitting in the middle. The intent was to have the priest hear one confession, then close the door and turn to another small sliding door that concealed the person on the other side. Given the acoustics of construction materials back then, while these double confessionals undoubtedly sped things up, they certainly affected the quality of the confessions. If one were inclined, it was not that difficult to hear the whispers from the other side. And if the voice on the other side was a bit muted—which invariably was the case—one could count on a priest who was hard of hearing to fill in the gaps.

Acoustics were always a problem in the confessional, but all privacy went out the window with priests who had hearing deficiencies. Not only did they insist *you* "speak up," *they* spoke up! There was always the unnerving possibility that a mortifying comment could blare from the confessional and ricochet off the walls outside. It was enough to make one want to skip the priest and just do the max: the Stations of the Cross!

4

Butterflies and Smoking Machos

BERNARD entered high school at less than five feet tall, weighing 114 pounds. His mother and sisters wondered if he were ever going to grow. His height had once prompted a friend of his sisters to exclaim, "Bernie Conners! You get smaller every time I see you." It seemed those around him were becoming taller, but the only thing growing in Bernard was his little-man complex. The difference in size between him and his classmates had not been as troubling in the earlier grades, but now it was affecting his ability to compete in athletics. And while grades had become less important to him, athletics were by then all-consuming.

He began to grow as a sophomore in high school, and from then until he was twenty he just kept growing, topping off at over six feet. Actually, he was a hair less but by stretching his neck slightly, he managed to reach seventy-three and a half inches. His college football roster listed him as six feet one and 185 pounds, both of which were slightly inflated.

High school at Vincentian Institute consisted of strong academics, competitive athletics, and a Roman Catholic education heavy on sexual restraint. Hell's fire was waiting for transgressors. The strict curriculum was administered by "Brothers" of the Holy Cross, a cadre of male teachers whose disciplinary measures might well have rivaled that of the SS in Nazi Germany. Or at least that's what Bernard thought at the time. There is no question that the Brothers' corps was well equipped to handle the burgeoning vitality of young males. (High school at VI was coeducational, girls taught by nuns and boys by Brothers.) The Brothers meted out pummelings on a daily basis. These were the 1940s, the years of World War II, when graduates were immediately conscripted. This early training by the VI Brothers proved helpful when alumni were later confronted with the rigors of drill sergeants at army boot camps.

The "macho honcho" of the VI cadre was Brother John. He was a tall, imperious man in his mid-to-late thirties, handsome, well built, with jet black hair and horn-rimmed glasses. He taught few classes himself, but seemed to roam the halls in his robes (the Brothers wore ankle-length black habits) and surface dramatically in classes where there appeared to be disciplinary issues.

Punishment by Brother John was swift and severe. Grabbing a student by the collar, he would launch him from his desk and administer whopping blows to his victim's back. For those sitting in front of the hapless student—no one dared turn around—the thumping sounds punctuating Brother John's visits had a sobering effect. Because of his brutish methods, like many overpowering persons, he inspired a certain awe and respect in those remembering him years later. No one would forget the most fearsome of all disciplinarians: Brother John "the Backbreaker"!

Bernard's first encounter with Brother John was fleeting. It was his freshman year and he had just purchased a yo-yo during lunch period at a small store near the school. It cost twenty-five cents—not an idle investment for him at this stage. He loved the yo-yo, with its shiny ebony surface and glittering zircons and, though yo-yos were forbidden during school hours, he sauntered down the hallway, practicing a yo-yo trick known as "walking the dog." From out of nowhere appeared a flurry of black robes containing the menacing figure of Brother John. Bernard quickly aborted the "dog walk" in a futile attempt to squirrel away the yo-yo. Too late! Never breaking stride as he approached, "the enforcer," as he was sometimes called, without a word, snapped his fingers and extended his hand palm up. It was the last Bernard saw of his yo-yo. He'd had it less than fifteen minutes. For a fourteen-year-old it was a sad day. He sometimes wondered what Brother John did with all the yo-yos he confiscated. Occasionally Bernard imagined Brother John behind the closed door of his office, amusing himself with a "walk the dog" or a "rock the cradle."

Few high schools could have provided better educations than VI. Although occasionally extreme in their disciplinary measures, the Brothers were religiously motivated and accepted their teaching duties straight from God. Student performance on New York State Regents examinations was of paramount importance.

Although religious and academic studies were the primary focus of Vincentian Institute, athletics were an important part of the curriculum. Many of the Brothers were good athletes, and they were friendlier and less threatening on the ball field, where they often joined the students. The athletic department featured a number of fine coaches during Bernard's time, some of whom went on to distinguish themselves in major sports. Among these was Joe Kuharich, who was head coach at Notre Dame and then of the Chicago Cardinals in the NFL. It was exceptional talent for a provincial school in upstate New York. Bernard performed well under such guidance, making all-star teams in football, basketball, and baseball.

The sport that remained his best, however, was boxing. He continued his unbeaten streak throughout high school. As undignified and boorish as it seemed to him in later years, fighting, both inside and outside the ring, was a part of his life as a youngster. Given his Butterfly affliction, he ought to have cowered in the face of such battles. But he had an antipathy toward bullies, which derived from the early years on the playground. His little-man complex somehow fostered an inexplicable spunk, and, once provoked, the smoking machos easily outmatched the shivering Butterflies.

5

Jews and WASPs

BERNARD was reared in a section of Albany called Pine Hills. It was a friendly middle-class neighborhood with many Jewish families, all of whom were exceedingly thoughtful and kind to the fatherless Bernard. Reared with such gracious neighborhood families as Heggleman, Bolz, Bennett, Pomerantz, and Schwartz, he was unprepared for the anti-Semitism he would witness in later life.

One neighbor was particularly helpful during his early years. John Boyd Thatcher, a Princeton alumnus and courtly mayor of Albany, lived only a few doors away and took an interest in Bernard. Doubtless the man felt compassion for the youngster, who was something of a waif with only a mother and a bevy of sisters. Mayor Thatcher and his wife, a charming woman of regal bearing, often took the young boy to games at Hawkins Stadium, home of the Albany Senators, a minor league baseball team.

In his junior year, Bernard's mother transferred him to the Albany Academy for Boys, a prep school that served the Capital District's patrician class. It was a quantum leap for Bernard both socially and academically.

The Academy, founded in 1813, was one of the oldest country day schools in the nation, counting among its alumni famous people such as Herman Melville and Andy Rooney. Steeped in tradition, it featured a military battalion that wore uniforms modeled on those of the Civil War era, and a faculty composed of erudite gentlemen, some with doctorates (unusual then for high school teachers). One in particular exemplified the reserve and dignity of the elite English public schools such as Eton and Harrow: English teacher Dr. Pike. Confined to a wheelchair, he depended on students to bring lunch from the school cafeteria known as the "buttery." It was a task that Bernard performed willingly. Not only was Dr. Pike appreciative, he was also a published author, and Bernard already harbored thoughts of becoming a writer.

The Academy excelled as a preparatory school: a high percentage of its graduates were accepted at Ivy League schools as well as at West Point and Annapolis. The headmaster was Harry Meislahn, a Princeton graduate who personified the typical English headmaster. Bernard was the first student Mr. Meislahn admitted during his tenure at the Academy. He was very kind to his new student, and Bernard was grateful for his thoughtful guidance. The headmaster saw fit to comment later on Bernard's application to Princeton that "Bernard has a great appreciation for the Academy and its faculty." It was an accurate comment borne out in the classroom. Bernard had great liking for his teachers, and he presumed the feeling was mutual. One "Master," as the Academy teachers were called, Mr. Midgely, made a particularly revealing observation about his student: "Bernard is an introvert pretending to be an extrovert."

Although the Academy would lose some of its traditional style during ensuing years, as did most of the prominent eastern prep schools, it still retained much of the dignity of the old English preparatory institutions. For Bernard, it was a significant change from the middle-class, rough-and-tumble VI to the WASP-oriented military academy. Nowhere was the difference more evident to Bernard than the stark change from Brother John "the Backbreaker" to Harold Meislahn.

While Bernard thought the "Masters" were gentle and supportive, it was Coach "Country Bill" Morris who became his father figure. The man's ability to understand the problems of young boys, while still motivating them to achieve top performance in athletics, was remarkable. For Bernard, for whom athletics were now consuming, there had never been anyone who could compare with Country Bill Morris on the athletic field. The record of his teams was stunning. There were only twenty-nine in Bernard's graduating class, yet Coach Morris was able to field competitive teams against much larger schools. There were times, however, when Bernard tried the coach's patience. With a shortage of funds at home, most of his wardrobe, other than school uniforms, consisted of material he filched from the locker room. T-shirts, athletic socks, jerseys, sneakers, pants all found their way to his house. One day Coach Morris said to him in his affable tone, "Conners, one of these days I'm sending a pickup truck to your house to get back some of my athletic gear!"

It was on the Academy football field during an inter-squad scrimmage that Bernard sustained his first football injury. A blow to his right knee sidelined him and prompted one examining physician to tell him, "You'll never play football on that knee again." Notwithstanding the devastating prognosis, Bernard would later be named on all-star teams while in college and the service, be inducted into his college hall of fame, and experience a brief stint with the Chicago Bears in the NFL.

Part II

6

Self-Pity

DURING Bernard's high school years, everyone was caught up in World War II. Newspaper and radio reports, movies, war bonds, rationing . . . the country was consumed by the war effort. The media conveyed the intensity of the battles in Europe and Asia. There were times when things were not going that well. It was possible to lose! All too often the report of the death of a son would arrive in the neighborhood, with the inconsolable grief that followed, and the gold stars on small flags in front windows that signified the loss of a loved one. The "Nazis" and "Japs" were the objects of intense enmity, and fervent patriotism gripped the country. Virtually all healthy males were drafted or enlisted directly from high school. Not to be in uniform at the time was to be the object of curiosity or even derision: "Was he a draft dodger . . . or 4F?" It was the latter designation that was of intense concern to Bernard during his last few years in high school. 4F was the classification for one who was rejected for military duty, most often because of physical limitations.

Throughout his early years Bernard had been gripped by an unreasonable worry about his health—particularly his heart. Although his heart was sound, his concern persisted, causing him considerable anxiety. Perhaps such concern derived in part from his mother's habit of often listening to his heart when he was young. Sarah, an occasional English teacher, had a modest income and eight children. With her only other son serving as an army officer, she doted on Bernard, refusing him nothing, paying his tuition at the Academy, spending hours helping him with his homework after the other duties that consumed her day. Whenever he asked for the impossible, which was often, she'd say, "We can do it. We'll find a way."

With little money to spend on doctors, Sarah relied on a massive medical tome that described all kinds of maladies. Perhaps it was something in her medical book that led her to listen to his heart so often. At any rate, it troubled Bernard. He constantly worried that a doctor would find something wrong, which would keep him off the athletic fields. His sister Alice, although incredibly strong and healthy, had some of the same anxiety. Her concern was cancer. She and Bernard sometimes commiserated about their perceived conditions. Bernard was truly worried that he might not pass the army physical, and be classified 4F.

It was not the case. Bernard was inducted into the service early in 1945, and sent to basic training at Camp Blanding, Florida, where his previous training at Vincentian Institute proved valuable. Few drill sergeants were more intimidating than "the Backbreaker." Yet the basic training at Blanding was formidable. The talk at the base was that American troops in the Pacific had been trained inadequately and were having difficulty coping with jungle warfare. The orders, therefore, were to toughen the recruits so that they could withstand the stress that would accompany the seemingly inevitable invasion of Japan. The most arduous part was the lack of sleep, and long marches in oppressive heat carrying an eighty-six-pound backpack.

Bivouacs in the Everglades were the worst. Each recruit slept on the ground with a fellow soldier, covered by a small pup tent that consisted of two small pieces of canvas. Trainees were cautioned by superiors to lie still and look around before arising in the morning: snakes sometimes crawled in next to the bodies at night to stay warm. Bernard saw one victim whose hand had swollen to the size of a catcher's mitt.

The pup tents were barely large enough to cover two bodies. Each solder carried a small canvas called a "shelter half" in his backpack, which when attached to a fellow soldier's shelter formed half of the tiny tent. One night Bernard was preparing to crawl into the tent when his buddy cuddled him with his arm around Bernard's shoulder, and pointed to the initials "US" on the tent, which signified government property.

"Look," said his partner, feigning a coy intimacy. "Us!"

For Bernard, who had been reared with six sisters in a house where privacy was of importance, army life could prove to be uncomfortably close living.

When not on bivouacs, recruits lived in huts that formerly had served as a Japanese prisoner-of-war camp. Generally, one slept no more than five or six hours a night, less if one worried about snakes. Lights went out at 10 p.m. and the bugle sounded reveille at 3 and 4 a.m. The quarters consisted of four metal bunks with bug-infested mattresses. Bedbugs thrived despite constant dousing with insect repellant. Trainees often slept out on the sand, rather than endure the bedbugs. They were so tired they could sleep anywhere.

Recruits got scant relief during the training. An occasional weekend pass offered a trip to a nearby town, aptly named Stark, which offered little entertainment for weary troops. Contributing to the soldiers' frustration were strong rumors that the Friday meals at the base were loaded with saltpeter, which supposedly diminished the sexual desire of young males headed out for the weekend. Rightly or not, the troops were suspicious of Friday's food.

Training was often dangerous. Although their superiors, wary of the unpredictability of recruits with M1 rifles, carbines, flamethrowers, and hand grenades, took every precaution, there were still casualties. Some in Bernard's company were wounded during training, and fatalities occurred in nearby units. With the thousands of shots fired during mock skirmishes, accidents were inevitable. One maneuver had fighter aircraft swooping low over recruits firing 50-caliber machine guns at simulated targets ahead of the troops. Watching the rounds kick up dirt ahead could be frightening. The infiltration course was particularly unnerving, requiring recruits to crawl on their stomachs across a wide field at night as machine guns fired 30-caliber tracers a few feet overhead. The purpose: to give recruits the experience of being under close enemy fire.

But the obvious question for most recruits was what if you crawled up on a snake with all those bullets whining overhead? Rumors of such encounters were rampant. Camp wisdom recommended staying with the snake, since a man could recover from a snakebite, but not from withering automatic fire. Optimists posited that with all the action, it was doubtful snakes were around. But men from southern rural areas were unconvinced. "Those mothers are nocturnal! They're everywhere at night!"

Training seemed to progress from one dangerous endeavor to another. Making bombs to blow up bridges and other targets was equally unsettling. Fashioning the bomb from the required ingredients was not difficult, but setting the fuse was another matter. Wires had to be bound together with pliers, which could trigger the explosion prematurely. Recruits were instructed to hold the device away from their bodies well over their heads. That way if it went off they might lose just their arms. . . .

Casualties that occurred during training were not all due to explosives. There were suicides. None occurred in Bernard's unit, although there was one suspected attempt when a trainee stepped out in front of a Browning automatic rifle. Severely wounded, the soldier survived. Suicides in nearby units, however, led to occasional counseling, in which the company would be assembled for group therapy from army psychiatrists. Most of this therapy consisted of detailing the psychological dangers of self-pity. And there was absolutely no shortage of self-pity at Camp Blanding; it was generally thought that anyone who wasn't feeling sorry for himself just didn't understand the situation. Everyone knew he was being trained for the invasion of Japan and that fifty percent of the Camp Blanding troops would be killed. The battle of Iwo Jima only a few months before had resulted in severe American casualties, most of which occurred the first few hours after landing. Such battles demonstrated the fierceness with which the Japanese would defend their homeland. Of approximately 22,000 Japanese soldiers defending Iwo Jima, 21,800 were killed or committed suicide. Reportedly only 216 ever surrendered. The projected number of Blanding troops to be killed during the invasion of Japan was said to be five out of seven. Nevertheless, the continuous therapy from the psychiatrists was, "Remember, don't feel sorry for yourself. That's the quickest way to a nervous breakdown, and that won't solve a thing. . . . It might get you out of here, but chances are it'll be in a box!"

7

Duking It Out with Windmills

"HEY, PRICK!" It was an ungracious greeting even by army standards, and one that a person would not readily acknowledge. Bernard glanced uneasily toward the speaker, a dark, brooding, heavyset figure who was standing with two other soldiers a few feet away. "Yes, he was addressing me," thought Bernard, turning away and pretending not to have heard. But it aroused the Butterflies as well as a few smoldering machos.

"Hey, prick!" came the voice again, louder, attracting attention from those standing nearby, and demanding a response. Bernard was considering how to answer and was about to say "Are you talking to me, prick?" when the sergeant in charge announced the break was over and the platoon was to assemble on the nearby road. The timing of the order was fortunate for Bernard. The previous week he had watched the person who had just spoken to him perform in the Thursday night boxing matches that were a popular part of the meager recreation provided for the 55,000 soldiers at Camp Blanding. The man's name was Tony Corello, an impressive fighter who had scored a technical knockout over his opponent in the first round. Corello's adversary, although a game competitor, was similar to many young men whom Bernard later would box in the army. They had little experience. For the most part, the fighters he came into contact with in the service were like people who suddenly decided they wanted to be figure skaters although they'd never done any skating. Perhaps they were attracted by the machismo nature of the sport and wanted to display their manliness. They'd come out of their corner like unmoored windmills, flailing away with wild, frenzied punches. By the end of the first round (if it went that long) they'd be defenseless and utterly exhausted. Invariably, the referee would stop the fight. The only challenge they posed was their landing a clumsy punch from nowhere that first minute. After that it was no contest.

Tony Corello was something else: a worthy adversary who would later have an impressive career as a professional boxer. He and Bernard would soon become associated in Camp Blanding's boxing program, often sparring with one another in workout sessions. Bernard on occasion would read letters to Tony from his girlfriend and help him write responses. Tony had had little formal schooling. (With infantry casualties high in the Pacific during this period, few were rejected from the service because of disabilities like illiteracy.) They had never faced each other in a sanctioned bout, since Corello was in a different weight class, ten pounds lighter than Bernard. However, they did stage an exhibition fight one Thursday night, a memorable evening for Bernard. Although it was billed as an exhibition match in which no decision is rendered and boxers pull punches, essentially putting on a show for spectators, Bernard was uneasy about the impending fight. He was well aware of Tony's fondness for grandstanding and was wary of what the man might do in front of several thousand fans.

"It would be like putting on a show with a cobra," Bernard thought. He was taller than Tony and found it relatively easy to hit him with a left jab, but he was playing it pretty much as they had done in previous sparring matches, taking the sting out of punches. That is, until Tony caught him with a terrific left hook on his temple. He had seen Tony land the punch on several occasions to knock out opponents, and he knew very well what he was capable of doing. Bernard never felt a punch like that one. Everything spun in his head. It was the closest he ever came to being knocked down in a fight, but he pulled Tony into a clinch and was able to hang on. There was no question about the left hook: it was intended to put him on the canvas. Fortunately, he recovered, and the rest of the fight was certainly no mere exhibition. Bernard connected with a few left hooks of his own, which brought roars from the crowd. Who would have won if it had not been just an exhibition? Bernard thought he would have since he was taller and heavier. On the other hand, if Tony had connected with a few of those left hooks. . . . At any rate, what the troops saw that Thursday night, particularly in the final minutes, was deadly combat.

Bernard was not sure why he pursued boxing in the service. Perhaps it was vanity. He had far more experience than most of his opponents, enabling him to do well, and it earned him a measure of respect from the troops. It was quite gratifying to hear the rumble of approval from the crowd when a fight first started and he connected with a left hook. Yet he never crawled into the ring, even in the service where the competition was poor, without suffering from rampant Butterflies. Such a martial sport hardly conformed with his alter ego.

In Bernard's first sanctioned fight at Camp Blanding, he faced an opponent from Manhattan named Connors. He knew nothing about him beyond the introductions before the bell. The man was rather tall and rangy and didn't look much like a fighter. Nevertheless, Bernard was green with fear as he crawled between the ropes into the ring. He sometimes thought his anxiety might have helped speed up his reflexes. The newspaper account said the bout was stopped after the first round, that his opponent was "outclassed." Perhaps. Bernard felt he was not bad, probably better than some others he'd fought.

Bernard thought much of his success in the ring was due to showmanship. He usually landed a few left hooks early in the fight, and this, coupled with his undefeated record, probably intimidated opponents. It worked well against fighters in the service, but against more experienced boxers, in matches that lasted longer, he was not as effective. Although he won decisions after he left the army, there were not the stopped fights (technical knockouts) that he achieved against the madcap swingers in the service.

Bernard would later find little support for his boxing ventures at home where his mother and sisters found boxing unrefined and socially embarrassing. Indeed, a prominent Princeton alumnus, helping with his application to that school, thought it unnecessary to include his boxing laurels on his application. But there would be critical moments in his future when his fighting skills would save him from misfortune.

8

Troopship

THE ATOMIC bombs dropped on Hiroshima and Nagasaki in August 1945 ended the war with Japan. "Operation Downfall," the grand plan for the invasion of Japan in October 1945, was aborted. "Operation Olympic," the attack planned for Kyushu, the southernmost island of Japan, which had been deemed the most suitable for landing, was no longer necessary. The bomb saved hundreds of thousands of Americans, many of whom would have come from Camp Blanding. Indeed, declassified documents would later reveal that American commanders estimated that over one million of our troops would have been lost.

As a result of Japan's surrender, rather than shipping out to the Far East, Bernard was soon aboard a troopship headed for Europe. For those on board there was little to do. It was a dramatic change from the exhausting, often brutal, indoctrination of previous months. Despite a few storms in the North Atlantic and the inevitable seasickness that accompanied them, life aboard the ship was uneventful. Everyone realized that were it not for the bomb they'd be aboard another ship heading for what could have been a

Stygian nightmare in Japan. The fighting on the islands in the South Pacific a few months before had demonstrated the ferocity of the Japanese military, and their determination to defend their homeland to the very end.

Boxing matches, card games, books, and movies were the principal diversions on the troopship to Europe; Bernard naturally became involved with the boxing. He had several bouts but, like most of the service boxers, the contestants lacked experience. He considered these fights little more than exhibition matches, and won all his fights easily. However, interservice matches were not as predictable. Twice he fought Harold Loemon, champion of the US Coast Guard, when they reached their destination in Italy. They were far from exhibition fights.

Bernard was sitting in his corner after the first bout, commiserating with his cornermen. He thought he had lost the fight—the first defeat of his career—when they announced the verdict: a draw! The decision was a total surprise. Bernard couldn't believe it. Nor could anyone else. It was a good fight, however, which called for a rematch. The night before the second fight, Bernard was able to spend some time with Loemon aboard the boxer's ship, which was anchored in the Adriatic. In the course of a relaxed and friendly conversation, they talked about their first match.

Bernard found Loemon to be a perfect gentleman, more genteel than most service boxers. Loemon allowed as to how he was surprised at the "draw" verdict in the first fight, but was gracious, not making much of it. During the second fight, however, Bernard had him on the ropes. It was quite bloody. Bernard didn't ease up much, realizing it was unwise—things can change quickly—but he recalled looking at the referee expecting him to stop the fight. He never did. The verdict: another draw! Bernard would never understand these two decisions. He hadn't the chance to talk to Harold Loemon following the match, but he presumed Loemon felt the same as he did: they each had lost a fight.

CHAMPIONSHIP BOUTS

Satiri	110	N.J. vs.
Sanders	110	Penna
Lee	125	Calif vs.
Miranda	130	Mass.
Cataldo	140	N.Y. vs.
Manginelli	140	N.Y.
Zinno	150	N.Y. vs.
Hamel	150	N.Y.
Loprett	180	Mass.
Esposito	175	N.J.

FEATURE BOUT

Conners, USA	157 lbs	vs.
Leemon USCG	157 lbs.	

Boxing championships.

9

Waltzing in the Alps

After landing in Naples, Bernard and his fellow soldiers rode a troop train to the Julian Alps, where pockets of recalcitrant Yugoslavian partisans were engaging in occasional unpredictable skirmishes with Allied forces. The long trip gave them a glimpse of the ravages of war. Bombed-out towns and cities, hungry people crowding up to the train at stops along the way begging for food, clothing, supplies, anything. . . . The soldiers were under instructions not to give them supplies, but no one obeyed. The average G.I. was incapable of refusing hungry children with their hands out.

Bernard's unit finally reached its destination in the Julian Alps in northern Italy near a small town called Tarvisio. It was cold, but the spectacular scenery and leisurely days made it reasonably pleasant. The food was good, prepared by a talented mess sergeant, but Bernard found it dispiriting to watch people from the nearby town rummaging through the garbage. Reveille didn't sound until 6 a.m.—a tremendous respite following the 3 and 4 a.m. awakenings at Blanding. Beyond guard duty and some moderate training, there was little to do.

Other troops stationed in Europe seemed to have found entertainment among the local women, so much so that venereal disease had become a major problem for the European troops. The army had instituted radio announcements to forestall its spread, including one rather bizarre spot that opened with the sound of a man sobbing, followed by a booming authoritative voice proclaiming, "That man can't go home. That man has VEE . . . DEE!" In the mountains of Tarvisio, VD was not a great concern, although the troops were routinely subjected to "short-arm" inspections, which amounted to lining up to have medical officers look at their sex organs.

What the troops mostly suffered from was boredom. "We've gotta do something to boost morale," the commanding officer was supposed to have said. "Gotta get these guys off their ass."

The morale booster came in the form of a get-together with local villagers, not only to improve relations with the surrounding populace, but also to give the troops something to which they could look forward. Anticipating a party certainly lifted spirits. All kinds of rumors started: there were going to be *women* . . . a band . . . 3.2 beer . . . dancing! For young men who'd been deprived of virtually any social activity for months, it was invigorating, the elixir for which the commandant had hoped. He apparently envisioned something similar to the well-chaperoned gatherings between young women and soldiers provided by the Red Cross and the USO back in the States. It was not to be.

The party was held in a large hall in Tarvisio and the turnout was exceptional. But the women . . . well, where they came from was anyone's guess—and there were lots of guesses. According to the scuttlebutt, the commandant had sent emissaries on buses into the mountains to round up mothers and daughters with the promise of food and a good time in Tarvisio. Needless to say, the women were not what the troops had expected.

Most were heavy, or at least looked that way in their bulky winter clothing. Female legs were covered in heavy woolen stockings bearing vertical colored stripes. One soldier remarked dubiously, "Man, there must be one pretty gal here. . . ."

No one danced at first. The soldiers leaned against the walls, disconsolate. Finally, not to be deterred, the women began dancing with themselves, thumping heavily around the floor to waltzes, which apparently were all the musicians knew. It was hard to get high on 3.2 beer, but everyone surely tried. It was a bitter disappointment for the troops. "Well, what the hell did they expect in the middle of the mountains?" huffed the commandant afterward.

With the war over, except for occasional skirmishes with the Yugoslav partisans (called "Jugs" by the troops), the Allied command made plans for the occupation of the defeated countries in Europe. One of the programs provided for two football conferences: the European Theater of Operations (ETO) and the Mediterranean Theater of Operations (MTO). After a tryout, Bernard was selected as one of the quarterbacks for the Eighty-Eighth Division in the MTO. It was a good brand of football, the team composed mostly of college players as well as a few who had played professional football. The coach (who was also one of the players) was a man named Dick Todd, who had been an All-American star in college. Although he and Bernard were both quarterbacks, he let Bernard play most of the time. Bernard found him to be very encouraging, always helpful, never shouting as many coaches do.

Bernard's team won its conference and played the 442nd, a regimental combat team composed of Japanese Americans whose slogan was "Go For Broke." They were smaller than Bernard's team but very good, as demonstrated by their undefeated record. The game was held in a large stadium in Rome, packed with troops. Before the game Coach Todd pulled Bernard aside and motioned toward several photographers from army newspapers who were gathered on the nearby sidelines. "Go get your picture taken," he said. One of the reporters indicated that they preferred Todd, but Bernard heard him say, "Take his picture. You'll hear about him."

During the photo session Bernard jumped in the air, posing dramatically as though passing. It was not received well in the stands, and a loud hooting from the stadium derided the phony display. One of the reporters sensed Bernard's chagrin, telling him to forget it, mentioning that Bernard had made the MTO all-star team.

Bernard never did see any of the newspaper articles or photographs, but was told that some articles appeared in an army newspaper called *Stars and Stripes*. They won the game but Bernard did not play that well, almost losing the game with a fumble toward the end. Even then, Coach Todd was supportive, commenting about his recovering the ball.

It was an occasion for celebration on the bus trip from Rome back to their base. The smell of alcohol permeated the vehicle and, as might be expected from some sixty young men celebrating their championship, behavior on the bus deteriorated. One incident, which Bernard would never forget, involved a lieutenant who was on the specialty squad, place-kicking for the team. The officer was in his late twenties and to Bernard had seemed older and more refined than many of the players. At one of their stops the lieutenant had managed to convince two young women to join them on the bus. Once underway, to Bernard's astonishment, the lieutenant proceeded to have sexual intercourse with one of the women, in front of a number of their drunken teammates who cheered him on as though applauding one of his placekicks. For Bernard, a relatively inexperienced teenager, it would remain a profound disappointment in a man whom he had previously admired. He would reflect later about the many desperate young women who following the war resorted to prostitution to provide for their families.

10

George Plimpton

At the conclusion of the football season, Bernard received an appointment to the Lido Training Center, a highly regarded academy on the island of Lido near Venice. General Bryant Moore, the division commander who would later become the superintendent at West Point, had started the Lido Training Center as an institution for advanced leadership training modeled after West Point. In fact, it was referred to as "Little West Point." It was here that Bernard was promoted to a prominent role and met General Moore, who urged him to apply to the United States Military Academy and to make the military his career.

At the Lido Bernard met someone who would be far more central to his future: George Plimpton. The two became roommates and instructors at the facility. Both were interested in writing. George had been an editor of the *Harvard Lampoon* and offered a writer's cachet, which impressed Bernard immensely. They often exchanged essays and short stories, and a close relationship developed. They did well as instructors and spent much of their free time socializing in Venice, occasionally with friends of George's parents who vacationed there after the war.

George had an endearing manner and a remarkable ability to adjust to whatever milieu in which he found himself. He was a courtly chap whose British RP (Received Pronunciation), a traditionally prestigious form of pronunciation at Oxford and Cambridge, projected the image of a dignified British officer rather than the US Army. Although his patrician bearing did not always blend in with the less restrained ebullience of barracks life, he was immensely popular with the troops. He certainly stood out. Even when speaking his pidgin Italian, he impressed the locals with his pronunciation, having captured the spirit of the language.

He and Bernard loved the Italian women, of course. Two in particular. They'd met them on the beach near the Palazzo del Mare, a fashionable resort on the Adriatic Sea. Paula Scoto from Bologna and Radiana Fiortino from Venice—both blonde and deliriously beautiful. It seemed they were always carefully chaperoned—an aunt, a relative, a family friend—much to George's and Bernard's disappointment. Chaperoned or not, it probably would have made little difference, given that period of their lives. Both behaved like gentlemen. The fact that they were in leadership positions and quite visible on the Lido provided little opportunity for improper behavior.

Bernard, second from left; George, far right.

Bernard took liberties with George's personal space. He often wore George's uniforms, taking things as needed from his roommate's wardrobe. George found it unsettling but was usually a good sport. Although his roommate was taller, Bernard learned that by just turning his trousers over at the waist, they'd fit quite nicely. Occasionally George would react. One night Bernard was dining alfresco with an Italian beauty at a quiet restaurant in Venice. George appeared and joined their table. After introducing himself and ordering a beer, George commented on Bernard's uniform.

"I see you're wearing my trousers," he said. Bernard sheepishly acknowledged the fact. "Well if they're mine I guess I can do what I want with them," said George. Whereupon, much to the surprise and delight of Bernard's date and adjoining tables, he emptied his stein of beer straight onto Bernard's lap.

It was a rare transgression. The overall conduct of the American troops enrolled at the Lido Training Center was quite good. They were at the academy because they aspired to be officers and gentlemen and it was reflected in their behavior. British soldiers, on the other hand, came to the Lido on rest leaves from their units. They were inclined to relax and enjoy themselves. Since the Americans were charged with maintaining order on the island, it sometimes caused some nocturnal confrontations involving American military policemen and the furloughed British, who did not always take kindly to the Americans' authority.

Once, late in the evening, two American MPs entered Bernard's office, escorting a hysterical young woman who had been severely beaten. Bernard was horrified and tried to console her, speaking soothingly and assuring her that she was going to be all right. In reality, he had to look away: the woman's face was disfigured, her front teeth knocked out. Between sobs and showers of tears, the woman said she had been assaulted by an English soldier.

After calling for an ambulance and medics to care for the woman, Bernard and the MPs drove to the Albergo Excelsior on the Lido, where British troops stayed on leave; it was a lavish resort once frequented by Mussolini. With information supplied by the victim, there was no difficulty identifying the English soldier, who had a pronounced speech impediment. Bernard proceeded to interrogate the subject under the watchful eyes of two British officers, who were not altogether comfortable about one of their troops being questioned by an American.

For Bernard the most surprising part of the interview was the British soldier's total lack of remorse or compassion for what he had done to the young woman. "She was nothing but a bloody whore!" he kept shouting, outraged that he had been called to account for brutally assaulting her. Bernard left the interview with a deep feeling of revulsion for the British officers, who seemed indifferent to their subordinate's brutal crime. The experience reaffirmed Bernard's sympathy for the many desperate young Italian women, who, suffering deprivation and humiliation following a devastating war, had turned to whatever means enabled their families to survive.

Until his appointment to the installation on the Lido, Bernard had spent considerable time training for boxing matches, but with the rigorous schedule at the academy there was little opportunity for extracurricular activities. It was with surprise, therefore, that Bernard read the following article in an army newspaper:

> **BOXING SHOW TO FEATURE CARD OF TOP FIGHTERS**
> A tremendous boxing show hits Trieste . . . the card really looks great. A large crowd is expected. . . . Special Service men are doing their best to seat the throng comfortably. . . . Roland La Starza, two-time Golden Gloves light heavyweight champ will be fighting in the heavyweight class for the first time. Attempts are being made to contact Bernie Conners, sensational young light heavy who can give anybody an interesting evening. Should Conners be available, he will go Friday night against La Starza.

Thoughts of fighting La Starza would have been worrisome for Bernard during the best of times, but having had little training and no bouts for many months, it seemed particularly daunting. Yet, after encouragement from friends, Bernard relented and agreed to the fight in Trieste, a large city in northern Italy. His first encounter with La Starza had been at the Lido where La Starza was a trainee and participated in sparring and training supervised by Bernard, sessions that involved little serious fighting. La Starza was an outstanding boxer, and later in his career would have two very close fights with Rocky Marciano for the heavyweight championship of the world. In fact, most of those in the media who saw the first fight thought La Starza had won the disputed decision. During the second fight, La Starza was ahead on all three judges' cards, when he lost on a technical knockout in the eleventh round.

Bernard's training for the La Starza fight amounted to a few sparring sessions with George Plimpton. Although George was a relatively good athlete (he would later box Archie Moore and Sugar Ray Leonard in exhibition fights), he was certainly no match for Roland La Starza. Because of the weight disparity (La Starza was fighting as a heavyweight), the fight was canceled that night in Trieste. Bernard spent a pleasant time with him in the locker room that day. He admired Roland and his pleasantly reserved and thoughtful personality.

Bernard would like to have boxed him that evening, but suspected the outcome might have proved unfortunate. In most sports, lack of training or having an off night may not be critical. One can survive. In the ring, however, there's no one to save you. It's absolutely the worst sport for the faint of heart—particularly those heavy body blows to the midriff, hangout of the Butterflies.

11

General Jitters

BERNARD received commendations for his performance at the Lido from General Moore and General John Lee, the commander of the Mediterranean Theater of Operations. It was during this period that General Lee, a West Point graduate like Moore, urged Bernard to consider West Point and to make the army his career. Such proposals were made in spite of what Bernard thought was a dreadful initial meeting with General Lee. The troops had been assembled in a large open area that served as a parade ground. General Moore and other top officers were conferring with General Lee in front of the troops when one of the officers motioned for Bernard to come forward. Bernard, standing in front of his battalion, at first was unsure the officer wanted him. The officer motioned again impatiently and called him by name.

Senses thoroughly roused, Bernard moved out to where the top officers were conferring. General Moore presented him to General Lee; whereupon Bernard saluted and stood at attention, as stiff and rigid as a cigar store Indian. Moore proceeded to tell the general that Bernard was an outstanding leader and was considering the army as a career. As he stood ramrod straight, listening to the general's effusive plaudits, Bernard became increasingly anxious. He was standing so stiffly that, to his dismay, his lip and jaw began to quiver.

"We need fine young men like you," said General Lee, following Moore's introduction. "You're thinking of West Point, are you?"

"Yes, sir. I'm contemplating making the army a career, sir," Bernard said, dropping his quavering voice an octave.

By this time the Butterflies were no longer confined to Bernard's stomach, but about to fly him off the parade ground. Perhaps General Lee was accustomed to quivering subordinates: later Bernard would learn that he had made a favorable impression on the general. Bernard knew that General Moore had been at one of the football games in which Bernard had starred and had commented to General Lee about Bernard's athletic ability and interest in West Point. Encouraged by Generals Moore and Lee, Bernard seriously considered continuing his military service. Shortly after his meeting with General Lee the following item was carried in the division newspaper:

> Bernie Connors, who is also due to leave soon to try for a West Point appointment, is the finest type of young soldier. He is the type of soldier the Army likes to put on recruiting posters—big, athletic and clean cut.

Collegiate football was on Bernard's mind at that time. While at the Albany Academy he had made several trips to West Point to play the Army plebes and had been impressed with their athletic programs. But during this period Army was regarded as one of the best football teams in the country. Could he play at this level? Indeed, he was uncertain he would even be accepted at West Point. This, plus a general homesickness, were strong reasons for Bernard's decision to leave the army. His mother was aging and her resources limited. Throughout his tour of duty he often sent his army paychecks home, since the army provided almost everything—food, clothing, shelter.

Not the least of Bernard's concerns about leaving at the time was a stray dog he'd befriended on the Lido. Always a passionate animal lover, he'd become attached to the dog and was determined to bring him home. With the help of one of the Italian girls he'd been seeing, he arranged to have the dog, which he'd named Lido, shipped to the United States. It was a laborious undertaking, but Lido would provide him with much joy for years to come.

George Plimpton elected to continue serving for another year in a program similar to the one offered Bernard. Saying goodbye to him was difficult. They had become close during those days. They had no reason to know that their future lives would become entwined in publishing *The Paris Review.*

Bernard valued the experience he had in the military, but they were uncertain times. One month he was facing what seemed possible death in the invasion of Kyushu, while a few months later he was waltzing with a girl from the mountains in the Julian Alps. They had been unpredictable days, and he was ready to head home to the comfort of his mother and sisters.

Such comfort did not await the scores of German prisoners of war who were interned at the Lido Training Center following the war. These prisoners performed support services, such as repairing structures, cleaning barracks, and cooking. They were treated well by the cadre at the center and many were reluctant to be repatriated, fearing reprisals from the Russian troops who awaited them at their homes in Germany.

Bernard became friendly with some of the POWs, one in particular named Hans Greip, who showed Bernard a clipping of himself starring in the 1936 Olympics in Germany. Bernard empathized with their plight. Bereft of family and loved ones, they were a tired, beaten-down crew with a dismal future.

Part III

12

Steeplejack

WHEN Bernard returned to the States and was discharged from the army, he succumbed to an indolent period, which confronted many veterans as they adjusted to civilian life. A popular government program referred to as the "52-20 club" (twenty dollars per week for fifty-two weeks) provided income for returning veterans who were unemployed. This well-intentioned law was predictably abused. Thousands of veterans declined to look for work as long as the government paid them for doing nothing. Bernard himself felt uncomfortable about taking a government handout, but ignored his conscience and took the money.

He was soon bored, however, and began looking for work. An opportunity came in the form of a newspaper ad for a painting job with a firm called Fuller-Holstein. It was a wholesome-sounding name and for some reason Bernard thought it might have something to do with farms—perhaps painting barns or the like. It sounded pleasant, no experience was necessary, and the advertised salaries were significant. Indeed, they should have signified that there was a catch: while the salary was high, so was the work. It entailed painting the tops of radio towers and tall stanchions that carried high-tension wires.

Bernard had arrived at the site with a former prep school friend named George Harder, a veteran who had applied for the job along with him. The owner of the firm, Mr. Fuller, a portly, affable man, greeted them and gave some perfunctory instructions about the job. They were to be employees of the Fuller-Holstein Company, a general contractor for steeplejack work. It entailed climbing one hundred feet or more in the air and painting steel framework with a slimy, black, oily steel preservative called fisholene, which had a dreadful odor of dead fish.

There were no safety precautions whatsoever. OSHA had not yet arrived on the scene. Although Mr. Fuller gave each of them a safety belt, he did so with the warning that it might be better not to use it since, when it was unhitched and dangling from a belt, it could come in contact with a high-tension line and, well, "that wouldn't be good." Bernard later read in a clipping shown to him by an older employee just how "not good" that could be: Fuller-Holstein had lost one of its men two years before when he painted too close to a high-tension line. According to the article, the electricity hit the metal on the man's paintbrush, pulling him against the wire. A fellow employee described the man as "a ball of fire" falling from the tower. The older man said, "I wouldn't paint that stuff for one hundred dollars a foot." Bernard and George Harder would learn later that they were the only ones who did the high-wire work—and also that the turnover, like the work, was high.

Within the first few minutes on the job, Bernard knew it was not for him. Butterflies it would seem are impervious to heights, fluttering blithely among treetops on their diaphanous wings. But in Bernard's abdomen, one hundred feet in the air, with no safety net. . . .

He had climbed up to reach the crossing spans that carried the high-tension lines, rarely looking down. To ensure no one, particularly children, would climb the towers, there were no steps or rungs, which meant climbing up by hand—a challenge, considering the slippery fisholene covering the strands. The high-tension lines on the side of the tower that required painting had been turned off, but the ones attached to the spans on the other side of the tower some ten feet away remained very much on. The steel cables carrying 140,000 watts of electricity had a distinctive hot odor and emitted a low humming sound, a constant reminder of the fate of one of Mr. Holstein's former employees.

Bernard glanced over at George on a nearby tower. He was clutching a steel girder tightly with one arm while painting with the other. It seemed he was painting right over his arm rather than risk taking a new grip. Bernard resolved to stay on the job until lunchtime and then quit, reasoning he could get paid for half a day. At lunchtime, however, when George suggested they finish the day to ensure being paid, he reluctantly agreed. By 5 p.m., Bernard had become a bit more adjusted to the heights and when George suggested they come back for one more day—the pay was really good—Bernard said he'd think about it.

But having slithered through the steel frames covered with fisholene (clothes had to be thrown away at the end of each day), Bernard was ambivalent about returning. As they walked from the site, they carried with them the reek of decaying fish. By this point their olfactory senses had been dulled by a day of exposure, which was not the case for the standing-room-only commuter bus that they boarded to go home. "My God!" . . . "What the hell is this!" exclaimed distraught passengers, crowding to the rear to avoid contact with the fisholene twosome. The following night, after surviving a second day on the job, a confrontation with these same passengers was avoided when the bus sailed by them without slowing. George was incensed. "That bastard! He saw us! I'm going to report this!"

he shouted after the disappearing bus. "You're right," said Bernard. "He saw us. We should have stood behind the sign until the bus stopped."

The job lasted but a short time. Both George and Bernard concluded that while the pay was great (Bernard was able to buy a used Ford roadster with the money), the work did not offer a promising future. Indeed, some of the towers they painted were in an Albany cemetery, where occasional funerals provided a memento mori.

13

Cool Kate

WITH MILITARY service behind him and the G.I. Bill offering veterans college tuition plus seventy-five dollars per month living allowance, Bernard turned his attention to education. Because he had been the beneficiary of considerable kindness from his headmaster, Harry Meislahn, a Princeton alumnus, Princeton seemed the logical place. He was aware that his football accomplishments in high school and the service were of interest to Princeton's coach, Charlie Caldwell. Although it was too late to be admitted for that school year, armed with generous comments from Coach Morris and Mr. Meislahn, he traveled to Princeton on two occasions to meet with school officials, including Dean Hermance, the dean of admissions, to apply for admission in the following academic year. About the same time, a friend from high school suggested they work out with the football team at St. Lawrence University in Canton, New York, where his friend was acquainted with the assistant coach. It seemed a good way to stay in shape, and Bernard would find it offered other opportunities as well. He learned that while college football rules at that time precluded freshmen from playing on the varsity team, in effect limiting players to three years of actual intercollegiate football, one could still take advantage of the G.I. Bill and its living allowance.

Bernard was uncertain when first arriving on the St. Lawrence campus. How would this affect his hopes for Princeton? The answer came quickly in the form of an attractive seventeen-year-old named Catherine Connors—the same last name as his but spelled with an "o"—whom he met on a double date shortly after arriving at St. Lawrence. Within a few weeks Bernard was in love. In the mind of a twenty-year-old captivated by newfound romance, thoughts of faraway Princeton, New Jersey, began to fade.

Bernard had dated several girls before then, high school sweethearts who were special. But there had never been anyone like Catherine Connors. He soon learned that her father's name was Bernard Connors, and then several dates later that her mother's name was Sarah, the same as *his* mother's. It was the start of an emotional relationship that increased in intensity with passing months. Any ambivalence about enrolling at St. Lawrence was gone with the wind that often swept the campus. And if the weather was often cold on the North Country tundra, it was more than offset by the ardent relationship that developed between the two classmates. Bernard enrolled in all Catherine's classes and often sat next to her when seats were assigned alphabetically. One professor took him aside one day and said, "I'm afraid I'm going to have to split you two up. The way you hold hands and whisper is distracting."

Things did not go well on the football field. As the quarterback of the freshman team, Bernard received considerable attention from New York's North Country press as well as the university newspaper. He enjoyed a good relationship with his freshman coach, an affable man named Chuck Patricia, who was popular with the players. This warm coach/player relationship did not carry over with the head coach, Paul Patten. The freshman team, which was exceptionally good, often scrimmaged against the varsity squad, and it was obvious to the coaches and spectators that the freshmen—many of them older veterans—were far superior. With little pressure from opposing linemen, it was an ideal situation for a quarterback such as Bernard, who liked to run as well as throw, and he made the most of it. But he sensed early on that neither his style of play nor the attention he was receiving sat well with Patten.

There were other circumstances as well that Patten had reason to disapprove of Bernard. One day Bernard was delayed with Kate and late for practice. Patten was waiting for him in front of several other players when he arrived on the field. Bernard stumbled through some excuse. "I'm sorry, sir"—he always used lots of "sirs" with the coach, a carryover from the military—"I had a car problem!" Patten didn't buy the reason. The coach took his measure for a moment and then said derisively, "Conners, you're bleeding! Take ten laps," dismissing Bernard with a motion toward the quarter-mile track that surrounded one of the fields. Bernard was puzzled by the bleeding comment until one of the players pulled him aside and said, "Hell, you've got freaking lipstick all over your face!"

But Bernard soon realized he didn't fit into the man's style of offense. Patten wanted a pocket quarterback who'd step up into the face of charging defensive linemen. Well, that didn't work for the Butterflies who were averse to being trampled by 270-pound behemoths. Bernard was fast and agile for about eighty yards or so; after that a lumbering lineman might catch him. But because of his speed and agility, he felt comfortable avoiding any pass rush by rolling out and throwing, or making long yardage by just running. His mobility and strong arm were his outstanding features while playing in high school and the service.

Practices at the college were often held at night under lights, and one night in order to keep Bernard in a drop-back position, the coach came up from behind and held him in the pocket in the face of blitzing linemen. Bernard didn't realize he was going to do it, nor did anyone else. Both of them were crushed. "Damn it, Coach!" Bernard exclaimed crawling to his feet. "You trying to get us killed?" He didn't say "sir" and the confrontation did little to help their festering relationship.

Patten also thought Bernard threw the ball too hard. Once he became very upset and lined up receivers, having them roll out fifteen to twenty yards and telling Bernard to throw at them as hard as he could. It was much too close and Bernard, afraid of breaking someone's fingers, took something off the ball. "Harder!" Patten kept yelling, his voice heavy with sarcasm. "Harder!" Obviously, his intent was to show the futility of throwing too hard.

And so it went. By the end of spring training in his freshman year—the period spent preparing the team for the following fall—Bernard was the fourth-string quarterback with little prospect of advancing. He was reconciled to the bench for the final spring game. Mortified, he was tempted to try to reestablish the contact with Charlie Caldwell at Princeton. Moreover, the St. Lawrence athletic director, Roy Clogston, had become the athletic director at North Carolina State and suggested to Bernard that they had a fine football program. The thought of leaving Catherine was intolerable, however. She had become the bedrock of his college existence—far more important than football. She was not only pretty with a lovely figure and adorable manner, she was also a straight-A student who would graduate Phi Beta Kappa, and would later achieve academic excellence at Columbia and Ohio State graduate schools.

Bernard continued his writing, publishing short stories in the university magazine, *The Laurentian.* His English teachers were supportive, including one in particular, Margo Burrell, who praised his work effusively. "Someday I shall be reading your stories in *Harper's,*" she wrote on one of his papers.

Although the G.I. Bill paid his tuition plus seventy-five dollars a month allowance, it hardly covered Bernard's living expenses. He worked at a number of jobs at various times to cover the shortfall. This included setting up pins in a bowling alley, working as a short-order cook in a restaurant, and waiting on tables. He finally inherited a sandwich business from two fraternity brothers who were graduating. It proved to be a lifesaver. Not only was he able to buy a better car, he could then send money home to his mother. The business consisted of selling sandwiches to students in the dormitories and fraternity houses that surrounded the campus. Kate, who had a radio program on the local college station, KSLU, provided advertising for the business. The ads were short and to the point, including the following song:

Hell-o everybody! Hell-o!
It's the sandwich man
On your ra-di-o
Hell-o everybody! Hell-o!
Cheese and ham
The sandwich man
Through rain or sleet or snow!

The sandwiches were no better than the advertising copy. One night standing at the bottom of the stairs in a dorm, Bernard was hit on the head with a sandwich by a disgusted customer hiding at the top of the stairs. A sneak attack, probably deserved: the item thrown at him consisted of the paper wrapper and two slices of bread, the actual ingredients inadvertently left out. Quality control was definitely lacking. Such *faux pas* in no way diminished the entrepreneurial spirit. Indeed, Bernard considered expanding the business to a nearby girls' school. Such was the whimsy of the sandwich man.

14

Cooler Mother-in-Law

"HE *LOOKS* like a boxer."

First impressions are important, particularly when it involves a girlfriend's mother. It was sometime after Catherine and Bernard had started dating, and Sarah Connors had come to St. Lawrence to visit her daughter. Catherine had introduced Bernard to her mother on campus. It was a short meeting and Bernard found the encounter intimidating. Mrs. Connors was a tall, attractive, exceedingly confident woman in her early forties, of few words, who gave little indication of being impressed by her daughter's latest boyfriend. After a brief conversation, the meeting was concluded, and she was off to pursue the main purpose of her trip to the campus: to insure that her seventeen-year-old daughter was ensconced in a suitable environment that conformed to Sarah Connors's parochial, ultra-conservative world.

It was a perfunctory meeting and Bernard didn't come away with the feeling she was thrilled with her daughter's new boyfriend. His impression was confirmed later by Catherine, who said that her mother thought he *looked* like a boxer. "That was it?" Bernard said, chagrined. "Nothing else?"

"Well, I can't remember right now," said Kate, always tactful. "I think she liked you. . . ."

It was less than a ringing endorsement, but Bernard was already learning that Catherine Connors was honest to the core. Unlike her new boyfriend, she was incapable of embellishing something just to avoid an awkward situation. This first encounter with Catherine's mother was the start of a cool relationship that would last many years.

Sarah was a woman of great character. There was not an ounce of disingenuousness in her tall frame. One knew exactly how she stood on everything, and she had no difficulty at all telling anyone just *how* she stood on everything! Once while talking to Catherine about Bernard she said, "He'll never have a dime!" Despite this, years later she wrote a big check for him to buy some soft drink companies. It was incredibly generous of Sarah. Bernard had few credentials to handle the soft drink business. Sarah must have thought at the time, "Well, here goes a small fortune!" Bernard did pay every dime back, though—at eight percent interest—even though she never asked for it. Although she was very good to him, Bernard felt she preferred Kate's many hometown boyfriends.

Regardless of her feelings, she was there for Bernard when he needed her. He did try to reciprocate years later when living alone became problematical for her. He earnestly tried to have her come to live with Catherine and him. She declined. Discomforting thoughts of sharing breakfast with Bernard may have contributed to her resolve to go it alone, until she finally passed away at ninety-three. She managed her waning years as she managed everything. Independent, confident, composed to the very end. A strong woman.

15

Quarterback No More

AT THE end of his college freshman year Bernard found summer employment at the Lake Placid Club in northern New York. It was a luxurious resort to which people came from throughout the world, many from New York City. Gregory Peck, the movie star, Sherman Billingsley, who owned the famous Stork Club in New York City, and Henry Kaiser, the shipbuilding magnate, were among the many prominent persons who took advantage of its well-appointed facilities. There were three golf courses, tennis courts, an enormous library, and a spacious theater. Thirty-three waitresses served guests in its large dining room and it was here that Bernard started as a busboy. The waitresses and busboys were mostly college students, and those in management treated the staff almost parentally. Employees lived in dorms on the property and had the use of the recreational facilities, provided they didn't interfere with the guests.

Bernard's roommate in the dorm was an engaging young man who interacted with members who had minor problems—sort of a low-level concierge. He was well equipped for the job. Personable, soft spoken, a certain hauteur including a patrician accent that would surface as the occasion warranted. To say that he was a trifle disingenuous at times would be charitable. But it worked. He somehow managed to appease the most obstreperous guests. Bernard recalled hearing him on the phone one night after he'd been awakened by an irritated lady who had lost her baggage. "I understand, madam," he said in a soothing tone as he slipped into his affected accent. "I too have had difficulty with my luggage." His "luggage," like Bernard's, consisted of a worn duffel bag. Yet in no time he had the woman apologizing for intruding on his evening. "Of course, madam. That's perfectly all right. I shall look into the matter the first thing on arising." After softly replacing the phone he said, "That old bitch! Doesn't she realize even those of us in steerage have a right to sleep!"

Bernard enjoyed his job in the dining room, particularly his association with the waitresses, many of whom were quite attractive. Whoever hired the staff had an eye for pretty girls. But later, when offered the position of assistant lifeguard on the waterfront, he didn't hesitate. When the head lifeguard left shortly after Bernard joined the crew, he was appointed to take his place. The lifeguard was in charge of the waterfront staff, which consisted of the lifeguard, the assistant lifeguard, a towel man, and a boat man who handled a number of sailboats and canoes. The waterfront employees were quartered comfortably by themselves in a boathouse on the lake. When the assistant lifeguard graduated from college and left, Bernard asked his boss, George Carroll, the secretary of the club, if he could hire his girlfriend, Catherine, as the assistant lifeguard. Mr. Carroll was an amiable, understanding man who treated employees like he was their kindly grandfather. Bernard sensed he was always a bit nervous around the water. If Mr. Carroll could have run a lakeside resort without the benefit of the lake he would have been happier. Bernard told him about Catherine, stressing her qualifications. At the time, she was the lifeguard at a park near

Lake Placid. Actually, she was an accredited instructor who had administered Bernard's tests and secured lifeguard credentials for him. "She'll have her own quarters on the lake," he assured Mr. Carroll.

Although dubious at first, Mr. Carroll finally assented. "All right, I guess it will be okay. I have confidence in you, Bernard." It was not a confidence shared by Catherine's mother. She was not inclined to let her daughter spend her summer alone on the beach with four young males. Sarah's reaction brought a bear-trap closure to Bernard's summer aspirations.

With the fall season, Bernard was back at St. Lawrence. Football continued to go poorly, Coach Patten having relegated him to only an occasional appearance. Several teammates, complimenting Bernard on his ability, asked him why he didn't just transfer to another school. One mentioned that he heard the Colgate coach had inquired about him after a game between the schools in which Bernard had excelled. His previous trips to Princeton had solicited some interest as well, but there had never been any assurances that he would be admitted. Both opportunities now seemed remote given his present position as fourth-string quarterback. It was frustrating for Bernard, and he was on the verge of quitting. The sandwich business, writing for the school magazine, studies, time with Kate . . . all were taking their toll.

One night under the lights while standing on the sidelines during a scrimmage he expressed his disappointment to Coach Patricia, who was now a varsity backfield coach. He asked if he could try out as a running back. At first Coach Patricia was dubious but, after a time-out on the field, with a cautious look toward Coach Patten, he sent Bernard into the game. It was the start of a new phase of football for a former quarterback. Bernard was determined to do well, and had an extraordinary night.

Although the running back position was new for him, Bernard adjusted to the role and with Patten's sober approval he was soon in the starting lineup. Playing directly behind a standout guard named Jack Barron, who consistently opened gaping holes in defensive lines, Bernard was soon being touted by newspapers as a leading rusher.

> In second place, only three yards behind, was the sophomore sensation, Bernie Conners, who started the season as a fourth-string quarterback. Conners picked up 233 yards rushing as a left halfback, and added 54 with forward passes for his total of 287.

It was a bittersweet accomplishment. The talent for which he had received the most acclaim to that point in his career was his ability to throw a football. But Patten's offense, built around a drop-back "pocket" quarterback, was loathed by the Butterflies. The coach wanted a controlled steady player at the key position, not some unanchored individual who ran all over the field and confused blocking assignments. He found such a player in Jack O'Loughlin, an outstanding athlete, popular with teammates, and a gifted leader as quarterback. Bernard understood. But he rarely threw the ball in his new position, and realized it deprived him of a promising career as a college quarterback. Yet he had few reasons to complain, receiving recognition after eight games as one of the country's leading ground gainers on the best small-college team in the nation. Before Bernard graduated, Paul Patten allowed somewhat remorsefully that they had made a mistake in not using Conners to his full potential.

Bernard received considerable press in his new position. The following newspaper article mentioned his change in position, although it miscast him as having been a third-string rather than fourth-string quarterback:

> **The outstanding star of a team not built on the star pattern, Bernie Conners, began his career as an unimposing third string quarterback last year. Conners now rates with the best in the country as a running back.**

Bernard sensed from his comments that the coach was somewhat ambivalent about the attention his running back was receiving. Patten fostered a team approach, which worked well and which received favorable write-ups in the press.

> Offense and teamwork were the watchwords this year, as 28-year-old Coach Paul E. Patten moulded a unit in which every man was a potential star but none was ever pushed into the limelight at the expense of the team.

At the time Bernard was receiving considerable press as a Little All-American, and he sometimes wondered how the coverage comported with Patten's team approach.

At the start of his senior year—a time when Bernard anticipated receiving considerable national attention—his football aspirations were thwarted. Patten's rigorous training methods were highly unusual. Fierce scrimmages were part of the daily schedule, routines resulting in many injuries. Bernard was no exception. As a running back he took far more hits than he would have as quarterback. The following article appeared in a North Country newspaper:

BERNIE CONNERS, S.L.U. GRID STAR FRACTURES ANKLE IN DRILL

St. Lawrence University's first undefeated, untied season in 50 years of college football vanished like fog in the morning sun Saturday, after a grueling, two-hour scrimmage had all but decimated the 43 man squad.

Worst news at the end of the Larries' blackest Saturday was that Bernie Conners, the Albany left halfback and Little All-America candidate, had broken a bone in his left ankle and will not play football this year. Conners led the team in scoring with nine touchdowns last year, and in yards gained 939 in 120 plays. He was the one man who could be depended upon, almost without fail, to pick up those precious extra feet needed for a first down or a touchdown, and his loss will cripple the Larries as no other casualty might do.

But there were no recriminations from Bernard. He still had Kate. Some years later, when Bernard was inducted into the St. Lawrence University Athletic Hall of Fame, he was asked to comment about his time at the university. The following appeared in one of the school's publications:

St. Lawrence was the bedrock of my life. It was here in my freshman year that I met Catherine Connors, whom I later married, a union that resulted in three children, two of whom also graduated from St. Lawrence. It was here that I received much encouragement to become a writer from my gifted English Professor, Margo Burrell. It was here, also, that I received what I consider to have been the most important testimonial in my life when Dean George Brown informed the FBI during my application to this agency that he would give me 'the highest recommendation of anyone in the Class of 1951.'

Although Bernard would never achieve his dreams as a college quarterback, he recognized that his perceived skills may well have proven deficient at a major college, whereas the lasting family values derived from St. Lawrence could never be diminished.

16

G-Man versus Army Officer

WITH GRADUATION from college came important new decisions. The Korean War was underway at the time and, as a member of the army reserve, Bernard faced a recall to active duty. Jack Barron, the close friend with whom he had played football, suggested he apply to the FBI. Jack had been accepted as a Bureau agent the year before, and supplied the application. Having already served in World War II, Bernard regarded the FBI as a preferable career choice. The accomplishments of J. Edgar Hoover and his G-men had been extolled in film and the press, and the reputation of the agency was at an all-time high. Bernard's preference for the FBI over the army was not understood by everyone. This was made clear to him years later in a meeting with General Westmoreland, who had commanded our troops in Vietnam.

A friend of Bernard's named David Traub, who had been a lieutenant general and comptroller of the army, invited him to meet General Westmoreland. Both Traub and Westmoreland had graduated from West Point and were stalwart professionals, particularly General Traub, who had rather strong opinions about the military. After Traub introduced him to Westmoreland, they were making small talk when Bernard allowed that the FBI had seemed a better career choice for him than the military after his college graduation.

General Traub took issue with Bernard's decision, citing the advantages of a military career. General Westmoreland, an amiable man, smiled, and they moved along to less contentious subjects. It was a pleasant meeting with Westmoreland, and Bernard was greatly impressed by the man's charm and overall demeanor.

Bernard did not mention it to Westmoreland, but shortly after college graduation he was reactivated in the army subject to his acceptance in the FBI to which he had already applied. He was sent to Camp Gordon, Georgia, where he served while waiting to hear from the Bureau as his application was being processed. Having undergone oral, written, and physical examinations, he had been advised by the FBI that a full-field investigation of his background was underway. He hoped that his military specialty, which at the time was criminal investigating officer, would enhance his chances of acceptance. Shortly thereafter he received notice of his appointment to the FBI, and the cancellation of his orders to active duty. Within a few weeks he was in Washington, where he was sworn in as a special agent.

Part IV

17

Introduction to J. Edgar

BERNARD was thrilled by his appointment to the FBI. Although he had little knowledge of what awaited him in the Bureau, stories of winter combat in Korea, where the casualty rate for lieutenants was exceedingly high, confirmed he had made the right choice. He occasionally heard news of individuals with whom he had previously served in the military who were casualties in Korea. Among these was General Bryant Moore, his division commander, who was killed in a helicopter crash.

Although not nearly as severe as the toughening-up process that troops had to undergo at Camp Blanding in preparation for the invasion of Japan, the FBI training for new agents in Washington was challenging both intellectually and psychologically. (Many of these activities were later described by Bernard in a novel, described by some critics as a "roman à clef," portions of which appear in the following text.)

Much of the pressure derived from the tenuous nature of a new agent's appointment. Some of the applicants during this period were individuals who preferred government service in the FBI rather than the military. Because of the large number of applicants, the Bureau was more selective than usual, and that was made clear at the inception of the training. The passing grade on all tests was eighty-five. Failure was not tolerated and the specter of a return to the military ensured Bernard was prepared. It was a six-day week with Sundays consumed by study, always trying to catch up. Each day began at 6 a.m., with evenings devoted to cramming for possible examinations in the form of blue pamphlets that were unannounced. One always had to be ready for the unexpected.

The days dragged by, each promising its own unique and sometimes traumatic experience. It was an exhausting schedule, covering subjects pertaining to all aspects of crime detection, federal criminal procedure, and counterespionage. Tours of the FBI laboratory and the local field office, as well as trips to remote sections of Washington where surveillance techniques or double-agent contacts were practiced, helped to break the monotony, but mostly it was long, tedious hours of classroom lectures and note-taking.

Instruction at the FBI Academy on the Marine Corps base at Quantico, Virginia, which came toward the end of the training, was demanding, but a relief from the daily classroom activity. Here agents were subjected to rigorous courses in firearms and defensive tactics—moves designed to ward off assailants or to handle recalcitrant subjects who posed physical threats. It was the latter training that Bernard questioned. Most of the instruction received to that point had seemed valuable and necessary, but the karate-like moves sometimes appeared impractical unless implemented by a highly trained tactician. The instructor in charge of the program was assisted by a hulking individual who had an extraordinary ability to propel himself into the air and to land with a resounding whack on the mat. The two of them were a symphony of movement, falling in and out of grips with the grace of a veteran dance team. Bernard appreciated the artistry but, as a former fighter, questioned whether the elaborate choreography would actually be effective in combat.

Overseeing the new agents' class was an affable man named Ed Timmons, an individual whom Bernard would come to like and respect. He was a tall, broad-shouldered man, with dark, graying hair, a swarthy complexion, and a kind, rugged face. Ed shared Bernard's belief that it was important to be liked by virtually everyone. One of his favorite comments was, "You can send a man away for twenty years, and if you handle it right, he'll think you're the greatest guy in the world."

The pressure mounted with the passing weeks. By the fourth month four agents had been rejected. No reason was ever given. One morning there would be an empty desk and Ed Timmons would simply say, "All right men, everyone move over one seat," and that would be that. Friends of the departed knew only that the man said he was leaving. Such departures made the study lamps of the remaining agents burn longer.

Bernard's Butterflies were particularly agitated by the thought of impending interviews with Bureau officials. The door in the rear of the room would squeak open, a man would enter, whisper to the instructor, and a new agent would gather his things for the unenviable trek to the Justice Building, where the Bureau executive offices were located. Generally, but not always, the agent came back. It seemed to Bernard that they should stand and shake his hand when an agent returned.

The daily format continued to be unpredictable. The class might be engrossed in study when suddenly in would come two men distributing blue booklets. Mimeographed sheets would soon follow, containing questions requiring comprehensive answers. There would be an hour or so of intense silence, broken only by the sound of scribbling pencils as elusive answers were cornered in weary minds and quickly tumbled into the blue booklets. As the days passed and the training gradually drew to a close, the meeting with the Director loomed as the biggest hurdle. It seemed any type of meeting with "The Man" was fraught with uncertainty, not only for new agents but for just about anyone in the organization.

"It looks like tomorrow's the day," said Ed Timmons one morning near the end of training. He paused and looked at the class apprehensively. Yes, tomorrow was the day when the Director would personally inspect the class and render his impressions of the twenty men who remained. If he liked what he saw, everything would be just dandy. If he did not, well. . . .

It was a somber group that left the classroom in the old Post Office building on Pennsylvania Avenue the following day. In their dark suits, hats, white shirts, and conservative ties they could well have been mistaken for a funeral procession during the short walk to the Director's office in the Justice Building. When they entered the building, a uniformed guard took them to a bank of elevators, where two elevators that had been reserved for the class opened as they approached. Bernard was amazed at the precision of everything: it seemed nothing in the organization was ever out of kilter. Nothing was late. Equipment never failed. No one made mistakes. The Bureau behaved as an elaborate, finely tuned engine comprised of many intricate mechanisms requiring a precise performance from each, lest the entire machine go awry. The man at the top demanded perfection and it was reflected at every level.

The men were carried smoothly to the eighth floor, a slight humming noise being the only thing that suggested they were moving at all. Following the counselor, they moved silently down an immaculate corridor, finally stopping before a door on which was printed in black letters, "DIRECTOR, FEDERAL BUREAU OF INVESTIGATION."

As they approached the entrance, Bernard could see a group of silent, formal older men just inside the Director's office, who appeared to be engaged in serious business. At the door a man stepped aside and motioned Ed Timmons inside. The class quickly followed the counselor into a large room with Edwardian furnishings. It was a cheerless ambiance. Although there were a half dozen Bureau officials standing about, Bernard's eyes riveted immediately on a figure in a dark suit. There was no mistaking Mr. Hoover. Bernard was introduced and received a clipped "Pleased to meet you!" from the Director. There was little fallout following the meeting—unlike one with a previous class Hoover had viewed with something less than enthusiasm. His withering appraisal had culminated in the comment, "They look like a bunch of floor walkers from a department store!"

During a break late in the afternoon that day, Bernard, deep in thought, was resting his elbows on a brass railing outside the classroom when a classmate appeared at his side. "Rough day," said the agent. Bernard looked at him briefly without answering. "Hear about the affair in the LA office?" continued the man. Bernard shook his head. "Seems three agents were renting an apartment together, and after they moved out, the landlord called the office about some mail or something. Anyway, he mentions that one of the agents had been peeing in bed."

"So?" Bernard looked up at him quizzically.

"So, now there's an investigation to see who peed in bed," the man shrugged. "You know, it could embarrass the Bureau."

The next day, although laden with several pistols and sets of credentials, Ed Timmons almost floated into the room. "Good morning, good morning." It was actually the best one in six months, and Ed was having difficulty containing his enthusiasm. Holding up a sheaf of papers he said, "Here we are, gentlemen, first office assignments." The class immediately fell silent with anticipation. Amid much groaning and joking, the list was read. Invariably the agents from the East were sent to the West, while those from the North received assignment in the South and vice versa. Few in the class were pleased with their lot. Bernard was assigned to Albuquerque, New Mexico.

Ed presented each agent with credentials, a Smith and Wesson revolver with six shiny silver bullets, and a firm handshake. Then, picking up his papers from the lectern preparing to leave, he offered what perhaps was his most sincere comment at the training school. "The best advice I can give you fellows is this. Remember, you're a second-class citizen and have damn few rights. You rarely get a second chance in this outfit. If you screw up, then you're all through. You've got to understand that as long as you're an agent, the Bureau owns you body and soul. As far as the agents themselves are concerned, you'll never meet a nicer group of men anywhere. The work itself isn't that dangerous, but when it comes to Bureau personnel policy, then gents, you've got the most dangerous job in the world. So good luck, and remember, don't embarrass the Bureau. The job you save may be your counselor's."

After this final admonition, Ed gathered his papers and was preparing to leave when a friend of his entered from the rear door. He and Ed spoke briefly and shook hands, and the man was on his way out when he paused and glanced at the ceiling. "I see they haven't installed the sprinklers yet," he said.

"Sprinklers?" asked Ed.

"Yeah," said the man. "That way the Bureau can piss on you all at the same time!"

Ed glanced nervously at the rear door, as hushed laughter rippled through the class.

18

Through the Looking Glass

ELSTON DOOLITTLE, special agent in charge of the Albuquerque field office, was a large man towering some six feet four inches above his size fourteen double E's with a frame that indicated problems with the Director's weight chart (a plan formulated at the seat of government to ensure agents remained trim). Doolittle was well aware of the precarious nature of his job, and his conservative approach to all phases of Bureau work had served him well. Nor did his cautious approach vary when it came to new agents. As did most special agents in charge (referred to as SACs), Doolittle likened his position to a man rowing a round-bottomed boat in turbulent waters, and a trait he appreciated in any passenger was the ability to sit quietly—a quality notably lacking in rookies. And so it was by reflex one morning that after his secretary had announced Bernard's arrival, the SAC reached into the drawer of his desk for the antacids.

"Well, now, it's good to see you," he lied to Bernard, resuming his chair after shaking hands. "How was your trip out?"

"Pretty good, sir," said Bernard. "Until we got over the mountains. Then it was pretty rough. I'm afraid I got a little airsick."

There followed a few minutes of somewhat strained conversation as the SAC sized up his new passenger. He was not pleased. A young, single agent had to be bad news. Somebody's wife might fall in love with him, or he'd end up getting some steno in trouble. It was times like this when Doolittle took comfort from his controversial policy of hiring only unattractive women. "Show me a plain-looking girl and I'll show you a good girl," he was fond of saying, "a good, honest, hardworking girl who isn't going to get involved with some agent and screw us all up and get us all transferred. Besides, they don't run off and get married as soon as you get them trained." Indeed, the Albuquerque steno pool and clerical staff had one of the lowest turnover rates in the city and, in view of Doolittle's policy, it seemed nothing was going to alter this accomplishment.

Bernard shifted uneasily as Doolittle paused momentarily to prop his huge feet on the desk in front of him. Leaning far back in the chair, he clasped his hands behind his head and regarded the fledgling agent thoughtfully between the V-shaped sights formed by his crossed feet. In this position, he delivered the Doolittle interpretation of the *Manual of Rules and Regulations.*

For the first few months things went according to Doolittle's plan for first office agents. Bernard accompanied older agents on assignments and occasionally handled routine investigations by himself. Predictably, he was caught up with the power of his credentials, a folded black leather case stating that he was a special agent of the FBI and empowered to conduct investigations in which "the United States is, or may be, a party of interest." They were signed by J. Edgar Hoover, and in the lower corner was a picture of Bernard. They commanded immediate attention, and Bernard, young and unaccustomed to such respect, enjoyed displaying them. One day, he was doing a neighborhood investigation, covering innocuous leads on a minor fugitive, when an elderly woman answered his knock. "I'm Agent Conners of the FBI," he said, showing the credentials. "I'm looking for a dangerous fugitive reportedly seen in this area." The woman studied his picture for a moment, then said, "No, young man, I've never seen him. He certainly is ugly though, isn't he!" Back in his car, Bernard took a hard look at his picture.

Bernard, handling rudimentary leads such as record checking and applicant investigations, had become acquainted with the other agents. There were nine assigned to the headquarters in Albuquerque—all old-timers who had finally made it to their office of preference. To a man, they demonstrated qualities essential to the operation of Doolittle's shaky boat, and they greeted Bernard with all the welcome of a late arrival in a crowded life raft. "Like a bunch of old grannies pickling preserves for a church bazaar," he confided to one of the young clerks, who promptly reported the observation to one of the grannies.

It was not until early one morning near the end of his fourteenth week in Albuquerque that Bernard received any significant assignment. Because he was the only single agent in the office, he had often been dispatched on routine leads to various parts of the Southwest, boring trips that usually entailed bumpy flights over mountainous terrain, which made him airsick. It wasn't long before stewardesses knew him, and often greeted him facetiously with airsick bags and cold compresses for his forehead. Bernard made the most of such contacts, compiling a virtual phone book of names throughout the Southwest.

His first significant assignment took him to Las Cruces, New Mexico, where he was greeted at the airport by the resident agent who covered that part of the state. Standing seventy-four inches to the brim of his broad Stetson, his hand outstretched, and a wide welcoming smile creasing his ruggedly handsome face was Bob O'Rourke, a third-generation New York Irishman who had found the Southwest much to his liking. The initial conversation and enthusiastic handshake reflected a genuine cordiality, and Bernard's impression was that, unlike the old-timers in Albuquerque, Agent O'Rourke was glad to see him.

"The car's over this way," the agent said, taking the bag from Bernard's hand and starting toward the parking lot. "I've got a surveillance going at the Regency Hotel, a prostitution case on a subject named Pinky Miller. He's running these high-priced prostitutes all over the Southwest. They know me at the hotel, so you'll have to conduct the surveillance. I've developed the bell captain as an informant. He's got you planted in the room next to the subject's girlfriend—a hustler named Cyndy Powers. Very special. Terrific-looking babe. The informant's fixed it so you can cover her room. Both rooms have medicine cabinets, and they're back to back, only the mirror on her side is two-way. When you open the cabinet on your side, you'll see a small screw hole. You can look through there and catch all the action. I've got a radio for you in the car. After each trick you radio the description of the john to me. I'll be a block or so away with a state cop. We'll pick up the johns and get statements from them. We want to develop any evidence we can showing Pinky is transporting her across state lines for purposes of prostitution."

The Regency was one of the foremost luxury hotels in New Mexico, but the wing to which Bernard was led by the informant was of an earlier period and had not been renovated. After a final comment concerning his availability, the informant was gone. Loosening his tie, Bernard sat down on the edge of the bed. The sound of a voice laughing in the next room caught his attention. Rising, he walked to the medicine cabinet, and cautiously opened the door. A small stream of light came through the screw hole in the right side of the interior. Bernard pushed his head into the cabinet and put his eye to the hole. At first, to Bernard it seemed like watching a pornographic movie, but after a few nights it became wearisome, as were most physical and technical surveillances. Other than an education in people's sexual proclivities, and a certain admiration for Cyndy Powers's contortions—it crossed his mind that she might make a good gymnast—he soon lost interest.

It was almost two weeks before Elston Doolittle became aware of Bernard's assignment. "God Almighty!" he hissed at Joe Holloway, his assistant agent in charge. "How long has that case been going on?"

"But, Chief, this isn't just an ordinary white-slave case. The thing has gotten real big. This guy Miller is an international pimp, and the Mexican authorities claim there's narcotics involved."

"If there's narcotics, why don't we refer it to the Bureau of Narcotics? We need more closed cases 'round here. Our statistics have been off for two months. At any rate, you shouldn't have put that young agent down there. I don't like this one damn bit. Remember, don't let them use any technical surveillance equipment. Does the Bureau know they've got a two-way mirror? Good Lord, here we are tying up all our manpower peering through mirrors at people screwing, and we're getting absolutely nowhere on our major cases."

The white-slave case was soon closed out and Bernard was assigned routine leads at the White Sands Proving Ground. It was during the early 1950s at a time when Wernher von Braun and other German scientists were involved in rocket development for the US government. Von Braun was one of the leading scientists in the development of rocket technology, first in Nazi Germany and then the United States. Many of the early rocket experiments were conducted at the White Sands Proving Ground. Such efforts did not garner the approval of all who were associated with the endeavor.

"It's crazy! Downright crazy," said the security officer at White Sands with whom Bernard coordinated his leads on assignments. "This whole place could go up like that!" He snapped his fingers sharply. "They don't know what they're doing out there in those bunkers. . . . Experimenting with all those explosives. . . . They send those telephone poles up, and by the time they realize they're out of control and blow the head off, it's too late—they're hundreds of miles away. A few weeks ago one landed fifty yards from the guardhouse down there."

"You mean the guided missiles?" asked Bernard, surprised.

"Guided! Ha! A few months ago one ended up in a graveyard over in Juarez. You call that 'guided'? We've had a helluva time getting it back from the Mexican government. Those lousy Krauts out there—you can't trust the buggers. Goddamn independent, too. You'd think they won the war! If I had my way, I'd pack the buggers up and send 'em back to Germany."

It was a postwar sentiment likely shared by others on the base. But Bernard found the scientists, although reserved, cooperative and reasonably pleasant. While not as stimulating as some of the work with Bob O'Rourke, he found the experience at White Sands intriguing.

Bernard returned to Albuquerque to find an air of anxiety had engulfed the place. "The Goon Squad's coming in," said an agent. "The inspection team." Elston Doolittle had called for a meeting that evening, and several of the agents had already assembled in the squad room. Suddenly, 245 pounds of lumbering Doolittle appeared in the doorway. Within a few seconds the agents quieted down and Doolittle, in a voice heavy with foreboding, was delivering his traditional pre-inspection talk.

"Most of you have probably heard rumors about the inspection by this time. Well, all indications point to a tough one. But as I've always said, if you're doing things correctly, then you haven't a thing to worry about, right?" He paused and looked searchingly about the room for affirmation of his statement. Never was a man's gaze avoided more collectively as some two dozen eyes stayed riveted to the floor. Doolittle continued, shuffling several index cards on which were written his pre-inspection notes. "Now, start reviewing all your cases. Remember, a delinquent case is a dangerous case. It's bound to attract attention. Get something in the files to make them current. Insofar as informants are concerned, I expect each man to have at least one Potential Criminal Informant and one Potential Security Informant by the end of the month. The next subject is weight. It goes without saying that I expect to be looking at some pretty lean bodies around here within the next few weeks. Those of you who are borderline, and that's most everybody, should stop eating right *now!* And don't rely on gimmicks to pull you through. This stuff about enemas and the like the night before a weight check just doesn't work!" Doolittle's eyes probed the group, pausing significantly here and there on a drooping jowl or lumpy midriff. "There's absolutely no reason why we should be criticized for something like excess weight. I've been told a person can lose as much as twenty pounds in one week if need be. The main thing is we want to put our best foot forward."

The agents sat hushed and solemn, listening attentively. Doolittle concluded, "Remember, men, those of you who have been doing things the way they're supposed to be done don't have a solitary thing to worry about. Just stay on your toes, stay out of the office, and let's get these guys out of Albuquerque as soon as possible!" With a final solemn look he walked heavily from the room.

A buzz of excitement filled the room as Doolittle's assistant, Joe Holloway, stood up and moved uneasily toward the spot vacated by his leader. He always seemed uncomfortable following Doolittle, sensing the anticlimactic nature of his presence. Also, he usually had to field a multitude of questions precipitated by the chief's remarks.

"Hey, settle down! Take it easy, will you?" Joe looked anxiously over his shoulder toward the door where Doolittle had made his exit. "You all know what happened during the Detroit inspection last month. Transfers . . . suspensions!" As the grumbling subsided, Joe launched his own pre-inspection talk. "Now, like the Chief says, if we've all been doing things the way we're supposed to, we got nothing to worry about." After a slight roll of his eyeballs he continued. "First of all, stay out of the office. If you've seen all the movies, then go to the library or someplace. The main thing is stay the hell out of here. Now, you guys with no informants, you better contact a few bellhops pretty quick. Don't use the coffee shop around the corner or the one near the garage. Make your overtimes as legit as possible. In this connection, make sure your wives know you won't be coming home until later so they won't be flooding the office with phone calls looking for you. If you got any old-dog cases, try to get them closed out before the inspection. If an inspector should stop you and ask if you have any problems, obviously you don't. And remember, fellas, above all else, if they nail you, then go down like a man. Don't go grabbing at straws and pulling the rest of us down with you."

When the inspectors arrived in Albuquerque a short time later they found the office "buttoned down" in accordance with Doolittle's wishes. A few write-ups for delinquent cases and insufficient informants, and the Goon Squad was gone, happy to be out of Albuquerque.

19

Underwater at "Acapulco"

ON FREE DAYS Bernard often spent time at a swimming pool in Albuquerque called Acapulco. Among its many amenities was an Olympic three-meter board on which Bernard practiced diving. He was not an accomplished diver, but having been a gymnast, he enjoyed working on competitive dives such as gainers, molbergs, and twists, albeit with little of the symmetry displayed by advanced performers. He often used the board to practice on late afternoons when most patrons had left.

It was on one of these afternoons that his practicing unnerved the superintendent of the pool, an easygoing man who was generally tolerant of his guests. The one dive Bernard never had the courage to try was called a "spot." This entailed completing a full gainer, a backward somersault above the board, then landing on the board, and finishing with a one-and-a-half forward somersault into the water. The challenge was to achieve sufficient height to complete the gainer above the board and to land back on the board with enough stability to spring the board once again to complete the one-and-a-half. The danger, of course, was contact with the board if the gainer did not go well. Bernard had practiced the gainer above the board on many occasions, but lacked the confidence to come back down on the board, electing to keep enough distance to miss the board and land in the water. One afternoon he was springing the board, completing the gainer, and coming ever closer to the board as he came down, when the superintendent appeared. "Bernard, you're making people nervous." His intervention may have prevented a calamity. Bernard didn't have the skills for such a stunt, and contact with a diving board could prove disastrous.

But Acapulco offered less risky ventures. It was here that Bernard became acquainted with a number of young women, most of them students from the University of New Mexico, who congregated at one end of the pool on weekends. Bright girls, they eventually saw through Bernard's claim that he was an automotive supply salesman, not long after a locker room attendant saw him packing a .38 revolver while changing into his bathing suit. His cover was blown completely when he was observed checking records at the university registrar's office. Thereafter his new friends peppered him with questions, often teasing him about his FBI work.

It was during this time when the FBI had instituted its ten most wanted fugitives program, which gained wide media attention. Number one on the list was a notorious bank robber named Fred Tenuto. One afternoon, Bernard was signing in as required on the Acapulco guest register when his attention was drawn to the signature on the register above his. He was astonished to see the name clearly written, unlike most of the other scrawled indistinguishable signatures: *Fred Tenuto!* Bernard stared at the signature for a second or two before he realized what was happening. Then he heard the laughter coming from the group. Apparently he'd been signing in under "Fred Tenuto" for some time without noticing it. "We finally had to print Tenuto's name in bold letters," said one of the girls.

A member of the gathering named Sheldon, a handsome chap slightly older than Bernard, was particularly unrelenting thereafter regarding the perceptive abilities of FBI agents. A Princeton graduate with a sharp, imperious manner, he was popular with the young ladies. Bernard found himself ill prepared to cope with the man's cutting wit. A low-level banking executive, he said he could understand why Tenuto robbed banks, given the FBI's ineptitude. Bernard's feeble rejoinder that Tenuto probably found banks an easy target, in view of the wimps working there, elicited a snappish reply from Sheldon. "Speaking of employees, don't all you FBI agents come from those Irish Catholic schools in places like Albany—like that St. Albans seminary or wherever you went to school." It was a derisive reference to Bernard's college, St. Lawrence. (St. Lawrence was in fact founded in 1856 not by the Catholic but by the Universalist Church.) The comment drew snickers from the University of New Mexico coeds. One told Bernard that Sheldon often made sarcastic remarks about him—statements such as "I saw Bernard the other day. He had his gun, prayer book, and a bottle of milk, and was going to catch a criminal." Although Sheldon outgunned him with his repartee, Bernard found the man's company stimulating, if occasionally unnerving.

But the long, sunny days lounging with pretty girls at Acapulco would soon give way to the harsh reality of working in the FBI. Life-threatening events were waiting. . . .

20

Close Call

WITH PASSING months Bernard was assigned more important cases, some in the field of counterespionage. One involved the surveillance of a Soviet KGB agent in Taos, New Mexico, a small artists' colony located near a Navajo Indian reservation north of Santa Fe. It was a picturesque little place, the main part of which consisted of a small square just large enough to accommodate a dozen benches and, at the center, a statue of a Navajo warrior sitting languidly astride a pony. Bordering the park on four sides were cobblestone streets. Across the street on one side was a post office and a variety of art shops and quaint little stores, some of which dealt in Navajo blankets, jewelry, and other items from the nearby reservation.

Most of the people who frequented the square were Native Americans. Enshrouded in their traditional blankets, they walked lazily about the park, or sat quietly under their blankets on the block-like stoops of the adobe buildings. More often than not the loudest sound was the buzzing of a honey bee or the soft peeping of a bird. With its slow, easy pace and restful atmosphere, Taos was an ideal retreat for someone in need of relaxation. But for someone charged with trying to conduct a discreet surveillance on a highly sensitive Russian agent, it posed problems.

The Russian agent was expected to pick up a document at the post office on a specified afternoon. Bernard and another agent were to stake out the post office, and to follow the KGB agent to his expected destination near Santa Fe, which was believed to have been the collection point for stolen documents from the Manhattan Project (code name for the atomic bomb development). Through contacts at the post office it was arranged that a blind in the front window would be raised to signal when the Russian came for the document. Not being "made" or identified in such a place was almost impossible. Particularly when much of the populace were Navajos who wore dungarees, moccasins, and blankets over their heads. In the crosshairs of a tail-conscious enemy agent, two white males would be of interest.

The answer, of course, was a Navajo blanket, dungarees, and a pair of moccasins, which Bernard purchased at one of the stores. Thus "disguised," he sat at the base of the statue in the center of the park from where he could see the front window of the post office in the distance. Although a bit warm in the sun under the blanket, it was reasonably comfortable, so much so that after a few hours, as so often happens on surveillances, he began to doze. Suddenly he found himself peering into the inquisitive black eyes of a Navajo youngster. As Bernard quickly pulled the blanket over his face, they were joined by another Navajo child, then another, all crouched in front of him, regarding him with suspicion. Cover blown, Bernard had to move. Years later, he captured the scene in a drawing he did for the cover of his first novel. It was rejected by the publisher!

Book cover drawing by Bernard.

As for the surveillance, it almost ended in fatalities. Bernard and his fellow agent lost the Soviet operator shortly after he left Taos. Rushing to catch him, Bernard, who was driving, attempted to pass a truck that was pulling a horse trailer. They were traveling fast downhill. Bernard sounded the siren in the Bureau car and started to pass the truck when it pulled directly in front of him. There were three men in the cab of the truck, and later they said that none had heard the siren, and that they were making a left turn into an open field when the crash occurred. All three ended up in the hospital as well as the agent traveling with Bernard. It was amazing there were no fatalities. The Bureau car was totaled. Bernard managed to get out by kicking open a rear door and pulling out his fellow agent behind him. The officials conducting the subsequent investigation stated that after viewing the Bureau car they were surprised anyone survived. Considering the magnitude of the accident it was surprising there were no recriminations from the Bureau in Washington. Those in the truck assumed responsibility, stating they had pulled to the right and then made an illegal turn to the left.

But it was the state police investigation of the accident about which Bernard was concerned. Shortly before he had been assigned to Albuquerque, the first office agent who had preceded him had reported a civil rights violation on the part of the chief of the New Mexico state police, and a sheriff and his deputy in Las Cruces. The first office agent had reported that the sheriff had told him how he, his deputy, and the chief of the state police had extorted a confession from a black subject in a rape-homicide case by tightening a bicycle padlock around the subject's testicles. The victim of the rape and homicide was an attractive nineteen-year-old waitress named "Cricket" Coogler, who was known to socialize with the sheriff who was called "Happy" Apodaca. The first office agent had pursued the case, which resulted in the conviction of and prison sentences for the three officers involved. (The case was later retold in a feature-length film documentary in 2001, narrated by the Watergate figure John Ehrlichman.)

When he first arrived in Albuquerque, Bernard was told to be careful in his relations with the state police, since the chief's prosecution had caused considerable resentment. The rumor in the Albuquerque office was that "the state police were waiting to get an agent in the middle." Although acutely aware of the situation, Bernard had developed a good relationship with the state police, often staying overnight in their various barracks while on the road. He was greatly dependent on their cooperation, particularly during apprehension of service deserters, many of which cases he was assigned at the time. Although generally not dangerous, the cases required two apprehending officers; if one entered the front entrance where the fugitive was staying, the deserter might well be leaving through the rear door. While the cooperation of the state police was less important in the Albuquerque home office, on the road where Bernard was spending most of his time, it was essential. Notwithstanding what he perceived was a mutually respectful relationship, Bernard was apprehensive as the state police conducted their investigation of his car accident. Fortunately, they concluded that the truck driver had violated the law and there were no citations issued to Bernard.

As time passed, Bernard's assignments became more complex and interesting. Much of the research and development of the atomic bomb took place in the region, and his work inevitably dealt with counter-espionage matters. Los Alamos Laboratory, referred to as Project Y, was started during World War II to work on the Manhattan Project. It was the scene of infamous espionage cases involving the Russian spies Klaus Fuchs and David Greenglass, as well as Julius and Ethel Rosenberg. Able Site in the Sandia Mountains was one of the principle repositories for atomic weapons, and was of intense interest to the Soviets. Later, Bernard would identify aerial photographs of the Able Site taken by Vilyam Genrikhovich Fisher, a Russian agent whose code name was Rudolf Abel. Abel was apprehended by the FBI, imprisoned, and later exchanged for Francis Gary Powers, the American U-2 pilot shot down over the Soviet Union.

Although Bernard's role in the Abel case was peripheral, he was able to stay abreast of the circumstances surrounding the subject's apprehension and prosecution. Abel managed to win the grudging admiration of interviewing agents for his totally composed manner. Considerable psychological pressure was applied, but he was true to his profession and yielded little information. Following his exchange with Powers he returned to a hero's welcome in the Soviet Union. A commemorative stamp with his picture was issued in 1990 honoring his service. Much to the chagrin of those in the FBI, Abel would later write a memoir in which he described Bureau agents as bungling and inept, stating he managed to destroy secret information when the apprehending agents permitted him to use the lavatory. Possibly so. What did not appear in his memoir is that, unlike their counterparts in the Russian KGB, FBI agents are trained to respect all subjects' rights during interrogations. The concept of using torture to elicit information is totally rejected by the FBI. There are reported incidents of Bureau agents disengaging from cases where waterboarding or other so-called enhanced interrogation techniques were contemplated. Like most FBI personnel, Bernard believed that euphemisms for torture do not justify the practice and it should be prohibited. As a practical matter, those who have utilized such methods have found it largely ineffective in yielding information.

With the passage of time, Bernard's thoughts turned toward home. The barren landscape of the Southwest had become tiresome. He missed the change of seasons and the lush green countryside of the Northeast. Concerns about Kate, as well as his aging mother, prompted him to request an assignment closer to New York. The weeks passed and it was approaching spring by the time his request was acknowledged.

There is not a marked contrast between seasons in the Southwest. Summer fades into fall; fall quietly slips into winter. Seasonal changes are almost imperceptible. That is, all but spring. Springtime, no matter the place, has an exhilarating effect and New Mexico is no exception. Wildflowers bloom in the sun-baked landscape and the sun feels a bit less intense than in summer. It had come on one particular evening in 1953, settling over Albuquerque, wonderfully balmy and fragrant. Bernard was sitting on a terrace at the University of New Mexico with a girl whom he had met recently at a sorority party, when they were unexpectedly joined by a fellow agent. He had news: a teletype had just come in from the Bureau. Bernard had been transferred to Chicago.

21

Chicago Nights with Cementhead

FATE HAD dealt unkindly with Henry O'Connor. It had bestowed on him those qualities of righteousness and fastidiousness that, together with a rigid abstemiousness, would have enabled him to become an ideal ecclesiastic, but then had provided him with the wrong calling. So instead of running a priory, he ended up as special agent in charge of the Chicago FBI office. O'Connor had started his Bureau career some thirty-odd years before as a stenographer and, in spite of the intervening years in which he had served in increasingly important positions, there was still about him the aura of the steno pool. Maybe it was the prim way he sat on the edge of his chair, or possibly the manner in which he crossed his legs. Whatever it was, it evoked a certain unease among agents.

All he had heard about O'Connor beforehand was a terse description from a fellow agent in Albuquerque who had known him: "If you don't drink or fool around with women, and you play bridge, then you'll make it with O'Connor. The agents call him Cementhead."

Indeed, O'Connor stressed comportment above all. "As you may have heard, Mr. Conners, we run a strict organization here in Chicago. I want that to be thoroughly understood by all new arrivals. Now, to start off you will be assigned to the espionage squad. Your record indicates you were involved in espionage matters at Los Alamos. Mr. Carl Horning is supervisor of the squad here. We're conducting a goodly number of surveillances these days, and you'll find the cases assigned to you deal pretty much with this type of Bureau work. Now, I touched on the subject of personal conduct. In particular I want to stress that Chicago has numerous temptations for a young man. Women, drinking—you know what I'm alluding to, Mr. Conners?"

"Yes, yes, of course," responded Bernard, uneasily.

"Oftentimes, when an agent becomes involved in some personal misconduct, it's because of alcohol or women. Do you drink, Mr. Conners?"

"No, sir," said Bernard. "Very little." Bernard was prepared to respond like a Trappist monk should the next question be about women.

Instead, Henry O'Connor sniffed a few times, picked up his pencil, put it down, pinched the end of his long nose, lifted each side of his buttocks, and then said, "Well, now, I think that should do it." The SAC rose and extended a slender hand. "My door there is always open and you should feel free to contact me anytime. Of course, if you feel there is something concerning our office—or anything, for that matter—that I should be informed of *personally,* then you may rest assured it will be kept *absolutely* confidential. Do you read me, Mr. Conners?" The message was clear.

"Yes, sir, I certainly do," said Bernard, as he shook hands and acknowledged the thin smile. If the Director wanted a martinet for the job in Chicago, then he had made the perfect selection in Henry O'Connor.

In addition to the special agent in charge and the assistant special agent in charge, the Chicago office was administered by three supervisors who headed up the espionage and criminal squads. The supervisor's position was a thankless one, caught between the fire from the Bureau and the disdain of the agents. The pressure was unrelenting and all three supervisors suffered from a variety of blinks, tics, and twitches, and were referred to as Winkin', Blinkin', and Nod. Bernard headed for the offices of these supervisors when he left O'Connor. The first individual he saw as he entered the squad room was an older agent who sat scowling at his desk, loading a pistol. "Could you please tell me where I can find Carl Horning?" asked Bernard. "He's supervisor of the—"

"Yeah," said the agent curtly, without looking up. "He's over there in Shaker Heights." The man gave a slight motion of his head toward the nervous supervisors at the front of the room.

Carl Horning was one of those rare people who were able to get along with both the agents and the Bureau. His manner was easygoing and, if it were not for the compulsive winking of his eye, which contorted the right side of his face, he would have seemed relaxed.

"Welcome aboard," said the supervisor, getting to his feet and shaking hands enthusiastically. "Glad to have you with us. I'll get Ken Hastings in here. He's single, too. He should be able to help you out with a spot to live."

Ken Hastings was a tall, angular individual in his mid-thirties with dark hair, rather prominent features, and a permanent frown. He shook Bernard's hand in less than welcoming fashion and, after a brief exchange with the supervisor, he had Bernard follow him. Soon they were seated in a Bureau car heading for the South Side of Chicago.

"You can hole up with me a few days till you get something," said Ken, apparently satisfied that the new agent would not make an objectionable temporary roommate. "Charlie Bryant, the guy who lives with me, is out of town."

"It sounds as though you people are pretty busy," observed Bernard.

"One day busy, the next nothing," said Ken. "This job is strictly feast or famine. Last week I had a lead on a satellite agent. Important case. The subject was in town for the day making a contact. I couldn't get even one agent to help me. Had to watch him myself. This week we've been bumping into each other in the office looking for something to do. Yeah, the whole thing gets a little monotonous after a while. I hope you like to walk because you'll be doing a lot of it on these surveillances. Man, how these guys love to walk. That's the way they dry clean themselves. Sometimes they have a partner trailing behind to see if they're being followed."

"Does the Bureau get worked up when you lose a subject?"

"All depends," replied Ken. "If it's an important subject and the Director says not to lose him, then you take your Bureau career in your hands if you do. A few months back three of us got letters of censure for losing a diplomat. They told us not to get made and not to lose the guy. Now, you tell me how the hell you can watch a KGB agent who's tail-conscious, with three guys, and not get made and not lose him. If you try to be discreet, then you take your chances. It's that simple. Not me anymore, though. No, siree. They say don't lose him, then I sit on him—close as me to you."

Bernard would spend several weeks sharing quarters with Ken Hastings on the South Side of Chicago. He did not, however, share Ken's lifestyle, which revolved around drinking, partying, and cavorting with airline stewardesses. This was not what Henry O'Connor envisioned for his agents, and it proved too much for the Butterflies. Although not ready for the monastic life prescribed by O'Connor, he realized that life in Ken Hastings's fast lane might land him on a troopship to Asia. Soon he was able to find a quieter place on the near North Side of Chicago.

Time passed quickly there. Kate and he remained in touch, but there were dates with two lovely girls during this period. ("Platonic relationships" was how he described them to Kate.) Such relationships were hampered somewhat when he was promoted to night supervisor, with responsibility for the entire operation during evening hours. He was in well over his head and in constant fear of O'Connor's or the Director's retribution should something go wrong. A lot did go wrong, but neither Cementhead nor the Director got wind of it. Although the night hours were demanding both physically and psychologically, Bernard found it far more interesting than the countless hours surveilling Russian KGB agents throughout the Midwest.

His greatest challenge was dealing with O'Connor and the SAC's disparate concerns about the morals of his agents. Such wariness became apparent one night when Bernard was on the phone coordinating a surveillance by two agents on a notorious fugitive named Nick Montos, one of the Bureau's ten most wanted fugitives. Believing that they had identified the subject, one agent had followed him into a bar on Chicago's South Side. Because of the importance of the case, Bernard phoned the SAC and apprised him of developments.

"They followed him into a bar?" exclaimed the SAC. "They're not drinking, are they?"

Bernard reflected on the absurdity of the agent sitting down at the bar next to a tail-conscious Montos and ordering a ginger ale, but said nothing. Montos was apprehended shortly thereafter without incident. No women. No intemperance.

Even the slow hours were interesting. Out of curiosity one evening, Bernard asked for the file regarding the apprehension of John Dillinger. Seven agents were directly involved in the shooting of the fugitive and each submitted a memorandum describing the action. Having heard many different accounts of the event by the media, Bernard was surprised by the agents' reports of what had actually taken place.

A brothel owner named Ana Cumpanas, threatened with deportation as an undesirable alien, agreed to assist the Bureau in Dillinger's apprehension. Wearing an orange-reddish dress for identification purposes, she attended a showing of the movie *Manhattan Melodrama* at the Biograph Theater, along with Dillinger, and a companion of his named Polly Hamilton. As planned, the two women came out of the theater with Dillinger walking between them. Melvin Purvis, the agent in charge of the Chicago office, was waiting outside the entrance with seven other agents and, when the trio emerged, lit a cigar signaling to the other agents that he had identified the fugitive. Dillinger looked directly at Purvis, presumably suspicious. As he walked away between the women, the agents converged on him, drawing their weapons. All seven agents agreed that the first thing Dillinger did was to shove both women away with his hands and then reach for a Colt automatic pistol in his rear belt. The agents fired five shots, three of them striking Dillinger. The fugitive staggered into a nearby alley where he expired without speaking.

For Bernard, the most surprising revelation in the agents' memoranda was that Dillinger's first reaction was to shove both women out of the line of fire before reaching for his weapon—a dramatic irony in that Cumpanas had set him up to be killed. The outcome was extremely fortunate for the Bureau. A more cautious approach may have been to have waited, rather than risking a shoot-out amidst people exiting from the theater. Indeed, two women in the crowd were wounded by ricocheting bullets.

Bernard had been in Chicago for two years when he received notice of his reassignment to New York. It was timely for him since he was receiving some pressure from one of his "platonic" dates regarding a more serious association. He sensed his relationship with Kate was fading and was anxious to return to New York where she was teaching school in Long Island. Bernard had heard she was dating and it was a source of concern. It had been a long time since he had seen her, and he boarded the plane for New York with great expectations.

Part V

22

Big Leagues

THE NEW YORK office was the big leagues of the Bureau. More happened to Bernard in two weeks in New York than two years in Chicago. A few years after his arrival he was put in charge of the night operations for New York and Long Island. Caught between the frivolity that sometimes accompanied the night life of New York agents, and the Director's iron-fisted personnel policy, he found it a challenging job. Not the least of Bernard's problems was knowing when to write up an agent for some minor transgression, and when to look the other way hoping the matter would not surface. If it did, Hoover's retribution was swift and final—Butte, Montana? . . . Anchorage, Alaska? . . . It was enough to give a young agent the hives.

To cope with the labyrinth of federal statutes that defined the FBI's jurisdiction, the New York office had amassed an organization larger and more complicated than any other five offices combined. Heading up this complex operation when Bernard arrived was an individual named Sidney Granville Cabot. As did Elston Doolittle and Henry O'Connor, Sidney Cabot had most of the qualifications that enabled him to keep his job as long as possible under the Bureau system but, unlike them, Cabot was neither overtly nervous nor worried about his role. He was cold, analytical, and precise. On one occasion during his tenure in New York he had fired three agents for inflating their overtime figures, and had done so in the same dispassionate way that he handled routine administrative matters. Of course, the firings had reverberations that shook the office. The fired agents were referred to in solemn terms as "The Three." Rumor had it that the Director wondered if possibly Cabot were not a trifle *too* severe with agents.

Cabot had four assistant special agents in charge, each thoroughly aware of Cabot's dispassionate treatment of subordinates, including them. No one was immune to his retribution. Cabot was thus able to keep his fingers on the capricious pulse of the New York operations. He knew where to find his agents when he needed them. On Fridays, for example: agents considered Fridays to be "bank robbery days," since banks had more cash on hand Fridays to cash paychecks; hence more robberies. It was an unpredictable day for agents. One Friday afternoon, Cabot created a mild civil disturbance when he walked into Central Park, a spot sometimes frequented by relaxing agents. Between agents ducking and pigeons flying, it was a memorable afternoon for elderly ladies who fed the birds. His track record against crime and subversion was only so-so, but Cabot's success at containing "the enemy from within," as he referred to his agents, had been remarkable.

But Cabot's vise-like grip did little to engender productivity on "the farm," the squad of older agents near retirement who conducted most of the record checks. Bernard was assigned to this section upon first arriving in New York. New arrivals were sometimes assigned there to familiarize themselves with the city. Bernard approached one of the older agents one day to get help on a routine record check involving a recent bank robbery.

"Are you Tim Kelly?" asked Bernard.

"You're lookin' at him."

"I'm Bern Conners. The supervisor gave me a lead on that note job pulled at the National Commercial Bank last week. He told me you'd take me over to the Twentieth Precinct so I could talk to the detectives handling the case."

"Yeah, yeah," answered Kelly, with a look that suggested his morning was being complicated. "Why don't you give a guy a little notice on these things?"

Bernard was unsure how to respond. Finally he said, "Sorry, but the subjects didn't give them much notice at the bank last week. I can come back later if—"

"All right, all right," said Kelly, puffing a bit faster on his cigar. The farm was also referred to as the "cigar squad"; the cigar was as much a part of the job as were the files that were kept strewn on top of the desks for effect. "I'll fix you up, only it's gonna take a while. You young guys are all alike," said Kelly, talking around the stogie that now jutted belligerently from the side of his mouth. "Everything's gotta be done quick. Now, let me tell you somethin', pally. The quicker you do somethin' around here, the quicker you're in trouble."

"Yes, you're probably right." Bernard slumped into a chair. "I just got transferred from Chicago. I'm trying to get my feet on the ground."

"Listen, you seem okay," said Kelly after a pause, apparently feeling he was now receiving the deference that should be accorded an older agent. "You're just in from Chicago, you say? Well, I'll try to set you straight on a few things around here. C'mon, get your hat and coat." He picked up some memos and stuffed them into a battered folder.

They arrived at the Twentieth Precinct before lunch. It was a dusty old red brick building located in Central Park, with the unkempt look about the exterior that was once common to New York City's public buildings.

"Was this place ever part of the zoo?" asked Bernard as they approached the entrance. "It looks like the same kind of building they have over there."

"Hah!" snorted Kelly. "If you think it looks like the zoo from the outside, wait till you see some of the inhabitants." Chuckling, the agent pushed through the front door.

Once inside, Kelly affected a tougher personality. "Casey and Flanagan in?" he said gruffly to the desk sergeant.

The sergeant glanced up briefly and, without answering, gestured with his thumb over his shoulder toward the rear. Kelly walked toward a door leading to the detectives' squad room. Inside, two large, puffy-looking individuals in shirtsleeves were seated at a desk. Both were smoking cigars and were wearing round porkpie hats with the brims turned up in front.

"What's on your mind?" asked one of the detectives.

"Conners got the note job pulled at the National Commercial last week. He wants to check a few leads with you."

"We ain't got nuttin'!" said the other detective, rising from his desk and walking toward a file cabinet at the other side of the room.

"Yeah, we been drawin' blanks on that fuckin' thing," said the other. "You guys got anything?"

"Naw, nothin'," said Kelly, giving Bernard a half wink. "Conners here can fill you in."

Bernard proceeded to outline in detail a few leads the Bureau had developed in the case. Both detectives listened apathetically and, when he had finished, one said, "First time I ever got anything from an agent."

"Yeah," said the other man. "You guys had a change of policy over there?"

"Listen, that's a lot of crap and you know it," said Kelly. "We gave you guys everything on that homicide last month. You're just sore 'cause you blew the publicity on it." The detectives were no help, and once outside, Kelly reprimanded Bernard. "You gave them everything you had. You shouldn'ta done that."

"Really? You mean they won't cooperate?"

"Cooperate! Hell, I figured you had more sense than that. You worked in Chicago. You should know better."

As they drove out of the park into Central Park West, Kelly looked at his watch. "It's almost twelve o'clock. We'll go over to Lila's for a sandwich."

"Is that one of those restaurants on Broadway?"

"It's no restaurant. It's a cathouse. Lila's one of my informants. She's a madam."

"You mean we're going to a whorehouse?" Bernard sensed a rustling in his abdomen. "Doesn't the Bureau frown on that?"

"Why should they? Hell, they put enough pressure on for informants, don't they? Where the hell you gonna develop informants if you don't go where the action is?" Kelly fell silent for almost a minute and then, "Besides, wait till you see Lila. Real religious. Goes to church every Sunday. Serves her girls fish on Friday. Just like an old Irish mother."

Within a few minutes Kelly was backing the Bureau car into a snug parking place in front of a long row of brownstones. After locking the car, they mounted the steps to one of the buildings and Kelly rang the bell. There was a long pause and Kelly finally said, "Lila's checkin' us out. She's got a periscope in the rear of the building—looks like somethin' that came off a submarine. She checks out all—"

He was interrupted as the door opened and a kind, elderly face appeared in the opening. "Timothy darling, how are you? I haven't seen you for weeks."

"Hi, Lila. We in time for lunch?"

"You certainly are. Just let me grab something to put on. None of the girls are here, Timothy. We were closed down, you know."

"No kidding?" said Kelly, removing the cigar. "What happened?"

"Oh, you know the detectives, Timothy. They're not like you boys, you know. I finally had to cut them off. Well, it wasn't two weeks after that before we were raided. Knocked the door open, came in snappin' pictures like it was a show at the Coliseum."

"Gee, that's rough, Lila," said Kelly with genuine sympathy. "When do you think you'll be back in business?"

"Oh, I'm not sure," said Lila hesitantly. Then brightening, "Maybe in about two weeks . . . God willing."

23

Riptide

BERNARD worked on a variety of cases during his tenure in the New York office, both espionage and criminal matters, some of them high-profile cases that received considerable publicity. Handling the press during the evenings when major cases broke was particularly challenging. Often the stories in the morning papers were distorted versions of the press releases he distributed the previous night. Particularly disturbing were the undisclosed sources constantly utilized by reporters to assert details that were little more than reporters' suppositions. As an apiring writer himself, Bernard valued the freedom of the press, recognizing its enormous importance to a free society. But his experience with reporters while in the FBI, coupled with his later involvement in publishing, exposed him to abuses of the system.

In most cases the laws provide redress in courts for those who have been damaged or victimized. For example, if a doctor removes the wrong kidney, or a manufacturer produces a product that harms a consumer, the plaintiff may recover damages. In libel cases, however, a plaintiff may sustain significant damages both emotionally and financially by mistakes of a publisher. But since the Supreme Court's 1964 decision in *New York Times v. Sullivan*, if the victim is a "notable"—a term vague in the extreme—then the injured party must prove "malice." This is one of the more unfortunate pieces of legislation dreamed up by constitutional lawyers. From a practical standpoint, how does one actually prove "malice"? A plaintiff must prove the defendant knew a statement was false and acted in reckless disregard. A high burden of proof. Successful libel actions are rare. The incontrovertible fact is that the media, as well as writers, have abused their position, and it has had a profoundly harmful effect on many institutions and innocent people. Everything in our society requires oversight and the idea that the press will "police" itself is unrealistic.

Much of Bernard's investigative activities took him to Long Island airports. Anonymous calls threatening bombs on airplanes were not unusual. For such matters Bernard often arranged to meet another agent at the airport and handle the case with the Port Authority. Although threats were generally baseless—they never did find a bomb—all leads had to be checked out.

Occasionally there were more tragic incidents with the airlines. Once an American Airlines plane crashed in the East River, killing a number of passengers. Another greater tragedy occurred when a United Airlines plane collided with a Trans World Airlines plane over Brooklyn, killing all on board. Although not directly involved in the investigation, Bernard spoke that evening with a number of agents who were on the scene. They related the horrific details. An eleven-year-old boy named Stephen Baltz, who reportedly wanted to be an FBI agent when he grew up, was traveling alone on the United plane and somehow survived the initial crash, landing miraculously in a snowbank. Although badly burned, with broken bones, he remained conscious. He tried to smile but his burns prevented it. His immediate concern was for his mother who he said would be worried about him, waiting for him at the airport. He described in unbearably poignant terms the moment in the plane just before the crash. "I was looking out my window and saw the snow falling on the city like a beautiful fairyland. . . ." He died a short time later in the hospital. Such tragedies held dreadful unforgettable moments for agents dealing with airline personnel and the families of victims.

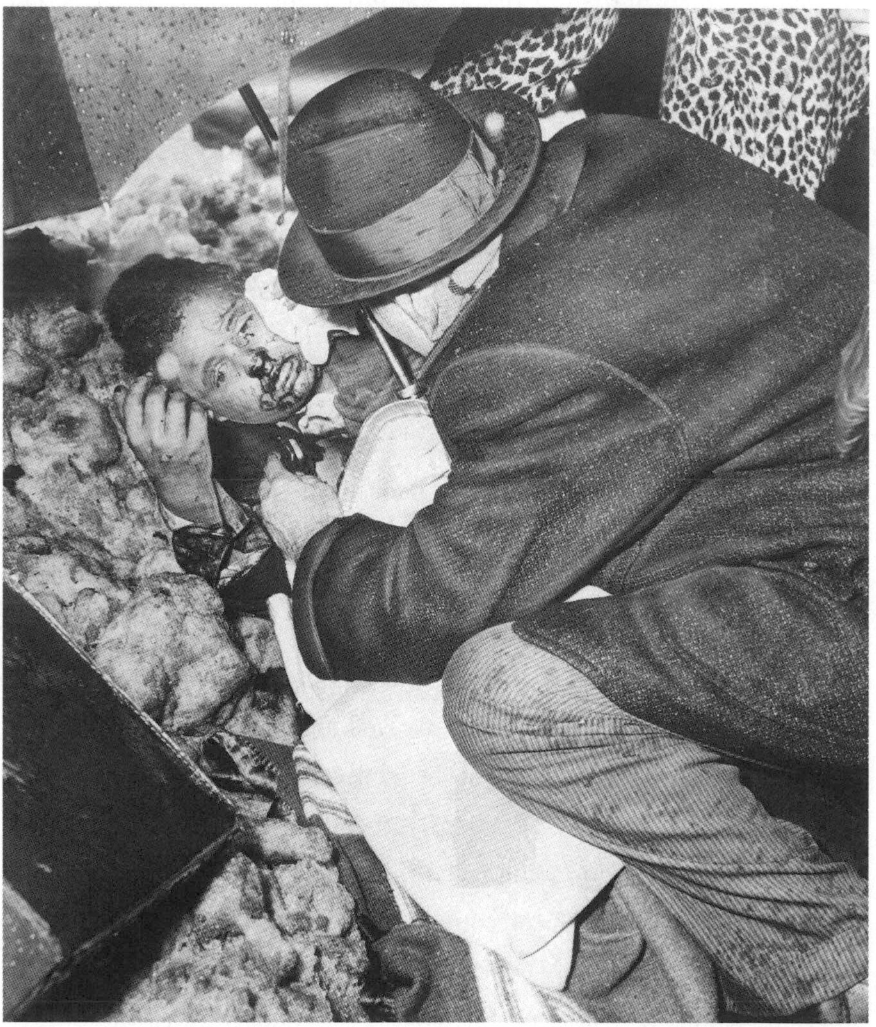

Crash victim Stephen Baltz.

Boy-Boy with Big-Boy and sister Rosalie. Big-Boy was a gentle horse, seemingly comfortable with the lavish affection bestowed on him by Boy-Boy's sisters.

Left: Bernard (far right) in grammar school. Less than five feet tall, he inspired little expectation that he would someday be able to dunk a basketball. Above: Bernard as an Albany Academy cadet. The Academy, at 200 years old, is one of the oldest country day schools in America. Among its prominent alumni writers is Herman Melville, author of Moby-Dick.

Some of Kate's progenitors, a traditional ancestry where God and country were held dear, and organizations such as the Daughters of the American Revolution were honored.

Kate with brother, John, and dog, Prince, during the serenity of their early years. John shared Kate's remarkable equanimity. They never heard their father raise his voice.

Kate as queen of Franklin Academy High School prom. An outstanding student, she received many academic awards, including Phi Beta Kappa.

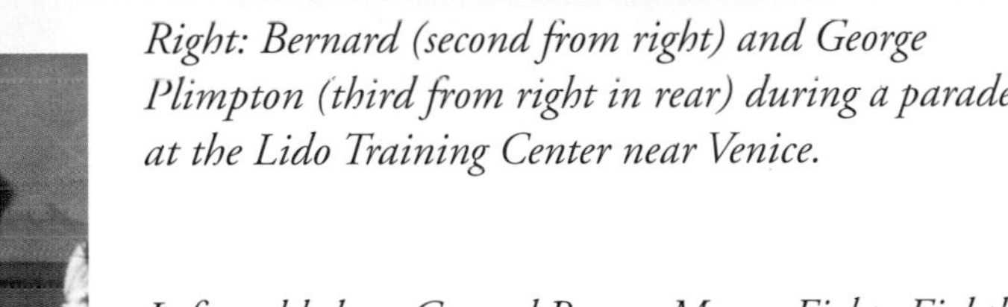

Right: Bernard (second from right) and George Plimpton (third from right in rear) during a parade at the Lido Training Center near Venice.

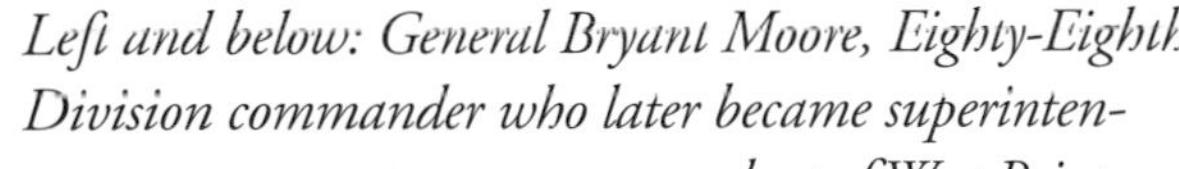

Left and below: General Bryant Moore, Eighty-Eighth Division commander who later became superintendent of West Point, spoke well of Bernard and encouraged him to attend West Point. General Moore was enormously popular with the troops. He would later die in combat in the Korean War following a helicopter crash. He was promoted posthumously to four-star general.

Above: Bernard (front row, middle) reviewing troops with General Moore (upper left).

George and Bernard with an Italian friend.

George on the Lido, administering first aid to Bernard's injured foot. Above Bernard is one of many Italian youngsters whom they befriended.

Above right and above: George and Bernard with Radiana on the Lido beach. Radiana was a beautiful Italian girl with whom George and Bernard became close beach companions. She was bilingual and instrumental in improving their pidgin Italian.

George playing the organ during a friend's wedding, which he and Bernard attended.

Bernard with dog "Lido" that he brought back from Italy. An animal lover, Bernard would later support charitable projects involving animals.

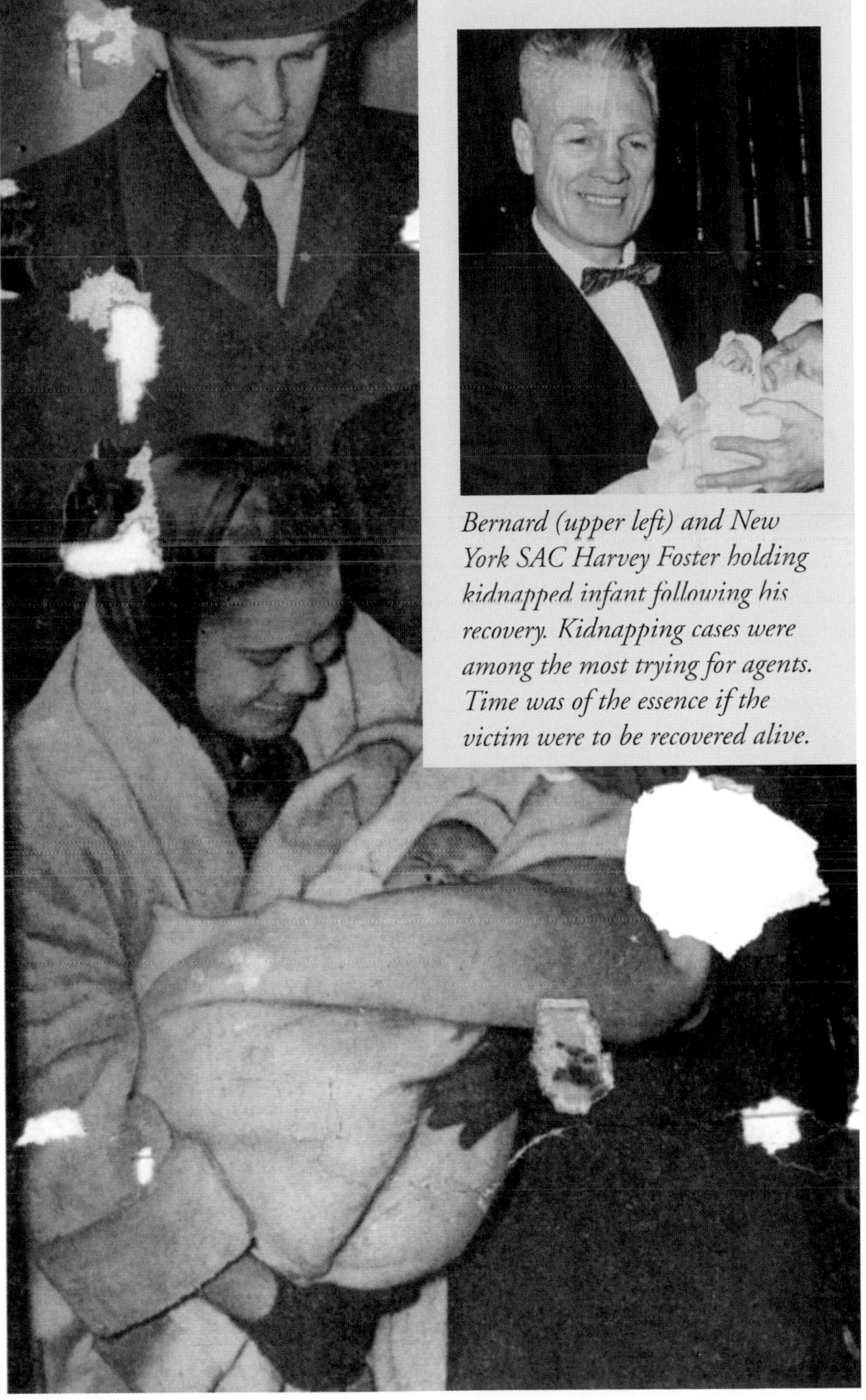

Bernard (upper left) and New York SAC Harvey Foster holding kidnapped infant following his recovery. Kidnapping cases were among the most trying for agents. Time was of the essence if the victim were to be recovered alive.

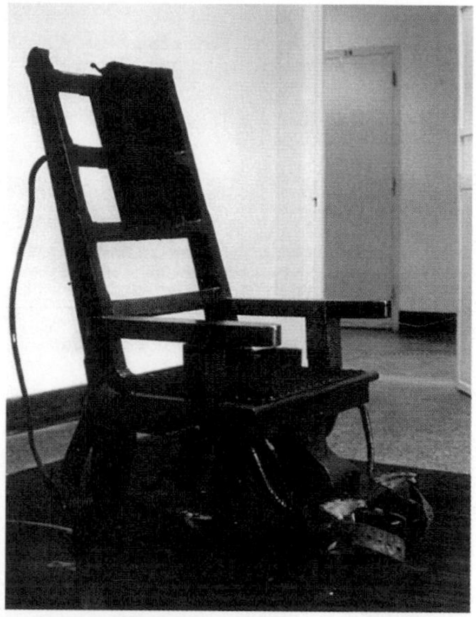

Left: Enclosed in a small closet in the execution chamber was the control panel. Behind one-way glass the executioner awaited a final sign from the warden before pulling the long, black lever that delivered a lethal charge of 2,000 volts to the chair. Right: Electric chair in which Ruth Snyder and Julius and Ethel Rosenberg were executed at Sing Sing Prison. To the right of the chair is the door through which the condemned prisoner entered the execution chamber from the "dancehall," the nickname for the holding cell. The first sight of the chair was usually a jarring moment for the condemned.

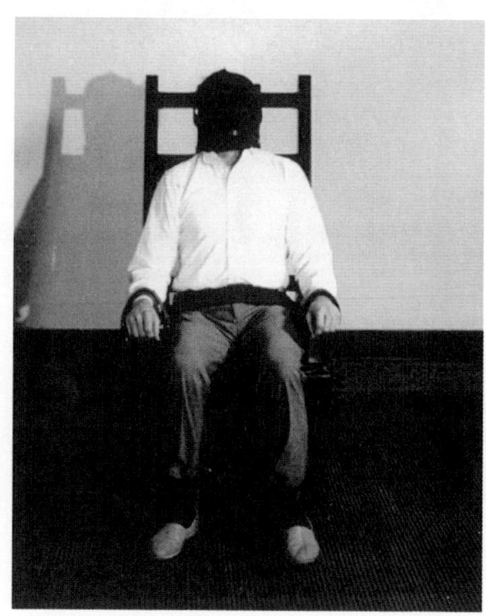

Bernard in the electric chair during simulated execution while researching Dancehall.

Bernard and Kate during freshman year at college. Her ground floor room during her freshman year facilitated many encounters, perhaps distracting at times to her roommate, Janet Tag.

Kate at a West Point tailgate party. Kate and Bernard were occasional guests of General David Traub, a prominent West Point graduate.

Kate while at Columbia University, and Bernard after being recalled to active duty. Photo taken on the Staten Island Ferry circa 1951.

Above: Kate with daughter Sarah and son Christopher.

Bernard relaxing with Christopher, Sarah, and recently arrived Jane.

Kate golfing.

Bernard's sisters Carol diving and Alice on horseback.

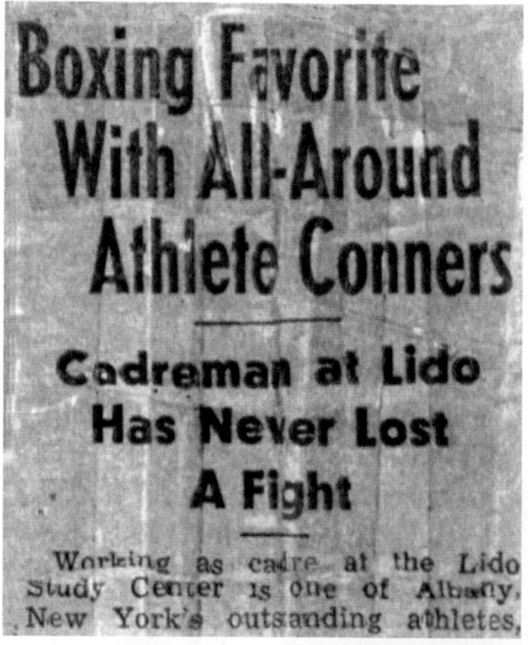

Boxing Favorite With All-Around Athlete Conners

Cadreman at Lido Has Never Lost A Fight

Working as cadre at the Lido Study Center is one of Albany, New York's outsanding athletes,

These Golden Gloves Victors Boston Bound

These [illegible] boxers are slated [illegible] to Boston for th[illegible]ional AAU Golde[illegible] s Tourney ne[illegible] won in th[illegible] Golden G[illegible]ght:

[illegible]y.

[illegible]rank Alva[illegible]e-nectady.

126—Roosevelt Flagg, Al-

349 Boxing Show To Feature Card Of Top Fighters

boxing show hits Trieste tomorrow night. With teams entered from every Division unit the card really looks great. A large crowd is expected at the Hangar and 349th Special Service men are doing their best to seat the throng comfortably. Trophies of all descriptions will be given to winning teams and individuals.

Roland La Sta[illegible] golden glove, light heavyweight champ will be fighting in the heavy weight class for the first time. Attempts are being made to contact Bernie Conners, sensational young light heavy who can give anybody an interesting evening. Should Conners be available, he will go Friday night against La Starza. La Starza will [illegible] however, come what [illegible]

The teams competi[illegible]

349th Inf.

Roland La Starza, C[illegible]

Athletic Blurbs and Trivia

Bernie Conners, S.L.U. Grid Star Fractures Ankle in Drill

Stellar Halfback Will B Lost to Larries for the Season

WATERTOWN TIMES

Canton, Sept. 18.—Visions St. Lawrence university's fi undefeated, untied season in years of college football vanis ed like fog in the morning s Saturday, after a gruelling, t hour scrimmage had all but de mated the 43 man squad.

Worst news at the end of t Larries' blackest Saturday w that Bernie Conners, the Alba left halfback and Little A America candidate, had broken bone in his left ankle and w not play football this year. Co ners led the team in scoring wi nine touchdowns last year, a in yards gained with 939 in 1 plays. He was the one man w could be depended upon, almo without fail, to pick up tho precious extra feet needed for first down or a touchdown, a his loss will cripple the Larr as no other casualty might do.

Bernie Conners One of Country's Leading Ground Gainers—Team Has Set New Scoring Record.

Bob Wallen, Jack Barron and Bernie Conners Display Best Form Against Colgate Outfit.

CONNERS REPORTS TO S. L. U. COACH

Brilliant Halfback May Be Ready to Play Against

BERNIE CONZERS—St. Law-
rence University left half back
and Little All America candidate.

St. Lawrence University

Athletic Hall of Fame

Bernard Conners '51
Football

One of the country's leading ground gainers in football and a member of the undefeated 1950 football team, Bernard Conners went on to an outstanding career as a writer and film producer after serving over eight years as a special agent for the Federal Bureau of Investigation.

Conners was the leading rusher and scorer for a 1949 team which won six straight games to conclude that season, starting a record 18-game winning streak. He missed all but three games of the undefeated 1950 season due to an ankle injury, but returned for the Clarkson game and played a pivotal role in a win over Rochester which concluded the perfect season. Conners rushed for 849 yards, averaging 7.1 yards per carry and completed four passes for an additional 90 yards to lead the 1949 team in total offense with 939 yards. He accounted for 54 points on nine touchdowns which also led the team. In addition to his football exploits at St. Lawrence, Conners was also a two-time Golden Gloves boxing champion.

The former publisher of The Paris Review, Conners is a best-selling author and owner of British American, a multi-faceted firm which includes real estate development, producing films and television shows, book publishing and the manufacture and sale of soft drinks. Among the movies of which Conners was executive producer was "Nuremberg", which received two Emmys in 2002.

Not all the trauma on Long Island involved Bureau cases. On one occasion Bernard was on a beach with three other agents when their attention was drawn to a figure on a nearby wharf that extended into the Atlantic Ocean. The person was shouting and pointing excitedly toward someone well out in the ocean who was calling for help. It was determined later that the person in trouble was a lifeguard at Jones Beach who had been caught in a riptide and swept out to sea. One of the agents immediately called authorities for help while the others looked frantically for rescuing devices.

Bernard, the only agent with lifeguard experience, hesitated, but then plunged into the ocean. It was one of those rash actions that sometimes overcame Bernard's worrisome self during perilous moments. Had he time to reflect or known of the riptide, he might well have remained with the other agents waiting for help to arrive. Newspaper articles would later describe Bernard in "heroic" terms as a "strong swimmer who saved the man's life." In reality the episode was somewhat different. Once in the ocean, despite the heavy waves pounding toward the shore, Bernard felt himself being carried out to sea and worried about the undertow. Reaching the victim, he supported the man, keeping his chin above water.

"Don't grab me!" yelled Bernard. "I'll stay with you as long as you don't grab me!"

The man appeared barely conscious but remained remarkably composed under the circumstances, his arms extended as though trying to float in the trough of the waves. Things went wrong quickly. Standard lifesaving methods were not going to work in the ocean's heavy seas. Bernard was soon in a life-threatening situation, swallowing salt water and gasping for air. He would later reflect on those moments, and think how unimportant the other man's life had become. He hung on to the man, but at the moment it was more for self-preservation. Bernard thought he may have pushed the victim under, trying to keep his own head above water. Rather than the "heroics" described in the papers, he might well have contributed to the man's drowning. Through the efforts of others who managed to reach them with ropes and lifesaving buoys (particularly a man who was never identified in the news articles), Bernard and the lifeguard were rescued. After being taken to shore, a respirator brought by the police was applied to the unconscious lifeguard. Bernard lay nearby exhausted, throwing up salt water.

Bernard's "heroics" earned him the following citation from J. Edgar Hoover:

OFFICE OF THE DIRECTOR

UNITED STATES DEPARTMENT OF JUSTICE

FEDERAL BUREAU OF INVESTIGATION

WASHINGTON 25, D. C.
September 7, 1956

Personal and Confidential

Mr. Bernard F. Conners
Federal Bureau of Investigation
New York, New York

Dear Mr. Conners:

I know you have received many comments on the part you played in the rescue of an individual from the Atlantic Ocean this past August and I just want to say how deeply impressed I was with the fortitude and courage you showed on that day.

Sincerely yours,

J. Edgar Hoover

Although the episode was covered in some detail in the newspapers crediting an FBI agent named Bernard Conners with saving the life of the Jones Beach lifeguard, Bernard never heard from the lifeguard. He was not surprised. How do you thank someone who almost drowned you?

24

Newlyweds

IT WAS OFTEN said that, although J. Edgar Hoover was a bachelor, he was married to the Bureau. Bernard, himself a bachelor, had no such marital aspirations. For him, Catherine Connors would be his wife; it was just a question of when. His transfer from Chicago to New York brought this destined event much closer. There had been other men and women in their lives since graduating from college—so-called social or passing relationships—but stories of Catherine's dates had found their way to Bernard. Of particular concern was Kate's association with another FBI agent, a former boyfriend from her hometown. She assured Bernard it was only a friendly relationship. But those "friendly chaps" could be the most dangerous. The man was popular, assigned to the FBI office in Detroit. And it seemed he was making frequent trips back to his hometown. Did he visit Kate much? Oh, yes. But it was the same old thing—"just good buddies." Once in college Kate invited the man to a big dance. For Bernard, it was a long weekend.

But there had been women in Bernard's social life as well. Particularly the two from Chicago, who had been beauty queens in college—one at

DePauw University, the other at the University of Michigan. Both were tall with lovely figures, one blonde, the other brunette. Bernard was dating them simultaneously and at times it was awkward. They commanded much attention from men. It was no small feat keeping admirers at bay. One of them came to New York to visit him, and Bernard took her to the Hamptons for a few days. She was a sensation on the beach, people mistaking her for a blonde movie star who was popular at the time. One chap with whom Bernard had a casual acquaintance was unrelenting in his attention. Bernard finally told him quite directly to ease off, but it fell on deaf ears. The man continued with his overtures, asking for her phone number. He was a tall, sandy-haired individual, confident with the ladies. Bernard found him exceedingly annoying, and a confrontation was avoided when she told the man she was involved in a serious relationship with Bernard. The man would later tell Bernard that he'd spared him the embarrassment of telling her that he'd seen Bernard with a different girl every weekend—an observation grossly exaggerated.

Bernard was dating frequently during this period, but they were passing relationships (most of the time) just like Kate's. He may have gone off the reservation on occasion, but Kate remained his primary interest. She was teaching math and science at Roslyn High School in Roslyn, Long Island, while Bernard was assigned to the Bureau's New York office. He spent a great deal of time in the Hamptons during the summer months and for a short time he and Kate began to drift apart; that is, until Kate surfaced with a tall, personable young man whom she had met in New York. It was too much for Bernard. A wedding date was set. She and Bernard were married during a downpour at St. Vincent Ferrer in New York City under the ambivalent eyes of Sarah Connors.

Life was exciting at 10 East 83rd Street in Manhattan, where the couple took up residence. It was a small penthouse apartment from which one could look across the street to the imposing entrance of the Metropolitan Museum on Fifth Avenue. With Kate's teaching salary augmenting their income they were able to furnish their quarters adequately, which was not difficult considering the apartment consisted of only two rooms. One of their more expensive investments was new carpeting—a purchase they made only after much discussion. The most attractive feature of the apartment was a fairly large terrace that encircled most of the penthouse where they sunbathed and entertained. Kate was a welcoming hostess, even when Bernard showed up unexpectedly at dinnertime with fellow agents. The agents loved her. She had an uncanny ability to make visitors feel as though she were thrilled to see them regardless of the time of day or night.

The couple would soon learn, however, that ground-floor and penthouse apartments came with security risks. Soon after moving in they were burglarized, losing the few valuables they had been able to accumulate that early in their careers. Some of Bernard's athletic awards, including his Golden Gloves boxing trophies, as well as a modest collection of Kate's jewelry were among the lost items. Fortunately, the new carpeting had been tacked down and escaped the looting.

Not long after the burglary, there was a more serious encounter. On occasion Kate would awaken saying she thought she heard someone on the terrace. Usually, Bernard would go out with his revolver and look around, but often he didn't take her concerns too seriously. One night after being awakened, more to placate her than out of concern about an intruder, Bernard went outside, not bothering to take his pistol. As he walked down the terrace he looked up and saw a foot protruding from one of the eaves. Without thinking he reached up, grabbed the intruder's leg, and pulled him down. There followed a bloody battle involving a Latin man with a shiv.

Bernard was able to subdue the intruder and take him into the apartment, where he bound him with the man's belt and a bathrobe sash. While they waited for the police, Kate noticed that the intruder, lying on his stomach, his arms and legs tied behind him, was bleeding on the new rug. Kate apologized to the assailant, then lifted his head to slide a piece of leftover carpet under him to save the rug. Following the encounter Bernard was glad that he had not taken his pistol with him to the terrace. Under the circumstances he could have shot the man during the struggle, and he did have a measure of sympathy for the intruder by the time the police arrived.

In spite of such tribulations, their residence at 10 East 83rd Street was considered very nice, even fashionable. Bernard was sure their neighbors regarded them as two mere itinerants on the roof, wondering how they ever ended up in the building. Especially since Bernard often failed to dress the part. About that time he was running surveillances on the Lower East Side, which required that he wear old clothes to blend in. There were days he didn't shave. Since surveillance work was highly unpredictable—when the subjects moved, you moved—Bernard found it best to carry a sandwich, which Kate made for him and put in a paper bag. It was summer and since he wore no jacket to conceal his pistol, he sometimes carried it in the paper bag with his lunch. No one in the building was aware that he was an undercover FBI agent; he looked more like a longshoreman. It raised eyebrows on the elevators. Although the residents were pleasant enough, they had trouble understanding the Connerses' lifestyle—particularly when one day they'd see Bernard in the elevator brown-bagging it to work in his scruffy Lower East Side drag, while another time he and Catherine might be gussied up in evening finery going to a black-tie affair.

One day a lovely couple, somewhat older than Kate and Bernard, invited them down to their apartment to play bridge. As they were about to sit down and play, Bernard allowed that his bridge skills had diminished somewhat. The truth was he had limited knowledge of the game, but talked Kate into accepting the invitation. With both of them working they had little social life. No one else in the building had ever offered an invitation. "Let's go, Kate," Bernard said. "I'm good at cards. You can teach me how to play!" She was still explaining the game to him when they went down on the elevator to their hosts' apartment. They were never asked back!

It wasn't long before Catherine became pregnant. The early morning trips by cab to 125th Street, where Kate joined fellow teachers, followed by long rides in the carpool to Roslyn, Long Island, were complicated even more by morning sickness. And the morning sickness was not confined to Catherine. Bernard could not understand why. How does a husband become morning sick? But there he was, just an observer, and feeling dreadful. Kate handled it as she did everything—with equanimity. She was overjoyed with thoughts of a baby and morning sickness was a small price to pay.

25

Unarmed in Harlem

An **FBI** agent's life in New York City was unpredictable at best. An agent could never be sure when he was off duty. There was no Bureau rule governing when an agent carried his pistol. The Director's requirement was simple: "An agent should have it when he needed it." Given the challenges in Manhattan and the outer boroughs, most agents believed they might "need it" at any time. This prophecy was borne out one night as Bernard and another agent were walking toward their car in Harlem. Suddenly a man in great distress rushed toward them shouting that a nearby business had just been robbed. Given their hats and suits, the man may have assumed they were police officers.

"He's back in there," the man yelled pointing to a dark alley. "He's gotta gun!" Acting on impulse they moved cautiously toward the alley.

"You got your pistol?" asked Bernard.

"Yes," replied the other agent. "You?"

"No," murmured Bernard.

"Jesus!" from his associate. "What'll we do?"

"We have to look in that alley," Bernard said, glancing after the man who had alerted them, now watching from down the street.

"No way!" said his associate. "No way I'm going into that fucking alley!"

If he had time to reflect on the danger inherent in the situation, Bernard probably would have been just as frightened. But caught up by the challenge of the moment, he was almost oblivious to the risks.

"Give me your gun," demanded Bernard.

The agent drew the pistol from his holster and handed it to Bernard. "No bullets," he said.

"What?" exclaimed Bernard, astonished. "Why the hell . . . ?"

Now at the entrance to the alley, followed by his associate, Bernard flattened himself against a side wall and proceeded cautiously into the passageway.

"FBI," Bernard shouted, pointing the empty pistol into the darkness at nothing. "One move and we'll blow your fucking head off!" Raffish language was considered appropriate at such times.

"Okay! Okay!" came a voice from the alley. "Easy! Easy!" An African American man, his hands high over his head, emerged from the darkness.

The two agents took the subject into custody and searched him for weapons. They found no gun. They then called the police, who arrived quickly and took charge. Bernard received a personal citation from the Director for his "performance in keeping with the highest traditions of the Bureau" that evening. Although gratified by the citation, Bernard was well aware that acts of courage under fire are sometimes embellished in the retelling. An award for rash stupidity may have been more appropriate.

OFFICE OF THE DIRECTOR

UNITED STATES DEPARTMENT OF JUSTICE

FEDERAL BUREAU OF INVESTIGATION

WASHINGTON 25, D. C.

April 27, 1959

PERSONAL

Mr. Bernard F. Conners
Federal Bureau of Investigation
New York, New York

Dear Mr. Conners:

I am taking this means to commend you for your excellent performance in detaining for the New York City Police Department one James Small, who allegedly had just robbed and assaulted a clothing store owner.

You and a fellow agent exercised splendid alertness and judgment in handling this situation. You certainly performed a real public service. Your performance was in keeping with the highest traditions of the Bureau and I want to express my sincere thanks.

Sincerely yours,

J. Edgar Hoover

Commendation letter from Hoover 4/27/59.

A less hazardous example of New York's pervasive criminal activity confronted Bernard a few weeks later. He was headed home one evening during rush hour on a crowded Madison Avenue bus, one hand holding an overhead strap. Glancing down, he saw a dark hand slipping surreptitiously under his unbuttoned suit coat toward the black FBI credential case in his shirt breast pocket over his heart. The hand belonged to a small African American, clothed in a white suit and white porkpie hat. At first the display of boldness struck Bernard as almost comical. He waited a moment as the man reached for what he apparently thought was a wallet, and then reached down and grabbed the man's extended arm. With his free hand, Bernard withdrew his credentials and flashed the large blue FBI letters at the astonished pickpocket. Reflecting on the time it would take to book the man at the police station, he hesitated. Then he said with a measure of amusement, "It's your lucky day. If it weren't so late I'd take your ass over to the Twentieth Precinct."

With profuse thanks and apologies, the man backed away into the crowd of gaping passengers, and left the bus at the next stop. But it was actually Bernard's lucky day. Had he not glanced down at the right moment, it would have been a banner day for the light-fingered little man—lifting an FBI man's credentials! For Bernard, the consequences could have been significant. FBI credentials bearing Bernard's name in the hands of a roving thief would not rest well with the Director. Bernard liked the snow. He was a skier. But Butte? Anchorage?

26

The Tragedy of Julius and Ethel

WHILE RUNNING the night operations of the Chicago and New York divisions of the FBI, Bernard was involved in major cases. Although his participation was not always as a street agent working directly on the cases, he had a detailed view of events as a flood of information washed over his desk during the normal course of investigations. In these affairs he believed the Bureau pursued its work honorably, particularly when it came to cases regarding violations of civil rights. Under federal statutes the Bureau was empowered to investigate such matters, which often included cases of police brutality. Since it investigated other agencies for violations of civil rights, it was vital that the Bureau keep its own house in order. Accordingly, internal civil rights investigations were closely monitored by supervisors. Notwithstanding the stringent rules of conduct that prevailed, adjudication of cases in rare instances could be different when referred to the US Attorney's office for prosecution. Bernard found one matter in particular very troublesome: the execution of Julius and Ethel Rosenberg.

Bernard believed Julius had been justly convicted under the Espionage Act of 1917. But he felt the indictment and conviction of Julius's wife, Ethel, was tainted by procedures employed for the purpose of putting pressure on her husband. The Bureau knew Julius had a great deal of information that would be valuable to counterespionage efforts that could be elicited over the course of a long prison term provided by the espionage statute. Very few of those who followed the matter expected the federal judge presiding over their case—the diminutive martinet Irving Kaufman—to roll himself up in the American flag and sentence them to death in the electric chair. The lead prosecutor, Irving Saypol, never asked for the death sentence in his closing argument. But others involved in the prosecution gave tacit support for the sentence, believing that Julius would ultimately crack with his wife facing the chair. It didn't happen. Neither copped a plea, which could have saved their lives. Both went to the chair proclaiming their innocence.

Visits by their two young children, ages six and ten, prior to the execution posed emotional challenges for their prison guards. The prison rabbi, Irving Koslowe, who ministered to Ethel during her final moments, is reported to have pleaded with Ethel to say she was guilty and to cooperate with the government to avoid electrocution—"if not for yourself, for your two small children." She refused, stating she'd rather be dead than to plead guilty to something she hadn't done. The execution was carried out at Sing Sing Prison in a grisly procedure described to Bernard by Bob Considine, a prominent reporter. Bernard was having lunch at the 21 Club with Bob and Toots Shor when Bob told them that he had been one of two journalists selected by media pools to witness the execution. He said that guards had to assist Julius, who appeared to be in a daze as they brought him into the chamber and strapped him to the chair. His execution was followed quickly by that of Ethel, who walked quietly into the room—paused to kiss a matron who promptly broke down crying—and then sat down calmly in the chair. Considine said she was remarkably composed throughout the ordeal. He gave a horrifying description of the execution, stating that the chair did not function properly and the process had to be repeated, producing a nauseating combination of smoke and odors. He said it was an experience he could never forget, and that when he got home he threw away all of the clothes he was wearing as well as his watch.

In the end, instead of obtaining priceless information, the Bureau ended up with two bags of ashes. Those responsible for this tragedy, Judge Irving Kaufman, Roy Cohn (one of the prosecutors who reportedly had illegal contact with Kaufman during the trial), and many others who approved of the executions have established their place in infamy. This includes Dwight Eisenhower, for whom Bernard had great admiration for his leadership in World War II. Eisenhower had the authority as president to commute their sentence. Instead, in his comments denying their pleas he lapsed into the subjunctive, stating that what they had done might result in the loss of many American lives. None of which, as it turned out, was true. Judge Kaufman spoke in a similar vein as he imposed the death sentence in a rambling jingoistic statement that included the following:

"I must pass such sentence . . . in this diabolical conspiracy to destroy a God-fearing nation . . . I believe your conduct . . . has already caused the communist aggression in Korea, with the resultant casualties exceeding 50,000, and who knows but that millions more of innocent people may pay the price of your treason. Indeed, by your betrayal you undoubtedly have altered the course of history. . . ."

It was a statement that had no basis in fact, one for which the judge would be severely criticized. Bernard's position brought him in contact with many federal judges during his career. As a group he found them honorable and competent. Kaufman was an exception. That he could have meted out the death sentence to this couple, in the face of what he must have suspected regarding Ethel's innocence, is beyond comprehension. Professor Yale Kamisar of the University of Michigan Law School reportedly said, "I'm sure the decision plagued him to his last day," adding that "Kaufman was someone whose desire for recognition was not easily fulfilled."

Perhaps the most absurd feature of the trial from Bernard's perspective was that David Greenglass, Ethel's younger brother, who actually did furnish information to the Soviets, received a fifteen-year sentence and was released after ten years because of his cooperation with the government. His testimony stating that Ethel had typed up his notes regarding the "lens mold" of the atomic bomb (an explosive designed to detonate the nuclear core by instantly bringing it to critical mass through implosion) was the critical evidence that was used to indict and send his sister to the electric chair. Years after his release from prison he recanted much of his testimony, stating that he had lied about his sister's involvement at the urging of prosecutors to save himself and his wife. In later years Soviet physicists would state that the Greenglass material was neither accurate nor useful, in fact worthless; Greenglass had only a high school education and the Soviets had already received valuable information regarding the atomic bomb from the British spies Alan Nunn May and Klaus Fuchs, the latter, as mentioned earlier, a physicist who worked on the Manhattan project at Los Alamos. A further irony in the case was that May and Fuchs were tried by a British court and received only fourteen years in prison for their far greater crimes. Many biographers of J. Edgar Hoover reflect that Hoover regretted the strategy of using Ethel Rosenberg as a "lever" in the infamous case and was opposed to her execution, feeling that the execution of a mother of two small children would result in dreadful publicity. In this case, his premonitions were accurate indeed.

A few years after the Rosenberg execution, Bernard appeared on a prominent New York City talk show in a one-on-one debate with Roy Cohn, the Rosenberg assistant prosecutor who also acted as Senator McCarthy's lead assistant during the Army-McCarthy hearings. It was a sixty-minute program and there may have been time to allude to the Rosenberg case, but it was never mentioned. While Bernard disliked Roy Cohn because of his role in the Rosenberg case, he had to admit that the man had a pleasant personality.

Their discussion was dignified and restrained. After the program, which was over very late, Cohn invited Bernard to join him for coffee at a nearby restaurant. The Rosenberg case never came up.

In an excellent book, *The FBI-KGB War*, Robert J. Lamphere, the FBI agent who supervised the Rosenberg case, stated:

"It is clear that no one in the hierarchy of the FBI who was at all connected with the Rosenberg case wanted a death sentence for Ethel Rosenberg. . . . When I heard that both Julius and Ethel Rosenberg had been sentenced to death, I was surprised and shocked."

Lamphere also described what happened the night of the Rosenberg execution:

"We had an open telephone line to [Assistant Director] Belmont in Sing Sing and, as the final minutes came closer, the tension mounted. I wanted very much for the Rosenbergs to confess—we all did—but I was fairly well convinced by this time that they wished to become martyrs. . . . Belmont telephoned us to say that the Rosenbergs had refused for the last time to save themselves by confession. Julius was reported dead to us at 8:05 p.m., and Ethel at 8:15 p.m."

27

Disorganized Crime

VICTOR RIESEL was a crusading reporter who wrote about mob activities in labor unions during the fifties. His relentless articles inspired the government to enact far-reaching legislation to control corruption in unions. The result for Riesel, however, was tragic. Sulfuric acid was thrown in his eyes under the orders of labor mobsters about whom he had been reporting. The attack was carried out on April 5, 1956, by a hoodlum named Abe Telvi.

Riesel had just left Lindy's, a restaurant on Broadway and 49th Street, when Telvi stepped from the shadows of the nearby Mark Hellinger Theatre and threw acid in his face. Riesel was rushed back into the restaurant where well-meaning patrons tried to wash the acid from his eyes. He was taken to a nearby hospital where doctors attempted unsuccessfully to save his sight. The crime would occupy front page headlines for over a year, and impel President Eisenhower to press for legislation to investigate unions. It was one of the more emotionally painful cases on which Bernard worked. He spent considerable time with Riesel following the attack. He recalled having lunch with him at Toots Shor's restaurant while he was recovering, at which time Riesel told him that he thought he might regain a small amount of his vision; that he could distinguish some light in one eye. Riesel wore dark glasses, and once during lunch removed the glasses to show Bernard his eyes as he spoke. Bernard was horrified at what he saw. What had been eyes were now two tiny burned-out orbs. There was nothing left that could ever provide vision.

As often happened with clumsy mob "hits," the Bureau soon identified Abe Telvi as well as the thugs who were behind the attack. All received prison sentences except Telvi. There was a big push to locate Telvi before the mob did. His handlers got there first. The Bureau finally found him a few weeks later on Mulberry Street—predictably, three bullets in the back of his head. Writers such as Peter Maas (*The Valachi Papers*) and Mario Puzo (*The Godfather*) tend to dramatize the crime families using terms such as "don," "capo," "consigliere," and "omerta" to create an impression of arcane sophistication. The only Mafia term Bernard could think of to describe these hoodlums was "oobatz," meaning "crazy." He found the so-called mafiosi to be desultory groups of barbarians involved in extortion, robbery, mayhem, and murder who wouldn't have the intellectual capacity to organize anything. He recalled that a friend named Steve Halpin, with whom he worked closely in the New York office, was assigned the job of determining the extent of organized crime in the New York area. It seems the Director had been quoted in the media questioning the nature and very existence of the Mafia. After months of investigation they finally concluded that there was, indeed, disorganized crime in New York.

Although Bernard would always be disturbed by the Rosenberg and Riesel matters, the most emotionally wrenching events in which he was involved were kidnapping cases. Once a child is reported missing, time is of the essence. A matter of hours often makes the difference in the fate of the victim. Errors of judgment can be fatal. Based on empirical data the mother is often the number one suspect in the absence of other hard information such as witnesses, phone contacts, or ransom notes. Once it is established that the child has been kidnapped elaborate procedures are implemented.

Bernard was involved in a number of kidnapping cases. The two most saddening were the Greenlease and the Weinberger cases. In both instances the victims were killed shortly after their abduction. In these situations the Bureau was able to apprehend their killers—a man and woman in the Greenlease murder, and a man in the Weinberger case. All three individuals were finally executed. Such cases weighed heavily on Bernard and with the passing of time he realized that his temperament was not suited to his role as an FBI agent. He had to conclude that the remark sometimes made about him by fellow agents was probably accurate. "He was a surgeon who was appalled at the sight of blood." More accurately, perhaps, his own blood.

Although he never considered the FBI job all that dangerous, there were moments. One midsummer morning in the Brownsville section of Brooklyn, he and another agent were doing a neighborhood investigation attempting to develop leads on a subject who had escaped from a Virginia penitentiary, killing a guard in the process. Since the case had gained widespread publicity and had achieved prominent fugitive status within the Bureau, the agents were cautious. The subject, described as "armed and dangerous," was likely to end up in Virginia's electric chair if captured. It was unlikely he would be taken without a battle.

Having already knocked on several doors searching for the subject, Bernard and his associate found themselves on a stoop, anticipating another innocuous interview. Bernard was about to ring the bell when a young boy delivering papers came up the steps and tapped on a front bay window with a coin, presumably looking for a resident. Bernard waited, reaching under his jacket in his breast pocket for his credentials. Suddenly, the door opened slightly and a dark African American face peered out cautiously. Bernard, reaching for his credentials, was about to identify himself, when the other agent, standing slightly behind him, shoved open the door. "FBI!" he barked, leveling his pistol at the man. There stood the killer, a pearl-handled automatic shoved in his belt.

Disarming the man, his fellow agent quickly put the subject in handcuffs and they took him to the Bureau car. It had all happened fast and Bernard, startled by his fellow agent's actions, which might have saved a gun battle, was confused.

"How did you know it was the subject?" Bernard asked.

"Christ!" responded the agent. "He's a prominent fugitive. He looked just like his picture. . . . A gun in his belt!" he added, shaking his head as though wondering how Bernard had made it through the FBI Academy. Although his part in the apprehension was marginal, it gained Bernard another personal citation from J. Edgar Hoover.

Back at the office during interviews with the subject, Bernard learned that the outcome might have been different.

"Why didn't you resist when you saw us?" he asked the subject. "You had your pistol—"

"I saw you had your hand on your gun," the man replied, referring to Bernard's reaching for his credentials. "I knew it was all over."

"Sure," said Bernard, drawing his credentials from his breast pocket. "I would've thrown these at you. We carry our pistol on our belt."

They both laughed. Bernard knew little about the man's background or the reason for his escape and killing the guard but, as happened on other occasions when dealing with subjects, he experienced a feeling of compassion for the man. He seemed to have an upbeat manner despite the grim future that awaited him. The man's sense of humor stood out later when agents were transporting him to the Federal House of Detention on West Street. As they were leaving their office at Sixty-Ninth and Third Avenue, two other agents joined them looking for a ride downtown. The subject, securely manacled, sat next to Bernard in the rear. As they started down Lexington Avenue, one of the agents said, "Drop me off at Fifty-Second and Lex." The other said, "I'm running late. Gotta get home. Drop me off at Grand Central."

"Yeah, me too," said the subject facetiously. "Drop me off at Thirty-Fourth and Lex!"

Bernard was the only one who laughed. But it was with a sense of compassion for the helpless manacled figure sitting next to him.

Part VI

28

Coast Guard Rescue

WITH EXPECTATIONS of a baby came compelling motivation for a new job. The demands and unpredictability of the Bureau coupled with a working pregnant wife inspired Bernard to look for a more sedentary lifestyle. It came courtesy of the president of Canada Dry, who offered Bernard a training position with his firm. The timing was right. After almost nine years in government service, Bernard was ready for a change in careers. He enjoyed working with his fellow agents. But the Bureau work was troubling, not only coping with the victims of crime such as kidnapping, but occasionally dealing with subjects of cases who themselves were in trouble because of circumstances over which they had little control. "There are many good people doing time," he would sometimes say—a comment that drew varied responses from his colleagues.

Bernard's final Bureau performance rating was "Excellent," reflecting six personal letters of commendation during his last eight months of service. Somewhat ironic was the excellent rating approved by Assistant Director John Mohr, who a few years previously had been unimpressed by Bernard's "breezy manner" and need of a haircut.

FEDERAL BUREAU OF INVESTIGATION
UNITED STATES DEPARTMENT OF JUSTICE

REPORT OF PERFORMANCE RATING

Name of Employee: BERNARD F. CONNERS #11102

Where Assigned: NEW YORK (Division) CRIMINAL (Section, Unit)

Official Position Title: SPECIAL AGENT GS-12

Rating Period: from 4/1/59 to 12/11/59

ADJECTIVE RATING: EXCELLENT
Outstanding, Excellent, Satisfactory, Unsatisfactory

Employee's Initials: BFC

Rated by: HOWARD L. GILLESPIE Signature: [signature] Title: SUPERVISOR Date: 12/11/5

Reviewed by: H. G. FOSTER Signature: [signature] Title: SPECIAL AGENT IN CHARGE Date: 12/11/5

Assistant Director DEC 16 1959

Rating Approved by: [signature] Signature Title Date

TYPE OF REPORT

( ) Official
( ) Annual
(XX) Administrative
( ) 60 Day
( ) 90 Day
( ) Transfer
(XX) Separation from Service
( ) Special

Report of Performance Rating — April–December 1959.

Although a large international corporation that was publicly traded, Canada Dry was run like a family business. Indeed, many of the officers were related either directly or through marriage to the president, a dignified Harvard graduate named Roy Moore, who presided over an executive group composed largely of Ivy League graduates. It was a major change from the stressful world of criminal justice and counterespionage, and Bernard found the move exceedingly pleasant. Although his Irish heritage was occasionally the pretext for good-natured kidding by his new WASP associates, his mostly warm acceptance in the executive suite was gratifying.

Following some initial training by the personnel department, which included a few trips to Connecticut where he underwent psychological evaluation to determine his aptitude for a variety of business endeavors, he was sent to Boston for further training. "You'll get along well with that element up there," commented the director of personnel, a Yale graduate.

After several weeks of training in Boston, Bernard was appointed branch manager of the Rhode Island division with offices in Providence. He and Catherine rented a house from a lovely widow in an upscale neighborhood in Barrington called Rumstick Point. Here Catherine settled into her final weeks of pregnancy, which were not easy. Catherine, who had beautiful, athletic legs, developed swelling in her left leg. It would recur through the years but she never complained. Her only comment was, "Oh, I don't care. I got Christopher." For Bernard, the arrival of his son was a thrilling experience. From the moment he first laid eyes on Christopher he was enthralled, and it never changed. He would be a joy to his parents during ensuing years.

Much of Bernard's work in Rhode Island dealt with selling soft drinks. There were periodic meetings with chain-store executives to secure authorization for some seventy-five different varieties of Canada Dry products, ranging from cooperative advertising to in-store displays. Much of the work entailed supervising salesmen in stores, often helping to stock bottles on shelves. Occasionally it was hard on Bernard's ego; he had become accustomed to respect with the FBI credentials, and selling Canada Dry soft drinks was entirely different. On one hot midsummer night he found himself in Bermuda shorts hawking soda like a carnival barker with some of his staff in front of a supermarket. He told a young lady who had just left the store that he was an undercover FBI agent on surveillance. She was unconvinced.

Because of its location on the water, Rumstick Point was popular with sailors. The Connerses were invited to join the prestigious Barrington Yacht Club and subsequently bought a forty-foot Rhodes auxiliary sloop named *Tempest*. Most of Bernard's sailing had been confined to small boats at the Lake Placid Club, and the change to ocean sailing was not without its traumatic moments. Docking their craft in strange ports was of particular concern to Bernard: one could cause damage with a boat that size, particularly under sail when the engine was off. He usually let Kate do the docking, since it didn't bother her at all, and she had little confidence in Bernard's nautical skills. Once land was out of sight, particularly in heavy seas, his Butterflies were as big as the jib. Kate, who was nerveless as a stone, referred to him as "Bernie Tuna, Chicken of the Sea!"

But there was an occasion when she thought he performed well. They had invited two couples, experienced sailors, to join them on a weekend cruise to Newport. Although the forecast was not good, bad weather did not seem imminent. It was. They ended up in a dreadful storm, with seventy-five-mile-per-hour gales, according to later news accounts. Bernard as skipper ordered his crew of four below deck, and lashed himself to the tiller. From here he watched anxiously as the bow would completely submerge, and then would take a deep breath as the waves crashed over his head. As the fury of the storm increased, with the help of his crew, he tied heavy canvas to the stern, letting it drag behind in the sea to hold the boat into the wind to keep from capsizing. Through all of this the boat was pounded relentlessly and soon the engine began smoking.

Finally, after an interminable period, there was an outline of land on the horizon. One of the crew, Julian Gibbs, who later became president of Amherst College, emerged from the cabin very concerned. "We've got to send up flares," he said. That was certainly all right with Bernard. So they shot up flares, and sure enough, within a few minutes a vessel appeared on the horizon. It was the Coast Guard, whose skipper proceeded to denounce Bernard. "Captain, what in hell are you doing out here? Do you realize the jeopardy you've put these people in?" Although Bernard was inclined to tell the man to go screw Davy Jones, a look at the smoke billowing from the engine portal convinced him that total subservience and gratitude were the better response. After securing their boat the Coast Guard towed them into a cove within sight of a mooring. "Captain," said the Coast Guard skipper, his voice laced with sarcasm, "Do you think you can manage to get your vessel in from here?"

After a few parting comments heavy with invective, they were gone. Silence and embarrassment followed. But the worst was still to come. Although the mooring could have been easily reached under normal conditions, the wind was still blowing hard, preventing the use of sail. This meant relying on power and the engine was not cooperating at all. Smoke was now enveloping everything.

"Maybe the portal to the engine is clogged," said Julian. "I've seen that happen. Seaweed clogs the portal and the engine heats up." It was a logical conclusion, but the portal was well below the waterline. To clear it would require someone going overboard. Given the weather and the way the sloop was heaving with the waves, there were few volunteers. Since Bernard was the captain, he decided he had no choice. In spite of protestations from Kate, he went over the side. Later, he would realize that this was dangerous because of the heaving of the vessel in heavy seas. Once underwater he managed to find the outlet near the bow. No seaweed. He surfaced, exhausted, and they pulled him up into the boat. "No seaweed!" he gasped.

"That engine's going to be on fire shortly," said Julian. "Where are the flares?" he shouted. "We have to send up more flares!"

"I'd rather drown!" Bernard said, watching the Coast Guard vessel, now a small speck on the horizon. "No way I'm bringing those guys back."

Bernard's potential humiliation at the hands of the Coast Guard was of little concern to the frightened crew and, in the face of what threatened to be an all-out mutiny, he sent up the remaining flares. Within a short time the dark silhouette of the Coast Guard vessel reappeared. An unprintable denunciation of the *Tempest's* captain followed. Notwithstanding the vituperation of the Coast Guard, Kate later stood by her man. "He was a real hero! The rest of us were huddled down in the cabin!"

The *Providence Journal* headlined the story: "COAST GUARD RESCUES FOUNDERING TEMPEST IN HEAVY SEAS."

29

Payne Whitney Yacht

THERE WERE happier cruises with the *Tempest*. Ocean sailing offered long days of solitary enjoyment, as well as engaging social encounters with new friends. One such experience took place while Bernard and Catherine were moored at the Ida Lewis Yacht Club in Newport, one of the great old world yacht clubs. Next to them was a magnificent vessel that overlapped the *Tempest*. They were having a cocktail, cooking dinner on the stern, when a man appeared above them on the yacht. He stood, arms folded on the railing of his boat, looking down at them for a moment or two. They were beginning to feel a trifle uncomfortable when he said, "Preparing for dinner, I see. Why don't you come over and join me?"

Although surprising, it was an invitation that brought little hesitation from the *Tempest* crew. After a few protestations about not wanting to intrude, they quickly climbed to the other deck and introduced themselves. The host was a charming Gatsbyesque man who appeared to be in his mid-thirties. After a few pleasantries, attention turned to his yacht. He explained that it had been owned previously by the Payne Whitney family.

"It's always had a three-man crew," he shrugged. "My wife and I had just been married when we bought it. We went on a six-month honeymoon cruise."

Kate and Bernard nodded appreciatively, waiting for the wife to appear. That didn't happen. Following drinks and dinner served by a crew member, they would learn that their host's marriage had ended abruptly. He and his recent wife had returned from their six-month honeymoon cruise and were promptly divorced. Anyone who has spent long periods with someone confined to quarters on a sailboat might understand. Indeed, such a voyage could prove instructive for those contemplating marriage.

There were other incidents involving the *Tempest*. When notice came of Bernard's transfer back to the corporate offices at 100 Park Avenue in Manhattan, the diminishing need for a sailboat, coupled with the promise of a substantial yard bill for storage and repairs, were sufficient motivation to place an ad in the *Providence Journal* offering the *Tempest* for sale. Responses came quickly, one from a courtly gentleman who seemed to be a square-dealing sort. "Would a short outing be in order to evaluate the craft?"

"Of course," replied Bernard, "and Sunday afternoon would be just fine." The short sail was accomplished quickly and the gentleman, who appeared knowledgeable, frequently dropping nautical terms during the sail, seemed keenly interested. They returned to the mooring a few yards in front of the Barrington Yacht Club terrace where several members were lunching. After securing the vessel, Kate, the gentleman, and Bernard went below to the cabin with the purpose of finalizing the sale. Well, it wasn't to be. They had no sooner sat down when, rather than making an offer, the gentleman explained with great suavity how he had enjoyed the trip but that unfortunately the *Tempest* would not meet his needs. Kate and Bernard, swallowing hard, were offering pleasantries about how nice it was to have met him when their guest suddenly excused himself and went above on deck. Kate and Bernard exchanged confused glances, and after a moment Bernard followed the man above. He emerged on deck to find their guest standing on the bow in broad daylight urinating. While such an act might be acceptable in the privacy of the high seas, standing directly in front of the old guard dining alfresco at the Barrington Yacht Club was another matter. Why he hadn't used the head in the cabin instead of flaunting himself in front of the audience on shore was hard to understand. Horrified, Bernard slunk back into the cabin. Kate, noticing his concern, asked, "What's the matter?"

"Oh nothing, I suppose," Bernard said. "But our guest's up on the bow relieving himself in front of the whole yacht club."

Bernard was quite embarrassed. Gaining membership at Barrington Yacht Club had required the young newcomers to Rumstick Point to put their best foot forward. This last display was something less. But such faux pas were soon forgotten, the *Tempest* was sold, and the Conners were off once again to adventures in Manhattan.

30

DeWitt and Lila Wallace of *Reader's Digest*

ONCE BACK in New York, finding a place to live was top priority. A new son made apartment dwelling less attractive, and it was decided that with Catherine's past earnings and Bernard's improved salary from the private sector, a house was in order. They proceeded to look in Westchester County. The happy end to their search came through the auspices of Harry Wilcox, an executive of *Reader's Digest* located in Pleasantville, New York, and a close personal friend of DeWitt and Lila Wallace, who had founded the magazine. Before long Mr. Wilcox had arranged for Bernard to meet Mr. and Mrs. Wallace at their magnificent Mt. Kisco estate, High Winds. Bernard sat with them in their large drawing room, quite intimidated, notwithstanding their gracious efforts to put him at ease. They were a suave, handsome couple in their late sixties. Over cocktails they inquired about his life, his experiences in college, the FBI, Canada Dry, and finally his marriage to Kate. Soon it dawned on Bernard that he was being interviewed, scrutinized really, to see if he and his family were suitable tenants for High Winds.

Bernard didn't recall always making great first impressions—Kate's mother? . . . Johnny Mohr?—but for whatever reason, Mrs. Wallace saw something that others had not. Perhaps it was their discussion about writers. She happened to hit on a few literary figures with whom Bernard was moderately familiar, such as Dickens, James, and Faulkner. Later, Mr. Wilcox told him that he had made quite an impression on Mrs. Wallace, and that she had said, "I want him for our guesthouse!" Kate, Christopher, and Bernard were soon ensconced in the Wallaces' beautiful estate.

It was a memorable experience. The Wallaces treated them with almost parental kindness, perhaps because they had no children of their own. They usually included the Conners in their parties, soirees that were limitless in their grandeur, hosting luminaries such as Dwight Eisenhower and the Duke and Duchess of Windsor. They were marvelous affairs and provided experience for entertaining that the Conners would later attempt to emulate. Nor was the Wallaces' hospitality confined to their parties. One Easter Sunday they took the Conners to dinner at a prominent restaurant. Kate was pregnant with their second child, Sarah, but looked lovely in a yellow spring dress despite the fact that the dress appeared to conceal a large beach ball. Midway through dinner, Mrs. Wallace caught Bernard's eye and motioned toward Kate. "Bernard, I don't think Catherine's feeling well." Bernard turned to see Kate swaying as though seated on a deck chair of a rolling ship. Before anyone could help, she and the beach ball had flopped onto the table. Despite some immediate concern and the replacement of dishes, Kate was soon sitting up as though nothing had happened. Bernard, chagrined, was apologetic. As for Kate, she hardly broke stride, continuing with her dinner. She would later pass it off with her customary indifference. "Oh well, it wasn't that bad. We had fun."

The few years Bernard spent with the Wallaces at High Winds were among his happiest. Their hosts appeared to have an unusual understanding of the couple at their doorstep: the strolling baby carriage, flying kites, skiing, pregnancy, gussied-up parties, and eventually talks of Bernard joining *Reader's Digest*. Things were progressing toward an executive position with the magazine, and it was with surprise and ambivalence that Bernard received notice of his appointment to division operations manager at Canada Dry's flagship operation in Hudson, New York. It was a remarkable promotion at Canada Dry, which could lead to a vice presidency. At the same time, he was uncertain how his close association with the Wallaces would be viewed by the magazine's top executives should he elect to join the *Digest*. Although interviews were pending, no specific offer had yet been made. After much deliberation, he and Catherine decided they could possibly resurrect the *Digest* connection if things did not work out with Canada Dry. They often wondered what might have happened had fate not intervened and taken them to Hudson. Leaving High Winds was a difficult decision. Although they remained in touch with the Wallaces, their departure marked the conclusion of a memorable chapter in their lives.

31

High Winds to Hillsdale

HUDSON, NEW YORK, was the site of the premier operation of Canada Dry. It was from here that the company originally shipped its products to satellite operations throughout the world. Soon after assuming his new position as division manager, Bernard purchased a small country house in Hillsdale, New York, a town near the Massachusetts border. It was a picturesque hamlet located in the foothills of the Berkshire Hills. Shortly after they had settled, Sarah was born. Bernard was ecstatic. Having been reared with six sisters, he felt no family would be complete without girls. And now a boy and a girl—a beautiful girl! The perfect family.

There followed a normal lifestyle with Bernard engaged in the Canada Dry operations. Weekends were spent with Catherine and their two children, Christopher and Sarah, occasionally playing tennis at a nearby club in Great Barrington, and skiing during the winter on the slopes of the Berkshire Hills. It was here also that Bernard resumed writing a novel, a roman à clef that he had started while in Rhode Island.

Always a passion since his early days with George Plimpton, writing occupied much of his free time. Although still in its embryonic form, the novel began to take shape. He intended the work to be a humorous, apocryphal FBI story containing anecdotal material woven around an espionage plot. As the work progressed, however, the story began taking the form of a lampoon. This was of some concern to Bernard inasmuch as he had positive feelings about the FBI. Since leaving the Bureau, he had come to realize that the overall quality of the agents and supporting staff were quite exceptional compared to the corporate world.

Nevertheless, he pushed ahead, writing in an improvisatory manner, rationalizing that it was a novel intended more as a caricature rather than as criticism of the FBI. Any comedic effort would inevitably have some parody, he reasoned. The storyline was somewhat contrived, revolving around the infiltration and control of the Bureau. The reader was led to believe that the Soviet KGB, operating through double agents, had successfully penetrated the Bureau at the highest levels, whereas the denouement, suggested later by a literary agent, reveals that, rather than the Russian KGB, it was actually the CIA that had infiltrated the Bureau under orders from the president who felt the Director had gained too much power.

Bernard's concern about embarrassing the Bureau diminished as he neared the completion of the book. After all, the Bureau knew of his writing ambitions: he had declared on his application that he aspired to be a writer. Indeed, had he not written speeches for Bureau officials to deliver at civic events and gatherings of law enforcement groups? Besides, the book probably had little chance of being published. It was extremely difficult for first-time novelists to get into print. Add to that the reluctance of any publisher to undertake a work that might subject them to the possible displeasure of J. Edgar Hoover. As one top editor of the *Washington Post* would later tell Bernard, there were many other newsworthy issues on which to devote resources rather than to offend Hoover. At the height of Hoover's power in the fifties and sixties, most of the media found it more propitious to extol the virtues of J. Edgar Hoover than to challenge his authority.

During the writing of the novel, Catherine displayed her usual cool, feeling Bernard was overly sensitive about possible fallout. She remained supportive throughout the process, occasionally reading parts of the manuscript and offering comments. One of her more singular contributions to the writing effort was preserving peace in a household composed of a struggling author and squabbling children, who now numbered three with the arrival of Jane (a bundle of delight who arrived twelve years after their marriage). She would later commemorate the publication of the novel with a handsome stand that held an enormous dictionary. A gold plaque bore the inscription:

To BFC
With Love and Noise
Sarah, Jane, Chris and Kate
March 31, 1972

Meanwhile, Canada Dry's financial structure rendered it a tempting target for acquisition. It came in the form of a successful takeover bid by the Norton Simon Corporation, a large conglomerate notorious for its takeover of vulnerable firms. Following the acquisition, the changes were swift and draconian. Under the control of the new president, David J. Mahoney, the former president of Good Humor, Canada Dry changed dramatically. As often happens in takeovers, there was an immediate purge of the executive team at Canada Dry, followed by a liquidation of much of the company's assets for near-term profit and cash.

Although Bernard was stunned by the inexorable changes that enveloped the firm, it provided him with the opportunity to acquire the company's most profitable operation in Hudson, New York. Thanks to Kate's request, a large check was forthcoming from her mother, Sarah. This, along with a consortium of banks, enabled him to become the owner of Canada Dry's largest franchise in the world, with operations in New York, New Jersey, Pennsylvania, Connecticut, Vermont, New Hampshire, and Massachusetts. As for members of the management team who headed up the takeover, they were soon gone, pursuing opportunities elsewhere. Mahoney, leader of this squad of raiders, would go on to become a prominent philanthropist and industrial leader. According to *Business Week* he was the highest paid executive in the United States in 1978. As for Bernard, although dismayed by some of the harsh changes in Canada Dry's top management, he realized that they enabled him to pursue his own entrepreneurial endeavor.

Becoming the owner and chief executive of a privately held company was a prodigious challenge for Bernard. Cash flow, from the inception, was a problem. Most of the company's operations were covered by ironclad union contracts. The Hudson division was governed by Local 812 of the New York Teamsters Union, a redoubtable organization that was said to have driven New York Coca-Cola into bankruptcy. Threats of strikes were omnipresent, particularly during the summer selling season. The union president was David Levinger, a formidable adversary, bolstered by his attorney and close associate, Leo Greenberg.

Bernard liked them both personally, but they were strictly arm's length, no-holds-barred when it came to negotiations. Even minor changes to improve efficiency were invariably the subject of intense protracted debate. Mr. Greenberg's manner of speaking was unusual, rather gravelly, and his words during negotiations were delivered in a slow measured drawl:

"Mis–ter Con–ners. . . . Here–we–are–again. . . . Wait–ing. . . . Al–ways wait–ing. . . ." He would sit in front of eight or ten grim-looking union representatives, summing up their latest offer to the union to call off its crippling strike. "Mis–ter Con–ners. . . . Here–we–sit. . . . Once–again. . . . A–gain! You–have–gone–to–the–well–and–come–back–with–noth–ing. . . . Noth–ing!" The words were always delivered with a sorrowful shaking of his head.

Bernard became adept at mimicking him. Home at night Kate would ask how things were going with the strike and he'd do his Mr. Greenberg imitation. They'd laugh, as only young people could laugh in the face of such dire conditions. But it was gallows humor. Corporate death by Local 812 was always in the wings. And now there was a family to consider.

What would he do? Bernard thought. Reapply to the Bureau . . . ? To *Reader's Digest* . . . ? By this time his mother-in-law's well was every bit as dry as the one to which Mr. Greenberg constantly referred. But he survived and somehow managed to buy sixteen other soft drink companies, as well as other firms, in the process. Along the way the description of their companies by creditors was well deserved: "Slow pay!"

Part VII

32

Wrath of the Righteous

BERNARD had completed the first draft on his novel *Don't Embarrass the Bureau* by the early seventies and had begun his search for a publisher. He thought there might be a mild reaction from the Bureau, but the response exceeded what he had anticipated. Friends in the FBI told him that the Bureau had secured a copy of the manuscript and that the Director had failed to see the humor in it. In fact, he was livid. Bernard would later obtain portions of his FBI file by means of the Freedom of Information Act (FOIA), and was surprised to learn the extent of the Director's displeasure. Hoover was kept informed about all developments, and the blue ink he scribbled in the margins of the memos was a clear manifestation of the degree of his concern:

> "I certainly would like to know who's behind this ..."
>
> —H
>
> "What is the X Agents Society doing about this?"
>
> —H
>
> "I don't like the way the X Agents Society is procrastinating."
>
> —H

A congressman named Sam Devine, one of many legislators who curried the Bureau's favor, expressed his dedication to the Director in a flattering letter and then, as if to prove his total loyalty, in his own handwriting scribbled in the margin, "Give me something to blast Conners on." Hoover, as seen in the following memo, gave his approval to the so-called "blast" with his customary "OK H" shortly before he died on May 2, 1972.

Within a few weeks, Devine was true to his word. After receiving information from the Bureau, he described Bernard on the floor of Congress as a disloyal employee who certainly did not speak for the vast

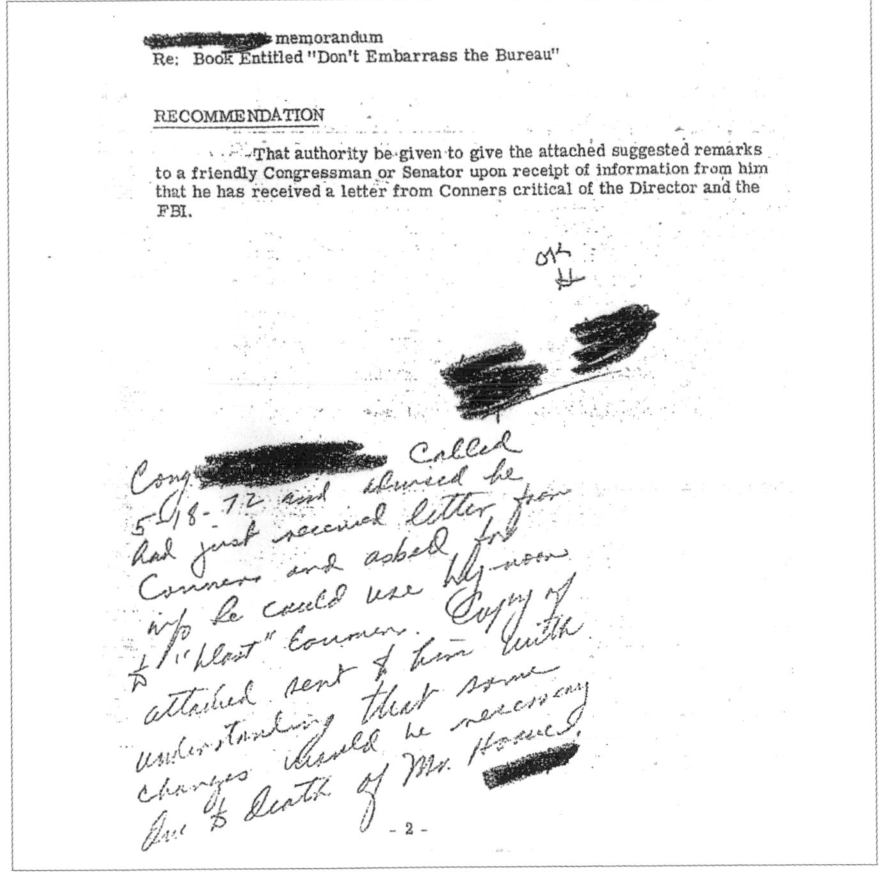

memorandum
Re: Book Entitled "Don't Embarrass the Bureau"

RECOMMENDATION

That authority be given to give the attached suggested remarks to a friendly Congressman or Senator upon receipt of information from him that he has received a letter from Conners critical of the Director and the FBI.

OK
H

Cong. called 5-18-72 and advised he had just received letter from Conners and asked for info he could use to "blast" Conners. Copy of attached sent to him with understanding that some changes would be necessary due to death of Mr. Hoover.

- 2 -

majority of agents. Considering the anger of the Director at the time, it was a rather benign rebuke. Knowing how the Bureau could react severely to criticism, Bernard was rather surprised that Devine's comments did not allege some subversive Communist activity on his part.

But Bernard continued to feel some remorse in his book undertaking. Hoover had treated him well during his tenure with the Bureau. Indeed, upon his resignation from the organization, Bernard had sent what was a customary letter expressing his admiration for the Director and the FBI and asking for an autographed copy of the Director's picture.

Bernard realized his novel did not cover all of the many good things the Bureau did, but believed those matters had been covered adequately elsewhere. His book was not an exposé but rather a fictitious spoof of the Bureau, and he thought Hoover should have been able to accept it for what it was. Yet, he certainly realized that if J. Edgar Hoover ever saw fit to acknowledge any criticism, however satirical, it would be with the absolute repudiation of the one offering the criticism. He would soon learn that he would be no exception to this policy.

33

Scribner's Acceptance and Rejection

BERNARD'S performance as division manager of Canada Dry's flagship operations in New York and New England had brought praise from top management, and he had been asked if he would care to recommend an FBI agent to work in the personnel department. Bernard's choice was an agent named Ed Hartnett, a West Point graduate and close friend who had worked with Bernard in the New York FBI office. Ed's personable qualities and business acumen had enabled him to adjust well to his new position with Canada Dry, and soon he became an assistant and close associate of Skip Walz, the director of personnel.

By this time, Bernard had purchased Canada Dry's operation and had come up with a title for his novel, *Don't Embarrass the Bureau.* He would later show the manuscript to Ed, who saw great potential in the work, and formed a public relations firm with Skip Walz to promote the book. A friend of Ed's named John McBride, a former newspaperman, was hired to write press releases. Hartnett's and Walz's involvement was short-lived, however. After learning of the Director's anger, they both elected to disengage. Their decision did not surprise Bernard, who about this time would like to have disengaged from the project himself.

Finding a literary agent to represent an unpublished author can be daunting; finding one who was prepared to withstand the scrutiny of Hoover was an additional challenge. Equal to the task was Oscar Collier, a respected agent with offices on Madison Avenue in Manhattan. Mr. Collier was impressed by the novel, but felt it was too long. He recommended that Bernard work with Darrell Husted, a highly regarded freelance editor and novelist with whom Collier had associated in the past. Bernard commenced working with Darrell and, although he was impressed with the editor's skills, he found rewriting challenging. Both Oscar and Bernard thought Darrell cut far too much from the novel. "This must go in toto!" was a phrase Darrell wrote repeatedly in the margins as he cut the manuscript by over one-third.

Shortly after Oscar Collier expressed interest in the novel, Candida Donadio, a prominent New York literary agent to whom Bernard had submitted the manuscript, called and asked to see Bernard. An interview was arranged and Bernard later met with her associate Mr. Gallagher. Bernard was favorably impressed by Mr. Gallagher, a relatively young man about Bernard's age who seemed knowledgeable about publishing. What's more, he really liked Bernard's story. At this stage of the writing it was the Soviet KGB that was infiltrating the FBI, but Mr. Gallagher said that as he read the manuscript he suspected it might be the CIA that was actually doing the infiltration. Well, voilà! It was a splendid idea and Bernard told him so. But he also told him of a competing agent's interest—Oscar Collier. Gallagher asked if he had signed on with Oscar. Bernard said he had not signed anything, but that Oscar had spent considerable time on the manuscript and that it would be awkward and unfair for Bernard to disengage. Mr. Gallagher looked at Bernard a bit perplexed and said,

"What are you, a writer or a priest?" They both laughed and that ended a pleasant interlude. But Bernard would remain grateful to Mr. Gallagher for his suggested denouement for the novel.

Had Bernard been more familiar with the editorial process, he may have resisted Darrell's cuts. But Darrell had good reasons for his excisions. "This is too expository. . . ." "This does nothing to further your storyline. . . ." "We can't have these digressions. . . ." were familiar admonishments. And of course he was right. Authors new to their craft often are carried away and overwrite. Theodore Dreiser's *An American Tragedy* is an example. Despite its success, it is doubtful this classic in its present form ever would have survived the contemporary editorial process.

Thanks to Darrell's editing skills they soon had a product with which Oscar was satisfied, and the book was submitted to several publishers. A number of prominent houses expressed interest and requested more information as well as interviews with the author. Bernard was particularly attracted to Scribner Publishing, because the former editor in chief was Maxwell Perkins, who had edited Fitzgerald, Hemingway, and Thomas Wolfe. Norbert Slepyan, a senior editor at Scribner, liked the book, but, as did many editors, had suggestions. Bernard did some rewriting in accordance with his wishes. During one of several meetings, Bernard mentioned that he didn't mind rewriting some passages, but could he be assured that Scribner would publish the work? He had been hearing from friends in the Bureau that the FBI had contacted some publishers who had received Oscar's submission and had conveyed Hoover's displeasure with the book. Obviously, such reports made him uneasy. He wanted assurance that after rewriting at Mr. Slepyan's suggestion, the publisher would not be intimidated and reject the book. Mr. Slepyan was effusive with his assurances. "Why of course we're going to publish it. I'd take it personally at this stage if we did not bring it out."

Things proceeded for a few weeks, during which Bernard had a meeting with Scribner's editor in chief, and assumed the novel was on its way to publication with this venerable publisher. Reality came in the form of a telephone call from Mr. Slepyan. Bernard was in a meeting with fellow board members of an art institute when a secretary informed him that Mr. Slepyan from Scribner was calling. He took the call to hear Mr. Slepyan, almost mournfully, inform him that they were not going to publish his novel. Bernard was stunned . . . but not totally surprised. He resisted asking Mr. Slepyan about his previous assurances of publication, sensing immediately by the man's tone that questions would go unanswered. Perhaps Mr. Slepyan did not know himself why Scribner had reversed course. Bernard suspected he knew the answer, but it was pure speculation. The publisher Charles Scribner was late in life; he would pass away a few years later. There were other books, other challenges. Bernard might have done the same thing if he were Scribner. Still, for Bernard at this particular time, even for a former boxer, it was a heavy body blow.

34

Publication and Reaction

REJUVENATION following the Scribner disappointment came from Bobbs-Merrill, a well-regarded house that had published distinguished writers such as William Styron, as well as a perennial best seller, *The Joy of Cooking*. Heading up the organization was a respected author and publisher named Eugene Rachlis who elected to publish the book. More editorial work followed. Bernard would learn that almost every editor has his own ideas about how a story should be told—ideas that invariably entail significant rewriting. Finally, *Don't Embarrass the Bureau* was published.

Promotion is important to the success of any book, and many authors become virtual shills in their publishing efforts. Bernard was no exception, and was uncomfortable with a process that entailed asking an embarrassment of favors. The following letter to George Plimpton was one of several that began appearing in the mailboxes of Bernard's friends after publication by Bobbs-Merrill and then Avon Books in paperback:

BERNARD F. CONNERS
40 OLD NISKAYUNA ROAD
LOUDONVILLE, NEW YORK 12211

June 13, 1973

Dear George:

According to Avon, my publisher, Don't Embarrass the Bureau seems to be "taking off" in paperback. It's number four on the New York Post best sellers list this week.

Right now, a review in the New York Times or some prestigious magazine could probably put it across. Last Sunday in the Times Book Review Martin Levin recommended it for summer reading, which of course helps.

If through some contact you could have it reviewed or mentioned, it would be grand and, of course, I should be forever grateful.

I hope this is not too presumptuous, but I've been urged by the publisher to contact any friends who might be in a position to help. They feel the book has significant possibilities.

Sincerely,

BFC/spc

Letter to George from Bernard 6/13/73.

Reviews were mostly favorable, although there were a number that expressed skepticism about the story line: "Why would the CIA infiltrate the Bureau?" or "The novel is essentially a roman à clef." One review by renowned critic John Barkham memorably concluded with the comment, "*Don't Embarrass the Bureau* is a conglomeration of espionage, comedy and sex in a verbal soufflé that never really rises." Shortly after the review appeared in the *New York Times*, Bernard was giving a talk to a large group of elderly women in Westchester. A woman from the audience stood and asked him his reaction to the Barkham review.

Bernard replied that he admired Mr. Barkham and thought his review was fair except for the reference to sex in the book. Bernard said there was no sex in his book, and that Mr. Barkham must have read the wrong book. "I know nothing at all about sex. Absolutely nothing!" Bernard said. And then, apparently carried away by his denial of sex, he added for emphasis, "I haven't had a sexual experience for eighteen years!" Bernard couldn't imagine why he had added the last sentence, but it drew a strong and appreciative laugh from the blue-haired audience.

Notwithstanding Barkham's remarks, the novel continued to receive good reviews, which launched it on numerous best-seller lists. Rather than criticism of the Bureau, most reviews described the novel as a fictitious humorous work. Following is a list of comments from leading newspapers:

"The novel proves as irresistible as it is frightening."
- Chicago Tribune

"A downright tantalizing suspense novel...a very exciting tale with unexpected shocks right up until the final page. Zingo!"
– Sacramento Bee

"...a fast-paced, exciting espionage story which demands being read from start to finish." – Women's Wear Daily

"A compelling, fast-moving story...It has humor, suspense and even sex...The book is educational and highly entertaining."
– Dayton Daily News

"A fast-paced...spy thriller...an intriguing tale of international espionage, murder, female impersonation and FBI infiltration."
– Chicago Sun-Times

"A lively and unusual story of intrigue with some fascinating FBI background...fast-moving, suspenseful, and provocative."
– Denver Post

"An impressive first novel...Story has more twists and turns than a tangled wiretap, plus an electrifying surprise ending." – The Cleveland Press

"An absorbing mixture of fact and fancy. Background on the FBI is fascinating. The story is intriguing, with a neat twist at the end."
– Hartford Courant

"A unique tale of internal espionage." – United Press International

"Don't Embarrass the Bureau is a tough, exciting book."
– Charlotte Observer

"Bernard F. Conners has done it in this thriller...you owe it to yourself to read this novel." – Bergen (N.J.) Sunday Record

"...downright humorous and frightening." – Cincinnati Post and Times-Star

"It's an exciting story, skillfully and believable told."
– Aurora Beacon News

"A novel which probably accomplishes more than its author set out to do...an intricate drama." – Louisville Courier-Journal

"Conners can write. His story moves fast. His characters are real." – Sacramento Union

"The book has a real feel to it...This book should be more than a passing first novel!" – Murfreesboro (Tenn.) News-Journal

The book inspired considerable movie attention, some from prominent film personalities. At one point Gregory Peck demonstrated his keen interest in a letter to Daniel Selznick and Joel Glickman, excerpts of which follow:

GREGORY PECK
1041 NORTH FORMOSA AVENUE
LOS ANGELES, CALIFORNIA 90046

August 14, 1972

Mr. Joel Glickman
Mr. Daniel Selznick
Goldwyn Studios
1041 North Formosa
Hollywood, California 90046

Dear Joel and Dan,

I have read DON'T EMBARRASS THE BUREAU and was quite intrigued by it. It certainly is a most unusual premise and continually surprising in its revelations. It has all the earmarks of a provocative, exciting film.

. . . I will be delighted to read the screenplay, and if the project at that point retains the promise inherent in the book would very much look forward to participating.

You know that I think highly of you both and would be happy to work with you. Good luck with the screenplay.

Best,

Gregory Peck

GP/bt

Gregory Peck letter 8/14/72

Such attention prompted Bernard to write his first screenplay, an effort described by one agent as "a script with lifeless, wooden characters." Notwithstanding such reaction, interest in a film continued to surface in the press:

BERNARD F. CONNERS

G-GIRL THROWS THE FBI A CURVE -- Who's Cricket? Author Bernard F. Conners, an ex-FBI agent, helps throw Director J. Edgar Hoover a curve with this one -- the mysterious Cricket, who may or may not be a girl in man's garb but who is nevertheless the Assistant Director in an explosive suspense novel "Don't Embarrass The Bureau" (Bobbs-Merrill). The book highlights behind-the-scenes revelations about the FBI and the bureaucracy of Hoover's "old gray battleship." Unlike the CIA or the Secret Service, and despite the recent passage by Congress of the Equal Rights Amendment, the FBI does not have women agents and Hoover refuses to hire any. Hollywood offers are being made for the book and suggested candidates have already been named for the role of G-Girl (?) Cricket, albeit for obviously different reasons: trim Candice Bergen, playing hands up, and Raquel Welch, who has both hands loaded.

Some movie offers, one of which was by a producer with significant film credits, suggested Bernard help finance production. George Plimpton was wary of the project as reflected in excerpts from his following letters:

GEORGE A. PLIMPTON
541 EAST 72ND STREET
NEW YORK, N. Y. 10021
PHONE UN 1-0016

September 18, 1973

Mr. Bernard F. Conners
40 Old Niskayuna Road
Loudonville, New York 12211

Dear Bernie,

I have sent the . . . material to Tim Seldes, my agent, who will have an opinion or two. I read part of it to Swifty Lazar, who is the west coast expert I have mentioned to you, and he was explicitly down on the project. . . .

Why don't we get together for a lunch sometime. I have some Paris Review news and besides I'd like to hear what you're up to.

Very best wishes,

George

GAP/mm

George Plimpton letter to Bernard 9/18/73.

GEORGE A. PLIMPTON
541 EAST 72ND STREET
NEW YORK, N. Y. 10021
PHONE UN 1-0016

October 10, 1973

Mr. Bernard F. Conners
60 Old Niskayuna Road
Loudonville, New York 12211

Dear Bernie,

The people I've talked to (my agent Timothy Seldes and his legal counsel) both think that it is "highly unwise" for you to get involved in financing a motion picture based on Don't Embarrass the Bureau. Of course, such people are notoriously conservative, but my own view is that they are probably right.

. . . Incidentally, the story editor for Clint Eastwood has been on my tail for the last couple of weeks looking for properties. I have advised her of your book.

I have a lot of Paris Review news which you should know about -- the most important being the likely move of the magazine back here -- the enormous cost of Dutch guilders being the cause. Do call when you next plan to come to New York.

Very best wishes,

George

George Plimpton letter to Bernard 10/10/73.

As George forewarned, interest from moviemakers eventually faded, and Bernard's script and its "lifeless characters" were soon consigned to Hollywood's graveyard of aspirations. But there was plenty of drama behind the scenes. Bernard would later secure his Bureau file and learn the lengths to which Hoover had gone to stifle publication of the book. John McBride, the press agent, was a skillful writer and his releases about the book were published throughout the country, mostly by smaller newspapers. As are most press releases, McBride's were designed to stimulate interest, and they were remarkably successful. Regrettably, from Bernard's viewpoint, they sometimes referred to the Bureau's alleged shortcomings at the time, such as no women agents. Probably worst of all, he committed the cardinal sin, characterizing J. Edgar Hoover as an elderly bureaucrat who should resign! Bernard cringed when he saw some of the releases, and expressed his concern to McBride. There was considerable discussion regarding the tone of the text, Bernard trying to soften the rhetoric, while McBride was doing what he was being paid to do: sell books. And this he was doing. *Don't Embarrass the Bureau* began to appear on best-seller lists, at one time reaching number two on the *New York Daily News* list.

This, of course, was having a corresponding impact inside the Bureau. Ed Hartnett called Bernard to say Hoover was displeased. Although he and Skip Walz had already elected to disengage, their concern was still evident. Bernard was surprised. "Ed," he said, "I think you may be overreacting. It's only a novel. It's comedy. I can't believe the Director is taking it that seriously."

Bernard would later discover under the FOIA a letter dated April 1972, sent to Hoover by the SAC in New York (O'Connor, who had been transferred from Chicago) that caused Bernard to swallow hard. It referred to a memo submitted by an agent who interviewed Hartnett that suggested Bernard had talked Hartnett into starting his public relations agency. This was not true. Hartnett had gone to lengths to convince Bernard that John McBride and the agency were the appropriate mechanism to promote the novel. How much Ed had actually said to the interviewing agent and how much was lost in Cementhead's translation is anyone's guess.

With the book appearing on best-seller lists, Bobbs-Merrill decided it was time for an author tour—a process Bernard disliked intensely. It consisted of traveling to the sixteen major book cells throughout the country, appearing on television and radio, as well as interviews with newspapers. It was an exhausting schedule, flying from one city to the next, doing shows at all hours of the day and night. Once Bernard counted fifteen different interviews in one day. Sometimes he was unsure if he were repeating himself, offering the same comments on the same show—or worse, contradicting himself. One of his first appearances was on a live national morning show in New York City. The publicity agent who had arranged the appearance was Valerie Jennings (wife of the newscaster Peter Jennings). Valerie was a lovely attractive person who did her job well. Bernard was exceedingly nervous appearing before what Jennings described as an audience consisting of several million people. It was beyond anything with which the Butterflies had had to cope previously. After the first unnerving few minutes he managed to compose himself and by the time it was over he thought he'd done well. In fact, he was in a state of such relief and mild euphoria when he walked off the set that he was unprepared for what happened next.

"Bernard, let's have a cup of coffee, okay?" said Jennings. Bernard, anticipating compliments for his performance, was unprepared for her critique. "Bernard, you were *terrible*," she said with lowered eyes. "I told these people you were going to be good. I have my reputation to think of!" It was probably the most honest assessment he had of his TV appearances. Jennings would later deny that she had been so blunt, but Bernard would remember it perfectly. They were in a green leather booth. Jennings lowered her pretty head, put her hands over her eyes and repeated in a voice heavy with remorse, “Bernard, you were terrible!”

But, throwing her reputation to the wind, Jennings later placed Bernard on many national TV shows. He was unsure about the effect of all this on her reputation, but her efforts certainly helped to put *Don't Embarrass the Bureau* on the lists.

35

Today Show

DONALD TRUMP'S brother-in-law, James Grau, was another person instrumental in gaining Bernard significant public exposure. James, an accomplished publicist, was married to Elizabeth Trump, whose manner was the antithesis of her brother Donald's. Friendly and reserved, she was a pleasure to be with. Bernard sensed Donald's great exuberance sometimes embarrassed his sister. Bernard would later have lunch with "The Donald" at the 21 Club and found him to be very cordial and entertaining—not at all like his sometimes intimidating TV personality.

James, an amiable former vice-president of NBC, used relationships at NBC to secure a half-hour interview for Bernard on the *Today Show* with Barbara Walters and Edwin Newman. This afforded a great opportunity to present the novel to millions of readers. As the day neared for his *Today Show* appearance, the Butterflies became increasingly restive. Bernard remembered the guards of the condemned inmates at Sing Sing telling him that they tried to have the condemned prisoner eat a good last meal as it helped emotionally to withstand the traumatic period before going to the electric chair. (He mentioned this bit of jailhouse lore to George Plimpton, who remarked, "I shall have to remember that when I'm going to the electric chair.")

A few days before Bernard's scheduled date for the *Today Show* in May 1972, James Grau called to announce that Hoover had just died. Bernard was stunned by the news. Grau, no admirer of the Director, had used the controversy with Hoover to promote the novel, and was devastated. "Wouldn't you know," he said dejectedly. "The last ratty thing he did was die!"

Bernard was staying at the Plaza on Fifty-Seventh Street not far from the NBC studio the morning he was to appear on the *Today Show*. With the Sing Sing guards' comments in mind, he awakened early and ordered a New York sirloin steak with all the trimmings from room service. Bernard forced almost all of it down in the hopes of smothering the Butterflies. It seemed to help.

Bernard arrived at the *Today Show* studio a half hour early and was greeted at the entrance by the frozen visage of their news and weather man Frank Blair. Bernard offered a hearty good morning and received only silence and a grim stare in return. It was a frosty welcome even by a weatherman's standards. Was he going to be "sandbagged" on the show? Would they attempt to embarrass the author of *Don't Embarrass the Bureau*? What if they were to read the totally sycophantic letter he'd sent to Hoover upon his retirement? A host of golden Butterflies clouded his vision as he walked past the stone-faced Blair onto the set.

Things warmed up a bit inside. Barbara Walters regarded him with an inscrutable stare while Edwin Newman, the anchorman, was more gracious. A guest who appeared with Bernard on the show was former attorney general Ramsey Clark—no friend of Hoover's, who had referred to Clark a short time before as a hapless "jellyfish." The show proceeded with Edwin Newman asking some rather benign questions, which prompted equally benign answers from Ramsey Clark and Bernard. The proceeding was very civil, with relatively little criticism of Hoover or the Bureau. Bernard left feeling he had covered his points regarding the novel while retaining his dignity.

As he walked out he noticed that the weatherman who had greeted him—or rather, who had refused to greet him—had abandoned his post. Bernard continued to wonder if Blair had been stationed there earlier for a purpose. No one without a motive would have been that uncivil. But the show had been a success. A full half hour on the *Today Show* was unusual for a novelist, and Grau was ecstatic. "That was just great," he said. "This will lead to lots of shows"—a remark that led to a host of new Butterflies.

Newspaper interviews were nerve-wracking for a different reason. No one knew better than Bernard that interviews with reporters could be unpredictable. He had learned the reporter's creed firsthand from handling press releases in the Bureau: "Never let the facts interfere with a good story." So it was with reservations that he approached his meeting with Sidney Fields, a prominent columnist with the *New York Daily News*. Fields had a readership of a few million people and the residual implications of his story could be significant. Anxiously, Bernard sat in front of him expecting a pretty thorough, perhaps combative interview.

"I understand you played football with the Chicago Bears?" It was the columnist's first question, but the very last one Bernard expected. After all, he was there to talk about his novel, not his brief experience with the Bears. "Yes, I played with the Chicago Bears," Bernard answered. "But I never played with the Bears while they were playing anyone else. I was with them about long enough to take a shower." Fields laughed, and seemed to like the answer. "Okay," he said, exuberantly, as though he sensed a good story line, "Let's talk about your shower with the Chicago Bears!"

Bernard never realized how uninspiring his athletic career was until that moment. To be reduced to talking about a shower with the Chicago Bears seemed frivolous at best, considering the real purpose of the interview: to discuss his book and how it came to be. Bernard admitted that it was a bit more than a shower; but he told Fields that he didn't even have his own locker, that he shared it with another back from some southern college. He explained, however, it was more than a preseason tryout. It was with the team at Wrigley Field after the start of the season.

Bernard didn't elaborate, feeling the book interview was being sidetracked. And from Fields's initial questions he sensed he had already investigated his background thoroughly. But had the conversation continued in that vein, Bernard would have told him that the owner and coach of the Bears, George Halas, thought Bernard was a talented quarterback and offered him a private option. One of the other quarterbacks at the time was George Blanda, a hall of fame star. Bernard thought he threw the ball better than Blanda, and he was far more agile. Butterflies, however? He was certain Blanda was a league ahead of him when it came to controlling his emotions—an important part of any athletic endeavor. The back with whom he shared his locker seemed to have some Butterflies of his own. He was nervous about being cut. "When Halas cuts players he always puts his arm around you," he said. Bernard thought the man probably spent as much time evading Coach Halas as he did tacklers. . . .

Bernard wasn't worried about being cut. His future had already been cast. It was either the FBI or the army. But Coach Halas was a kind man. He gave him many opportunities and the offer of a private option was unusual at the time. In some ways he reminded Bernard of his high school coach Country Bill Morris. "He was very nice to me," Bernard said, concluding his remarks about his brief experience with the Bears. "I have fond memories of Coach Halas."

Bernard found Sidney Fields to be likeable with a pleasant sense of humor. His story appeared in the *New York Daily News* the following week:

DAILY NEWS, MONDAY, MAY 15, 1972 • 44

ONLY HUMAN

FBI Without Tears

By SIDNEY FIELDS

Bernard F. Conners, an ex-FBI agent, is 45, plays semi-pro football, runs a multi-million dollar bottling business and is the author of "Don't Embarrass the Bureau," a novel which will be published on Friday.

A blunt, deliberate man, Conners served the FBI for almost nine years and is the first ex-agent to write a book about it who was neither disgruntled nor resentful. He was always on cordial terms with the late J. Edgar Hoover and received four personal citations from him. When the Warren Commission which investigated the assassination of President Kennedy, criticized the FBI, Conners dispatched a letter to Mr. Hoover condemning the criticism as unwarranted.

"But I was as aware of the weaknesses of the Bureau and its director as well as their strengths," said Conners during a trip here from his home in Loudonville, N.Y., where he lives with his wife Catherine and their three children. His wife was a college classmate.

As an FBI agent Conners served all over the country and was involved in major crime and espionage cases. He helped track down the kidnapers of Bobby Greenlease in 1953, the 6-year-old boy who was killed before the kidnapers even sent the ransom notes. He helped apprehend the kidnaper of Peter Weinberger, also killed.

Night Supervisor

He played a minor role in the arrest of Soviet master spy Rudolf Abel and a major one in the case of Ethel and Julius Rosenberg, convicted and executed for transmitting atomic bomb information to the Russians. Conners was promoted from agent to field supervisor. Before he left the Bureau he was night supervisor of the New York and Chicago offices.

"I'm indebted to the FBI," he said. "It was fine training and experience and I was associated with a group of extraordinary men. I left because I was getting married and I didn't want to be hunting people who were in great trouble."

Conners was twice a Golden Gloves champion and served in the U.S. Army from 1945 to 1947. He now plays quarterback for the Hudson, N.Y. team, in the Empire Football League. In 1949, when he was star halfback for St. Lawrence University, he was one of the leading ground gainers in the country. Before graduation in 1951 he filed his application to join the FBI. After graduation the Chicago Bears picked him up.

"But I was with them for only eight days," he said. "The Army recalled me. I was on my way to Korea when the FBI hired me."

At Albany Military Academy and in college Conners wrote for the school papers, always wanted to write more and began his novel in 1954, but put it aside until 1969 because "I was trying to make it on the outside."

Editors who saw some things he had written urged him to write a non-fiction book about the FBI because it would sell better than fiction by an unknown.

"But I want to be a novelist," said Conners. "I'm already at work on my second one."

"Don't Embarrass the Bureau" is a suspense novel which deals with the FBI on two levels: It's extraordinary power and how it touches everyone from the ordinary citizen to the Congress and even the President. And the minutiae

Bernard F. Conners: Novel on FBI

in an agent's life, the things the public rarely, if ever, hears about, the day to day problems the agent faces, everything from piecing together the tenuous threads of a crime to avoiding the slightest thing that would embarrass the Bureau. Did Conners ever do that?

"If I had I would have received a personal letter of censure from Mr. Hoover, in funeral black. He had an incredible phobia about anything that would sully the Bureau and the punishment didn't always fit the crime."

When Mr. Hoover took over the FBI in 1924 it had 600 agents. It now has 8,586, plus 11,015 other employes. Not one agent was ever convicted of a crime.

"Mr. Hoover conducted the Bureau with great propriety," Conners said. "He was a man of character and moral purpose. We were lucky to have him. He stood up. But we have no assurance that his successor will. And he made no provisions for a successor."

Pertinent Question

Conners posed another pertinent question: Will the awesome power built up by Mr. Hoover over a 48-year tenure be used dangerously in the hands of a lesser man? "Such power for one man is not in the best interests of an open society," Conners insisted. "It should be curbed. And I've always felt that the tenure of the FBI director should be limited."

He recalled the crack of Martha Mitchell, wife of the ex-attorney general, when she introduced Mr. Hoover as "The best boss my husband ever had." There was more bite than comedy in it.

And he voiced another fear: the use of the sophisticated surveillance equipment used by the FBI to collect a vast amount of information on a vast number of people, a practice that Conners considers a deterrent on free expression and inimical to the best interests of an open society.

"The worst thing about a dossier is not what's in it as much as the implication of being in a dossier at all," he said. "Mr. Hoover did a good job of controlling all that information. But will his successor be able to do it?"

36

Minor League Football

ALTHOUGH service in the military and FBI had prevented Bernard from pursuing a football career, he maintained a strong interest in the game, working out as time permitted. Sometimes that meant little more than throwing passes to Kate in Central Park. (The soft lofted passes during these sessions would have pleased his college coach, Paul Patten.)

His unlikely reemergence in organized football took place years later in a minor league composed of teams from cities such as Albany, Brooklyn, Syracuse, Scranton, and Wilkes-Barre. At first, it was his intention to merely work out with a team from the lower Hudson Valley north of New York City, but before long he was pressed into service as one of the team's quarterbacks.

Although the minor leagues, Bernard regarded it as a good brand of football consisting of players in their twenties and thirties, many of whom had played in college and some with NFL experience. The majority of players on Bernard's team were African Americans led by a talented black quarterback named Ace. Although a mixed racial group that worked well together as a team, Bernard sensed some sensitivity from a few black players. The blacks congregated in their own locker room, and it was soon apparent to Bernard that they preferred Ace as their quarterback. It was understandable because the team had performed exceedingly well during prior seasons under his leadership, ranking near the top of the league.

The head of the team was a white coach named Frank Hamblet, who did an excellent job of maintaining rapport among his diverse group of players. He handled the quarterback issue as well as could be expected, alternating Bernard and Ace during quarters of the game. This reduced role was all right with Bernard, who was approaching fifty years of age. He liked Ace, who was always supportive in their competitive positions, and soon developed a friendly social relationship with Ace and his wife, Betty. Bernard sensed a trifle coolness from some of the players when he first joined the team, perhaps because of his age, but believed any hostility to be short lived. Regardless of any continuing aloofness by a few, he was soon comfortable in his role. The team had an outstanding record. Bernard made the league's all-star team as quarterback, and was later inducted into their hall of fame.

...nnors has had a year to learn t...
...kings offensive system and has had ...
...team running smoothly in practice.
has an excellent throwing arm and c...
be expected to fill the air with footballs
this season is his performances of last
year are any indication. He had one of
the best pass completion and yardage
records in the EFL circuit.

Bernard found the languorous, easygoing style of his black teammates appealing, and he often kidded them about their heritage and their complaints about perceived discrimination. He occasionally made comments someone else might have considered insensitive. One night in the locker room following a game, one of the receivers was telling Bernard about being wide open and not getting the ball. "You never throw to me!" he complained.

"I know, I know," said Bernard, winking at his teammates. "You think it's 'cause you're black, right?"

Bernard suspected some of the players used drugs and alcohol in their locker room. Games were often played on Saturday nights. Bernard recalled one cold November night coming to the sidelines during a time-out to confer with Coach Hamblet.

"Coach," said Bernard, shaking his head. "When I stick my head in that huddle, it smells like a gin mill."

"I know, I know. . . ." murmured the coach, indicating little desire to pursue the subject.

Bernard liked his teammates and sensed it was largely mutual. He thought his long association with black athletes, as well as conducting investigations in Chicago and Harlem, provided him with a unique insight to problems confronting African Americans not always understood by the white community. He believed that few fair-minded people who spent time visiting homes in the lower Bronx where children often live with a working mother would fail to understand the problems facing a black family. In many instances elder siblings are acting as parents. Some children skip school and spend nights on the streets with gangs where they are subjected to narcotics and other vices. Growing up black in America is not easy. In Bernard's opinion, the mothers who strive to hold it all together in the face of enormous challenges are true heroines.

37

Al Capp Cabal

THE **FBI** had many informants in the media. These covert relationships were not confined to the news media, and included many prominent personalities in the entertainment field. This was brought out vividly during the House Un-American Activities Committee proceedings during the early fifties when a galaxy of Hollywood stars informed on their associates. Bernard was well aware of the Bureau's efforts to develop such informants, and while in Chicago was assigned for a period of time as the office contact man developing sources of information in a variety of fields.

Because of his Bureau experience, Bernard was ever alert to the possibility of a TV or radio show designed to discredit him and his novel. With this in mind he became suspicious upon receiving an invitation to appear on Al Capp's television show. Al Capp, a cartoonist who became famous for his cartoon strip *Li'l Abner*, hosted a Sunday night TV show. He was a combative personality with decidedly right-wing views who delivered acerbic comments on contemporary issues. Capp had also been the target of controversial charges of sexual harassment, which led to much criticism.

Bernard was hesitant but, feeling it was a large national audience that would enhance awareness of his novel, he accepted the offer.

A few days before the show was to air, Bernard learned that he was being set up in a scheme designed to discredit him. According to Hartnett, Capp planned to read the obsequious letter Bernard sent to Hoover upon his retirement as well as present whatever else they might dredge up to embarrass him. Hartnett did not think it wise to appear on Capp's show, and the Butterflies concurred. Bernard called Al Capp's office four days before the show and explained to a dismayed producer that his schedule had been altered. "Perhaps we could do it at another time," Bernard suggested, adding facetiously that he trusted the cancellation would not impede the careful plans they had made for the show.

As the day of the airing drew near, Bernard began to have second thoughts. He remembered an occasion during his boxing career he had an opportunity to fight an outstanding boxer in a TV event. He declined, offering the promoters a variety of reasons, but the actual reason was the Butterflies. It bothered him ever after that he did not have the nerve to take the fight. And so it was with *The Al Capp Show*. He thought he would forever regret that he'd been afraid to take on Capp. Bernard finally decided just to appear at the NBC studio unannounced. They'd be less prepared, he reasoned, and he'd have an opportunity to confront them, challenge their motives, and assert that he was aware of their intentions.

When Bernard told George Plimpton he was going to be on *The Al Capp Show*, George thought it was a terrible mistake and tried to dissuade him. George invited Bernard to his apartment before the show the night of the performance to have a drink with him and his wife, Freddy Espy. George and Freddy sat side by side on a couch shaking their heads mournfully in anticipation of Bernard's undoing at the hands of Al Capp. Their admonitions did little for Bernard's confidence, but the scotch and soda they served him bolstered his resolve. After a gallows-like farewell, he was on his way.

The night had an unpredictable ending, however. Bernard entered the NBC studio announcing his arrival to a page only to learn that the show had been canceled. He left the studio with surprisingly ambivalent feelings: greatly relieved but, on the other hand, somewhat disappointed. It was probably just as well. George's scotch combined with Bernard's Celtic macho spirit, when confronted by Capp, may have made for an undignified performance.

It was inevitable that some would see the novel as the product of a self-serving author. But there was less of this than Bernard had anticipated; moreover, many agents befriended him in the face of the Director's disapproval. Bernard's high regard for the Bureau agents and their Director was evident during his media appearances. Yet as the publishing process unfolded he was occasionally contacted by critics of the FBI who were alleging all manner of wrongful activities by the Bureau. For the most part he was able to avoid such traps. With the possible exception of some of John McBride's provocative press releases, any criticism of the Director was restrained. Still, some critics of the Bureau attempted to enlist him in their efforts.

In one such instance, he was at his house in Lake Placid when he received a telephone call from a British author named Anthony Summers, who said that he was writing a nonfiction book about J. Edgar Hoover, and would like to come to Lake Placid from Manhattan to discuss it with Bernard. The man was a reporter for the BBC and the author of books that included *Goddess*, a biography of Marilyn Monroe, as well as *Conspiracy*, about the assassination of John F. Kennedy. Bernard questioned whether it would be worth his time to come all the way from New York City, and he asked Summers about his book. Summers replied that it would be a fair, objective work about the Bureau, but during the conversation mentioned that he had information about Hoover's homosexuality. Bernard, surprised and skeptical, said, "Anthony, I don't know what your sources are, but we're used to hearing such charges about Hoover. If Hoover were gay, don't you think we'd be aware of it?" Bernard proceeded to tell him that it would be difficult for anyone to conceal such a lifestyle from associates in the Bureau, and that he doubted that Summers would find any agents who thought Hoover was gay. He then asked Summers the sources for such information.

Summers replied with a number of individuals who had furnished the information, none of whom Bernard considered reliable sources. One was the wife of a prominent individual with mob connections who claimed she saw Hoover in drag at a party with Roy Cohn. It all seemed preposterous, and Bernard told him so. He said he would be glad to talk to Summers if he came to Lake Placid, but he doubted if he could be of much help. It was a civil conversation and Bernard concluded the call with an invitation to an impending *Paris Review* book affair.

During Bernard's conversations with Mr. Summers prior to publication of his book, the British author had assured him that his work was to be a fair scholarly assessment of the Director providing for many achievements of Mr. Hoover and the Bureau. He confirmed as much in an excerpt from the following letter:

P.O. Box 2540
Manassas
Virginia 22110

ANTHONY SUMMERS

Phones: 703-368-4621
703-968-0263

Mr. Bernard Conners,
610, Old Niskayuna Road,
Loudonville,
New York 12211

31 October 1988

Dear Mr. Conners,

Thank you very much for your patience on the telephone last week, and I am really sorry I could not get to your book party. I still hope to get up to see you for a lengthier talk - some time in the next couple of months.

Meanwhile, may I ask you to send me copies of a few selected pages from your Freedom of Information File . . . .

You have my assurance that my treatment of Mr. Hoover will be fair and balanced - and that I have well taken your positive points about the Bureau.

I look forward to hearing from you, and hope we do get together at some point.

Sincerely,

Tony S

Although Bernard was sanguine about Mr. Summers's overall intent, he remained dubious about the information the British author had related during his phone call, particularly the materials dealing with Mr. Hoover's alleged homosexuality. Consequently, he delayed his response, finally sending Summers the following letter:

BRITISH AMERICAN

BERNARD F. CONNERS
CHAIRMAN

(518) 786-6000

April 14, 1989

Mr. Anthony Summers
Still Point
Dromore, Aglish,
Cappoquin, Co. Waterford
Ireland

Dear Mr. Summers:

Please forgive my delay in responding to your letter. I have been caught up with a number of matters, and find myself behind in most everything.

I have reviewed my F.O.I.A. file with the Bureau and, alas, I doubt there is anything there in which you would be interested. However, in all candor, I must confess that I should probably be reluctant to divulge information which I felt was not in the Bureau's best interest. I have restrained myself from doing so in past years, as I felt it was not in the best interest of our country.

I believe I told you that, although I felt Mr. Hoover may have been unfair in some instances, I feel he built an extraordinary organization which has had a beneficent effect on our country. And, of course, I think the agent corps is the finest of its type in the world. I realize that all of this may not comport with what you may have heard, but in my old age I find my esteem for the Bureau continues to grow.

I wish you the best of luck. I am sure your book will be a fair scholarly treatment of the FBI. If your travels bring you to this region I shall be delighted to see you.

With kindest regards, I am

Sincerely,

BRITISH AMERICAN BOULEVARD • AIRPORT PARK • LATHAM, NEW YORK 12110

Bernard's response letter to Anthony Summers 4/14/89.

Bernard read Summers's book when it was published. Parts seemed well researched, containing information about accomplishments of Hoover and the Bureau. However, the homosexual material Bernard thought absurd and detracted from what could have been an interesting source of information. During his reading, Bernard found himself admiring much of Hoover's achievements, while being resentful of specious passages demonizing the man. As he read some of the bogus charges, he experienced the guilt feelings that occasionally gripped him about having parodied the Director in portions of his own book.

Notwithstanding his continuous repudiation of slanderous comments about Hoover's lifestyle, Bernard once failed spectacularly. It was on a popular morning television show in Los Angeles in front of a large live audience where Bernard was promoting his second novel, *Dancehall*. The host was a well-known national broadcaster with a pleasant, witty manner. Although Bernard enjoyed his show on occasion, at this particular moment he was nervous. The host, probably sensing Bernard's uneasiness as they waited to go on, said, "You'll be fine. We'll just talk a little bit about your novel. What's the title, *Dancing* did you say? Great book!" "*Dancehall*," Bernard corrected, keeping his eye on the red light on one of the cameras, which indicated they were about to go on the air. This was the part Bernard disliked most about shows, waiting interminably, it seemed, before going on the air. One of the producers held up a card that said "10 seconds." The last ten seconds were the worst part for Bernard, hoping he didn't sneeze or develop a tick at the last second. A live audience always made it worse—all those faces. Where did they get so many people that early in the morning?

And then they were on. "Tell me, Mr. Conners," the host was now saying. "Was J. Edgar Hoover gay?" Bernard was stunned. *Dancehall* had nothing whatever to do with Hoover. Bernard almost asked him to repeat the question as he desperately tried to come up with an answer, thoughts racing through his mind. He'd been set up. No question about it. All that pre-show nonsense about *Dancehall*! But the audience was riveted now. Here was a former FBI agent who certainly had the goods on Hoover. Finally, Bernard stiffened and responded in a husky voice, "I'm glad you asked me that, sir. To my knowledge there is not a scintilla of evidence to support homosexuality on the part of Gay Edgar Hoover."

For a second there was stunned silence, and then the audience burst into laughter. "Did you say *Gay* Edgar Hoover?" asked the host, jumping on Bernard's mistake. Now, flustered, Bernard compounded the problem by denying he had. But the host wouldn't let up. "He said *Gay* Edgar Hoover!" he practically yelled, turning to the audience for support. "Didn't he say *Gay* Edgar Hoover?"

"Yes! Yes!" affirmed the audience.

It was all downhill from there. Bernard became frosty toward the host, and slunk out of the studio. He never believed Hoover was gay. But even if he were, given the strong character of the man, Bernard didn't think it would have affected the Bureau in any meaningful way.

38

Hoover's Reaction

AFTER READING the many harsh comments about Hoover made over the years by former FBI officials and Justice Department leaders, Bernard became less contrite about *Don't Embarrass the Bureau*. His book seemed mild compared to the caustic appraisals of some top Bureau officials and others who worked closely with the Director, little more than a mild teasing often undergone by prominent persons. Bernard noted that, unlike his novel, which was published prior to Hoover's death, most of the negative comments by these individuals came after Hoover died. Few people, whether in government or the media, were eager to take him on since his retaliation could be deadly. Hoover's reaction to Bernard's novel was an example of the man's bizarre sensitivity that surfaced during his later years.

Although Bernard anticipated that the Director would not be pleased, he was unprepared for the sustained personal attention he afforded the novel. In Bernard's opinion, Hoover's interests would have been better served by his ignoring the book, or, if he felt compelled to speak of it at all, to characterize it as an insignificant, banal piece of fiction that hardly deserved comment. Instead, the information Bernard obtained through his FOIA shows that the Director followed the matter personally and assiduously, noting the progress of the affair in his own handwriting on the bottom of reports that were submitted to him on a continuing basis. Following are a few sample excerpts from these memoranda followed by Hoover's quoted comments and initials:

Memorandum dated 7/27/71:
It is recommended that the New York office attempt to ascertain the status of this manuscript and whether or not it has any chance of being published.

"OK"— H

Memorandum dated 9/8/71:
… the New York office will remain alert to the status of Conners' manuscript …

"Let me have summary on BF Conners"
H

Report dated 2/18/72:
"I don't like this hedging the ex-agents are engaged in."
H

Memorandum dated 2/24/72:

This should give the ex-agents society additional ammunition toward expelling Conners.

"I doubt it."

H

Memorandum dated 2/28/72:

"I certainly would like to know who is financing this."

H

Given Hoover's psychological challenges during his advancing years, about which many have commented, it is understandable that his reaction to parody would be extreme. FOIA requests have divulged volumes of statements by notable people who were in a position to observe him closely during these later years.

Congressman Don Edwards, a former FBI agent who was chairman of the House Subcommittee on Civil and Constitutional Rights, stated that Hoover's actions against those who did not measure up to his idea of worthy citizens tarnished our role as a free society.

Nicholas Katzenbach, who served as attorney general during the sixties, believed that Hoover served admirably, but stayed too long and that his age increasingly affected his judgment. According to Katzenbach, Congress, the press—everyone—was aware of it, and that it was almost impossible to overestimate his sensitivity to criticism. It went far beyond natural resentment to criticism one feels unfair. The most casual statement was sufficient for Hoover to write a complaining memorandum to the attorney general impugning the integrity of the critic.

William Sullivan, who had been number three man in the Bureau as head of the domestic intelligence division, testifying under oath before a congressional subcommittee investigating whether the Director used files to intimidate people, stated: "Well, anyone who wrote a book or was writing a book, or we knew was going to be critical of Mr. Hoover and the FBI, we made efforts right then and there to find out anything that we could use against him."

Unsettling as these comments might be to a writer, out of fairness and honesty, it must be stated that J. Edgar Hoover's dedication to the Bureau and the contributions he made to the country are a matter of record. On balance, these historical accomplishments far outweigh the more regrettable decisions he sometimes made later in life. Nevertheless, in some measure the preceding remarks serve to illustrate the challenges which confronted Bernard in the publication of his novel.

39

Writing Ethics

WITH THE DEATH of J. Edgar Hoover in 1972, changes in the Bureau were swift and remedial. In 1975, the US Senate Select Committee on Intelligence, chaired by Senator Frank Church (the Church Committee), focused on irregularities within the CIA and FBI that indicated Congress had been remiss, indeed naïve, in its oversight of these branches. Notwithstanding such criticisms, some of which were based on counter-espionage activities during the Cold War years, most impartial assessments give the FBI credit for its continuous regard for human rights while discharging its mandate during difficult years.

Some might find Bernard's esteem for the Bureau and its Director to be puzzling, especially since he was a recipient of Hoover's recriminations. Many authors are uncomfortable writing about organizations with which they have been intimately involved, sometimes caught between a need to be factual and a reluctance to air the family laundry. As a writer, Bernard was no exception and the issue constrained him from disclosing much information regarding the Director's reactions to his novel.

After learning of Hoover's efforts to have him removed from the Society of Former Special Agents, Bernard had elected to disengage voluntarily rather than compromise those who supported him. He retained his friendships within the Bureau and, while he learned that some in the FBI hierarchy such as Mark Felt (the alleged "Deep Throat" of Watergate infamy) were involved in suppressing his novel, he was gratified by those who remained friendly over the years. On one occasion he hosted an affair for the respected former director Judge William Webster at his club in Loudonville. He found Webster to be an intelligent man, and often thought he should have received wider recognition on the national scene for his wise leadership.

U.S. Department of Justice

Federal Bureau of Investigation

Office of the Director — Washington, D.C. 20535

June 13, 1985

Mr. Bernard F. Conners
British American
550 Broadway
Menands, New York 12204

Dear Bernie:

While our departure was somewhat hurried by the airplane connection, I do want you to know how much I enjoyed the lovely luncheon which you provided us during my stay in Albany. It was very thoughtful of you to host the leading law enforcement officials of the community and as you know from your experience that nothing but good things come out of such opportunities to meet under such circumstances.

It was a great pleasure for me to meet you and to hear of your long association with the FBI, both in and outside. I especially want to thank you for the signed copy of "Dance Hall," the paperback copy of which I will be taking with me on my trip to London, and I know I will enjoy reading it.

If business or pleasure brings you to Washington, I hope you will let me know so we can make arrangements for a visit to the Bureau.

With warm regards and many thanks,

Sincerely,

William H. Webster
Director

A popular former director, Judge Louis Freeh, who continues to receive wide civic praise after leaving the Bureau, graciously sent a blurb for one of Bernard's books.

Louis J. Freeh
Senior Vice Chairman

www.MBNA.com

MBNA America Bank, N.A.
Wilmington, Delaware 19884-0315
(302) 432-1490

December 18, 2001

Mr. Bernard F. Conners
Chairman
British America
4 British American Boulevard
Latham, NY 12110

Dear Mr. Conners:

In response to your request for a quote, I submit the following:

"Well-written and researched book, *Tailspin* reads with the excitement and detail of a fast-moving case. Mr. Connors' work is a fitting tribute to the heroic and able efforts of the men and women of the New York State Police."

I wish you much success with this book and in all your future endeavors. If you have any questions, please call me. My telephone number is 302-432-1485.

Sincerely,

Louis J. Freeh
Senior Vice Chairman
Administration and Legal Affairs

Another close friend, Paul Daly, formerly a prominent official in the FBI as well as the Drug Enforcement Agency, remained one of Bernard's most trusted and valued confidants for over thirty years. Mr. Daly had extensive experience on Capitol Hill and was often referred to by peers as "the smartest lawyer in the FBI."

Although several former Bureau officials had approached Bernard, offering to sponsor him for the Society of Former Special Agents, he remained ambivalent. He enjoyed the company of FBI friends in New York, and saw no reason to expand his presence on the national scene. He was aware that a prominent member of the Society had been very critical of him. The man's hostility derived from a confrontation at an FBI party in Manhattan shortly after Bernard left the Bureau. Bernard could not recall how he incurred the man's anger, but suspected it had been a combination of alcohol and Bernard's undue familiarity. The individual was a short, brusque man who at the time was a supervisor in the New York office. Perhaps he thought Bernard disrespectful. In retrospect, Bernard realized that the bravado he sometimes exhibited to mask his shyness could be misconstrued. There were those like Mohr who were unimpressed with his "breezy" manner.

Whatever the reason, the man suddenly became enraged and shouted, "How would you like to be knocked on your ass?" Bernard was shocked and speechless. His physical confrontations had long since been confined to the ring, and the idea of fighting a man half his size was bewildering. He measured the man for a moment, unsure how to respond. Regaining his composure he said, "Well, I guess that'd be pretty embarrassing. So, no, I wouldn't like that at all."

Cooler heads intervened. Bernard's fear of an unhinged windmill coming at him, reminiscent of his army days in the ring, was averted. Although further confrontation was avoided that night, Bernard would learn of his adversary's continuing efforts through the years to discredit both him and his novel. Indeed, the man's vitriol appeared to have no bounds. Bernard would learn years later that the individual had planned to ambush him on *The Al Capp Show*. The man was no stranger to controversy. Several years later he shot and killed a young man who allegedly tried to rob him.

Bernard would never understand his adversary's animosity, but it has long since been interred. Reflecting on the regrettable experience, Bernard took heart from a remark by Winston Churchill. Asked how he handled his many critics, the great man responded with a pithy comment: "You outlive the bastards!"

Even after his adversary's aspersions were confined to the grave, Bernard remained uncertain about joining the former agents' society. Because of such ambivalence, Bernard was deeply moved when in early 2013 he received letters from the chairman of the former agents' society, a distinguished gentleman esteemed for his dedication to both the FBI and the society. The letters expressed the leader's appreciation for Bernard's support of both the Bureau and the society, and urged Bernard to consider membership, "joining with so many who share our admiration for your accomplishments and success."

Kate liked the letters and thought it would be great to join the society. She was fond of the agents and shared their passion for the American flag, admiring how they started their meetings with the Pledge of Allegiance, as she did at her DAR gatherings. (She was sometimes disappointed when their country club displayed the flag at night without a spotlight.) She often hosted parties for both the Bureau and former agents. From her days as a teacher on Long Island to her role as chatelaine at the Connerses' estate, her hospitality was there day or night. "I like the agents," she was fond of saying. "They're my kind of guys!"

The following picture appeared in the society's magazine, the *Grapevine.*

The chapter met in May at Bernie Connors' home in Loudonville, NY. All current and former employees of the Albany Division were invited. The guest speaker was Tom Constantine, former head of both the DEA and the New York State Police.

Part VIII

40

Saving *The Paris Review*

"You've saved *The Paris Review*!" George Plimpton was beaming. Bernard had just agreed to become publisher of the magazine. His rise in the organization was not due to any literary merit. He had started off as business manager, then executive manager and, finally, after writing a big check to enable the magazine to continue publishing, he was anointed "publisher." His predecessor, Prince Sadruddin Aga Khan, after a few decades of keeping the magazine in print, had finally concluded that there was more future in oil.

It was not the best of times for Bernard to have undertaken the salvation of the magazine. Many of his soft drink companies were still in their embryonic form, but his longtime friendship with George, whose dedication and efforts on behalf of the magazine were unrelenting, eventually overcame his better judgment. George was thrilled and proclaimed to everyone how Bernard had "saved *The Paris Review*." Norman Mailer seemed particularly grateful. George sent the following fulsome letter to Bernard from Chicago to express his gratitude. Since George's handwriting is virtually indecipherable, a printed version is presented in addition to the actual letter:

4 Jan 1972

Dear Bernie –

Of course the check was one of the grand things that has ever happened in our topsy-turvy history. It came at a time when the magazine's future was very much in jeopardy; indeed I do not believe it could have survived without such an injection. In the name of all of us, I want to thank you exceedingly. You will go on the masthead in the next issue in some exalted fashion – though I don't think there's a rank high enough to match your qualities of generosity, and (I might add) timing! Horray for you! In the nick of time!

. . . In the meantime, a grand New Year to you. You have certainly started it off for others in a grand style!

As ever,
George

GEORGE A. PLIMPTON

4 Jan 1972

Dear Bernie –

Of course the check was one of the grand things that has ever happened in our topsy-turvy history. It came at a time when the magazine's future was very much in jeopardy: indeed I do not believe it could have survived without such an injection. In the name of all of us, I want to thank you exceedingly. You will go on the masthead in the next issue in some exalted fashion – though in fact I don't think there's a rank high enough to match your qualities of generosity, and (I might add) timing! Hooray for you! In the nick of time!

. . . In the meantime, a grand New Year to you. You have certainly started it off for others in a grand style!

As ever,

George

The Paris Review had a distinguished literary background. Founded in 1953, it consistently introduced the important writers of their era. *Time* magazine described it as "the biggest little magazine in history." Perhaps one of the magazine's more distinctive contributions to literature was its "Writers at Work" series, which contained interviews with some 250 prominent authors, including Hemingway, Eliot, Celine, Faulkner, Pound, Bellow, and Mauriac. For Bernard, one of the more startling comments on the writer's craft was that made by William Faulkner during an interview with *The Paris Review* editor Jean Stein: "The writer's only responsibility is to his art," said Faulkner. "Everything goes by the board: honor, pride, decency, security, happiness, all, to get the book written. If a writer has to rob his mother, he will not hesitate; the 'Ode on a Grecian Urn' is worth any number of old ladies." Bernard considered this a facetious remark, but worth bearing in mind when dealing with writers.

Bernard enjoyed his long association with *The Paris Review*. He and George Plimpton remained close friends, sharing many experiences until George's death in September 2003. Bernard had dinner with him at Elaine's restaurant in Manhattan two nights before he died. George was in great spirits at the time, planning a *Paris Review* party. They often dined at Elaine's. It was always exciting and unpredictable. Bernard recalled one night waiting for him at the bar. When George arrived a man detained him at the door for a moment. George then came to Bernard and said, "Lewis Lapham would like to join us for dinner, is that okay?" "Of course," Bernard said. Lewis Lapham was editor of *Harper's* magazine.

George and Bernard walked to a table in the rear with Lewis following some distance behind. Suddenly there was a disruption toward the front of the restaurant. Bernard turned to George behind him and asked what happened. George in his unflappable manner said, "Larry King just struck Lewis!" They sat down and were joined shortly by a disheveled, red-faced

Lewis. "What was that all about?" Bernard asked, to which Lewis replied in an offended tone, "All I said to him was 'hello'!" George would later say that King and Lapham were antagonists and Lewis had done something to which Larry King had taken umbrage. Bernard couldn't imagine what Lapham had done that would have caused such animosity, but it seemed an inappropriate time to ask. Within seconds, Elaine, quite displeased, was at their table. She was not one to conceal her feelings, and for a moment Bernard thought Lewis might receive his second battering of the evening.

"What's the matter with you, Lewis?" she snapped, her voice loaded with invective. "It's always the same with you. There's always something!" Their table was near a rear fire exit and Elaine made it clear that the next transgression would find them out the fire door. Bernard found Lewis to be a pleasant, interesting personality, but the initial imbroglio tarnished the evening. It was Bernard's first encounter with Lewis Lapham, and a regrettable way to begin an acquaintance with a noted literary figure. Because of the man's prominence and engaging manner, Bernard would like to have become more acquainted with him, but it was not to be.

Bernard was fond of Elaine Kaufman. She was a large woman with dark hair and rather smoky, dark eyes. She rarely minced words when she became angry. Many notables received her harsh denunciation and were drummed out of her restaurant—including Norman Mailer. One always knew where one stood with Elaine. She was an intimidating woman, and Bernard tried not to offend her. Indeed his diffident, sometimes obsequious manner with her once drew a sharp response: "Get rid of that little boy act, will you!" But they became good friends and she treated Bernard well, joining him for dinner, introducing him to luminaries, occasionally dining with him at the Russian Tea Room and 21 Club.

He sometimes discussed her business affairs with her. In turn she offered advice on publishing matters. Bernard often went up to Elaine's following parties at George Plimpton's—usually in good company. He hired the same driver and car in Manhattan for a number of years. The man was a pleasant, elderly chap with a German accent and a shock of white hair beneath his chauffeur's cap. He drove an old classic limousine that creaked a bit, but had great style, the sort that whispers old elegance. Bernard was often in the city on Tuesdays and Wednesdays, usually on publishing or film matters, and adopted a routine that worked well with the driver. The man charged relatively little and Bernard treated him deferentially, sometimes taking him into Elaine's.

They usually followed the same pattern. The driver picked up Bernard at his Fifth Avenue apartment or the 21 Club, they'd stop off at places like the Four Seasons, then frequently to George's apartment on Seventy-Second Street overlooking the East River. Many times they'd end up at Elaine's for a late dinner. It was a handy arrangement when George was having a party. His apartment would have famous people from the world of entertainment and, after a scotch or two, Bernard would have enough nerve to ask someone to join him for dinner at Elaine's. In retrospect, he thought he could have accomplished much more in the city if it weren't for the Butterflies. On the other hand, they were like a constant chaperone. He may have ended up in some difficult circumstances were it not for the fluttering guardsmen. Bernard did ferry many celebrities to Elaine's and elsewhere. Everyone was impressed with the car and driver. They'd roll out of George's ready to look for a cab, and there the tall, white-haired man with the cap and distinctive accent would be holding open the car door.

George Plimpton afforded Bernard entrée to an elite segment of Manhattan society. George had interests that covered a broad spectrum of New York's *haut monde* and Bernard found himself mingling with people such as Jackie Kennedy, Tom Brokaw, Truman Capote, William Styron, and Mike Wallace.

Often, there were a host of marquee names at the parties, particularly *Paris Review* Revels. Bernard might be talking with some grande dame and turn, only to bump into Woody Allen or Kitty Carlyle Hart. Not all of the encounters were as satisfying as he hoped. Kitty had come to Bernard's house in Loudonville one evening, and was singing a song accompanied by a pianist in the music room surrounded by several guests. Bernard may have disengaged for some reason and apparently it offended Kitty. The incident provoked a coolness from Kitty, which never dissipated.

Once, at a large, special, black-tie dinner at George Plimpton's place, Bernard was seated with about eight other guests, including Kitty, when George, who was at another table, rose and delivered one of his entertaining talks. At the conclusion of his remarks, as he sometimes did, he introduced Bernard as the publisher of *The Paris Review,* and asked him to speak. Bernard, surprised and totally unprepared, rose and allowed that he really had nothing to say, but that he did have a great trick. With both hands he took the edge of the white tablecloth on which rested a glittering array of candelabras, dishes, and silver, suggesting he was about to perform the old stunt of snatching the tablecloth from beneath everything on the table. "This works most of the time," he said, gently pulling on the edge of the table cloth as if practicing. Of course, everyone immediately recoiled from the table, startled—and then laughed when they realized he was joking. That is, all but Kitty, who remained stone-faced and unamused.

Whether in East Hampton, Manhattan, or Bernard's own house in Loudonville, *Paris Review* Revels were always exciting, with fireworks, balloon rides, helicopters. . . . George was particularly fond of fireworks. Mayor Lindsay actually had made him Fireworks Commissioner of New York, although the title didn't help much when the local police took him away in handcuffs after a fireworks display done without a permit at one of their parties in the Hamptons.

There were other, more dignified affairs, such as the dinner hosted by the French ambassador in Washington, D.C., to pay tribute to *The Paris Review* on its fiftieth anniversary:

L'Ambassadeur de France
et Madame François Bujon de l'Estang
prient Mr Bernard Conners

de leur faire l'honneur to attend a dinner
le Wednesday, June 5th at 7:30
Black Tie

R.S.V.P.
Tél: (202) 295-3713
Fax: (202) 295-3750

2221 Kalorama Road, N.W.
Washington, D.C.

An Evening of Celebration

to pay tribute to George Plimpton on the occasion of the 50th anniversary of *The Paris Review*, founded in Paris in 1952 and which has made an extraordinary contribution to the arts and letters.

The evening will feature poetry reading, the music of Chopin, and in the garden, a petit fire works display by Mr. Plimpton himself, the Fire Works Commissioner of New York City.

On another occasion, George's fiftieth birthday party, permission from LaGuardia Airport was granted to stage fireworks on Randall's Island. This enabled guests to see them from George's apartment overlooking the East River. It was quite spectacular . . . legitimate and no arrests. For Bernard the parties were memorable affairs with a prevailing sense of anticipation. Cocktails, fascinating conversations, newfound friends, pretty faces. . . . Mostly, perhaps, great expectations often unfulfilled.

41

Shoot-Out at *The Paris Review*

BERNARD had been involved with *The Paris Review* for several years when he and George elected to resurrect *The Paris Review* Editions in 1989. This was an endeavor attempted years before by *The Paris Review* and Doubleday to publish hardcover books by quality writers in the high tradition of the magazine. Although the books achieved considerable approval from critics, the Doubleday effort soon fell victim to an unsustainable bottom line. Undeterred by this sad outcome, George and Bernard undertook a similar publishing endeavor, with Bernard's British American Publishing assuming a position similar to that of Doubleday. The venture was described in the following article:

Plimpton to Edit Paris Review Imprint at British American

George Plimpton, longtime editor of the *Paris Review*, has joined with his former publisher, Bernard F. Conners, to launch a new publishing house, British American Publishing, which will include the imprint Paris Review Editions. The first list will appear in the fall of 1988. Simon & Schuster has agreed to handle worldwide distribution and subsidiary rights sales.

Plimpton will serve as editor of Paris Review Editions, which will publish fiction, poetry and nonfiction of literary quality. Novels by Charlie Smith and Larry Schainberg are scheduled to appear under the imprint. "At the magazine," Plimpton said, "we think of this as a remarkable opportunity to further our literary tradition."

Conners, a novelist and ex-FBI agent, is owner of British American, a diversified company whose enterprises include real estate development and soft drink manufacturing. He will be publisher of the new house, which has offices in Latham, N.Y., and New York City.

Richard E. Snyder, chairman and chief executive officer of Simon & Schuster, said, "We are very pleased to be part of this new venture and proud to be associated with the distinguished *Paris Review.*"

In addition to the Paris Review imprint, British American Publishing plans to publish approximately 12 titles a year. These will include works of general interest in fiction, nonfiction and poetry. In nonfiction the company intends to cover applied science, current events, cooking, health, sports, journalism and popular culture.

Kevin T. Clemente has been named president and chief executive officer of the company. He is the former vice-president of Clarity Publishing and has 15 years' experience in the publications printing field. The managing editor, Susanne M. Dumbleton, has a Ph.D. in medieval literature and is editor and cofounder of Washington Park Press, issuing regional literature.

For a few years the new British American Publishing effort was successful, turning out works by gifted authors (including four named "most notable books of the year" by the *New York Times*, one becoming a finalist for the prestigious National Book Award).

Simon & Schuster provided excellent distribution for the books under their chairman, Richard Snyder, and president, Charles Hayward. But this valued relationship ended abruptly when Hayward left to become president of Little, Brown. Constraints imposed under the new leadership at Simon & Schuster resulted in significant losses for the British American/*Paris Review* partnership. Under their legal arrangement at the inception of the project, George Plimpton had received a small ownership position in British American Publishing, and Bernard received a modest ownership in *The Paris Review* magazine. As so often happens in such undertakings, loss of revenue from Simon & Schuster resulted in cutbacks at British American Publishing. Kevin Clemente, the gifted president of the publishing company at the time, faced a continuous challenge from George in view of such reductions. Clemente was a handsome, urbane man who somehow retained his composure in the face of George's tirades, as reported in the following memo to Bernard:

I informed the Paris Review that I had notified Charlie Smith's agent that we were passing on the Smith book. James told me that he felt that my calling the agent and informing her of my decision was "rude, and underhanded". I informed James that I did not agree with this assessment of my actions and that I most definitely did not appreciate him speaking to me in this manner.

George called; enraged. I told him that I felt that we had to pass on the book because it was not financially feasible. He asked me if I was telling him that I was going to be the one to make this kind of decision. I told him that it was my responsibility to see to it that the company survives and that sometimes this would involve making a difficult decision on a book such as this.

George told me that he was livid and shaking he was so mad. He told me that I had no right to call the agent before calling him. I told him that I did not see any purpose in calling him first since the decision was already made. I told him that I called James immediately after speaking with the agent. I asked him if he would have been any less angry if I had called him first. He said no but that if he was unable to talk some sense into me they could take their business elsewhere.

He then said, "Kevin, you are an idiot. He told me I had no right to do what I had done and that I had embarrassed both him personally and the Paris Review. He then said, "Let me ask you a very direct question, what makes you think you know enough to make a decision like this." I did not have time to answer this because he immediately launched into a tirade what our original deal was about them bringing out good books not money makers. I told him that unless we took care of business we would not be around to publish any kind of books. He said, "so you are quitting?" "What about everything Bern said about keeping the company going and that there will always be a BA Publishing." I told him that this was the exact reason why I had to make tough decision such as this. I told him that I had to look at the business over the long term not just one book.

I attempted to explain to him that it was not us but the agent who decided to take Charlies book elsewhere. I also told him that I was disturbed and disappointed that he felt that he had to resort to calling me names and that in point of fact I was not "an idiot" but in fact very competent. He relented somewhat and told me that my decision was idiotic and that this is exactly what he would tell you.

Still enraged he terminated the conversation.

Memo informing The Paris Review *of notification to Charlie Smith's agent.*

During this financial pinch, some *Paris Review* bills, including expense vouchers that were paid by British American, received more thorough scrutiny by the British American staff, and there were occasional differences in opinion between the publishing company and the editorial staff at the *Review*. Once British American managing editor, Kathleen Murphy, sent the following spoofing note to *The Paris Review* editors regarding some expense account charges:

November 30, 1989

James Linville
Jonathan Dee
Jay McCulloch
The Paris Review
541 E. 72nd St.
New York, NY 10021

Dear Editors:

We'd like to take just a second out of your really busy (and much more important than ours, by the way) day to talk about the understandings of the understanding we understood stood between British American Publishing and The Paris Review.

Now we really don't want to nitpick, but about that lunch James, and Anita Brookner's $1500 introduction fee Jay... well, it's a little sticky, you know? I mean, James, fifty bucks for lunch for you and an agent... well let's just be downright honest with one another: we think it's just too low. What does fifty bucks get you these days in New York? A little radicchio and some mozarella? Is that any way to treat an agent who might submit a manuscript worth, say 700 copies? Shame on you. To make our point, we're enclosing a check for a thousand dollars, and we want it spent by Christmas. Enough said.

Jay -- Anita Brookner's a nice lady, right? And you want to be able to hold your head up in The Russian Tea Room, right? We certainly do. You didn't say anything about this little fee before, and we're a little miffed about that. So quit selling the broad short and pay her 3 grand. Throw it around a little -- we've got a reputation to uphold. We've enclosed that amount in cash to make it a little easier for you.

So, I hope we're all on the same wave length now. No more penny pinching. We've got a business to run. To hell with the bottom line. We're here to have fun, right?

Love,

Kathleen

PS -- BF feels really bad about Bart, so he's enclosed his American Express.

The letter may have caused a trifle huffiness among the staff at *The Paris Review,* but they were all good sports. The issue quickly gave way to more pressing matters. Despite a few shoot-outs—probably inevitable among editors—they all remained good friends and had fun. Kathleen Murphy was an attractive young woman, witty, and a remarkable athlete. She would later have her own TV show in Manhattan, and Bernard often thought she would have a career in film. Although she was a gifted editor, Bernard would not have been surprised to see her name surface somewhere on a marquee.

When reflecting on this period Bernard continued to be impressed by the talented young people at *The Paris Review* who struggled to keep the magazine going during turbulent years; not only the staff, but the many interns who passed through the small offices on Seventy-Second Street, some on their way to prominence in the publishing world. Both George Plimpton and Bernard were grateful as well to the legions of readers who supported the magazine, never asking for a refund when the famous literary quarterly sometimes came out *three* times a year.

Sustaining both the magazine and the new venture with British American Publishing was a daunting task, and led to the following exchange of letters between Bernard and George Plimpton:

BRITISH AMERICAN

BERNARD F. CONNERS
CHAIRMAN

(518) 786-6000

January 23, 1987

Mr. George A. Plimpton
541 East 72nd St.
New York, NY 10021

Dear George:

I called yesterday, but heard that you were in California. You used good judgment, indeed, and escaped in the nick of time. It is just dreadful here with all the snow.

I reviewed the numbers for the Paris Review with my financial people, and the consensus here is that something rather dramatic must be done to have the magazine continue on a sound basis.

It has survived by virtue of donations ($553,000 worth, to be exact), and I believe it will be difficult to sustain it on this basis, particularly with the trend of the last 2 years during which time it has lost $175,000. The contribution of $70,000 by the publisher this past year is particularly significant in that these are after-tax dollars which equates to more like $140,000. Inducing people to make contributions which are not tax deductible will be increasingly difficult, in my opinion.

Our publishing effort (Paris Review books) will lose a significant amount without the magazine and, to add the deficit from the magazine may not be practical. Even by making our publishing

Continued . . . .

BRITISH AMERICAN BOULEVARD • AIRPORT PARK • LATHAM, NEW YORK 12110

Mr. G. A. Plimpton
Page 2
January 23, 1987

company a Sub S corporation, it will be hard the first few years. The new tax laws render losses less attractive than they have been heretofore.

We should discuss the matter of the magazine in detail before proceeding. I should appreciate it if you would call me as soon as you can.

With best regards.

Sincerely,

BFC/pm

BRITISH AMERICAN

GEORGE A. PLIMPTON
541 EAST 72ND STREET
NEW YORK, N. Y. 10021
—
PHONE UN 1-0016

Dear Bernie —

The warmest New Year's greetings to you from all of us --from your old sparring partner especially.

I enclose the first page of a letter I started to you last month when you told me you felt uncomfortable continuing with the Paris Review. It lacks a page detailing your financial support to date. But I hope it suggests how truly grateful we are for all that you have done. Harpers is doing an anthology of the best work from the Review, everything to be in its hands by mid-February, along with an introduction in which I'll be able in ~~XXX~~ some small measure to describe your assistance and how beholden the magazine is to you. . . .

Very best wishes,

George

42

The Hampton Sisters

OWNING SOFT DRINK companies could be challenging. Intense competition, insufficient cash, constant battles with unions, strikes, government regulations, personnel problems, banking relationships. . . . Along the way Bernard managed to buy sixteen different soft drink companies throughout the Northeast, mostly through cash flow. Most of it was accomplished by holding up glass company payables. It frustrated container companies, but the payables had become so great they could ill afford not to keep British American supplied. Despite the problems, British American managed to stay in business for over forty years with diversified holdings in real estate, soft drinks, publishing, and film.

Along the way Bernard wrote five books, three screenplays, and a smattering of poetry. Following *Don't Embarrass the Bureau* was *Dancehall*, a best seller that received splendid reviews and was published in many foreign countries.

Ex-Gridder Uncorks Success As a Canada Dry Ground Gainer

By ED MANOGUE
Times-Union Business Editor

Bernie Conners is one of the nation's leading ground gainers. That's what the sports columnists wrote when he was with the St. Lawrence nUiversity football team in 1949-50.

Now, the same Bernard F. Conners, a native of Albany, is a ground-gainer in the business world. He is president and chief executive officer of Tri-State Canada Dry which this past week acquired two New England bottling companies.

This means his multi-million-dollar firm now has the largest Canada Dry holdings in the United States.

Tri-State Canada Dry has more than 500 persons on its payroll and facilities in Albany, Hudson, Poughkeepsie, Liberty, and in Burlington, Vt. The two new ones are Canada Dry Bottling Co. of Springfield, Mass., and Canada Dry Bottling Co. of Hartford, Conn.

Operations Consolidated

And all of this acquisition, Conners explains, has been in the past year.

This new bottling empire is seeing changes. Conners points out that the bottling operations ae being consolidated at the Hudson "master plant" with the other facilities becoming distribution terminals. Of the 500 employes, more than half are with the Hudson operations. And looking back, the original Canada Dry operations in the United States were in Hudson.

BERNARD F. CONNERS

Included in the operations there is a machine shop engaged in the manufacture of bottling equipment and conveyor materials for several major bottling companies.

Conners has appointed James J. O'Hare of Boston as president of the new acquisitions in Hartford and Springfield. O'Hare had been vice president and general manager of First National Stores of Boston, a chain he has been with 23 years. The tow New England Bottling firms were formerly owned by Adm. Ian Eddy. (U.S. Navy Retired), and Joseph Dworman of Worcester, Mass.

Serves 6-State Area

Conners, 42, a 1944 graduate of Albany Academy and 1950 graduate of St. Lawrence University, excelled in athletics in the Albany area and was well known in Golden Gloves boxing competition.

After college, he was with the Chicago Bears and in the Army before joining the FBI. His assignments included duties as a special agent supervisor in the FBI's Chicago and New York offices.

He later joined Canada Dry at its New York City headquarters and served as division operations manager in New York State and western New England before heading Tri-State Canada Dry.

He and his wife, Catherine, and their children, Christopher, 7, and Sarah, 5, reside at Collins Lane, Hillsdale. His sister is Mrs. Alice Dibble of Loudonville.

"Strong stuff...Well-written." – The New York Times

"Fast-paced...Engrossing." – The New York Daily News

"...a real winner...should tempt the most discerning reader of fiction." – The Cincinnati Enquirer

"An excellent suspense thriller...a fast-paced entertaining read." – Gannett Newspapers

"Intrigue, passion...suspenseful, well done." – Publishers Weekly

"Dancehall is, at heart, a thriller." – Richmond Times-Dispatch

"...impossible to put down!" – The Houston Chronicle

"Strong and authoritative writing teamed with unrelenting suspense...a thriller in elegant attire." – The Denver Post

"Conners has written a compelling suspense novel which is likely to be in demand." – Library Journal

"DANCEHALL is a tour de force worthy of a comeback effort in the world of modern storytelling." – The Star-Journal

"This one deserves to be read...the work of a profoundly powerful writer." – The Desert Sentinel

"A good strong style...a masterpiece of suspense." – Worcester Evening News, England

"A prestigious novel...a thumping climax." – Coventry Evening Telegram, England

"Much more than an excellent mystery...an impressive work." – Die Welt, Germany

"A sophisticated story, brilliantly written." – Passauer Presse, Germany

Dancehall *Reviews.*

Dancehall received considerable interest from movie studios including the following letter from the president of Columbia Pictures.

Columbia Pictures Industries, Inc.

Richard C. Gallop
President and
Chief Operating Officer

January 2, 1985

Mr. Bernard F. Conners
Chairman
British American Operations, Ltd.
423 Loudonville Road
Loudonville, NY 12211

Dear Bernie:

We recently made a trip through the Pacific, and I was thrilled to see that the paperback version of Dancehall was on every Quantas flight we took in the in-flight library. My travelling companion, Patrick Williamson, who is in charge of all our international operations, read the book and was absolutely enthralled by it. I would love to give him a copy signed by the author. If you will permit me to purchase a hardcover copy from you and would be good enough to inscribe it, I would greatly appreciate it.

Best wishes to you and Katie for the New Year. Now that you have a place here in New York, I hope we can get together soon.

Sincerely,

Richard C. Gallop

RCG/kg

A subsidiary of The Coca-Cola Company

711 Fifth Avenue, New York, New York 10022/212-751-4400

Francis Ford Coppola acquired *Dancehall,* and planned a major motion picture. When the rights expired, the book was optioned by an independent film company.

Bernard's third book originated when he and his son Christopher visited a small estate called Grey Gardens in East Hampton, Long Island, during the late seventies. They came to the house at the request of Edie Beale, who had resided there with her mother, Edith Ewing Bouvier Beale, until her mother's death in 1977. The Beales were first cousins of the First Lady Jackie Bouvier Kennedy, and the Beales had been the subject of unflattering publicity when the health department found them living in squalid conditions and threatened to evict them in 1977. Jackie Kennedy came to their aid, spending some $30,000 to clean up Grey Gardens. When Edie expressed an interest in selling their estate, Bernard and his son, Christopher, went to the residence intent on negotiating a purchase. They had driven past Grey Gardens a number of times, evaluating the premises. The location was superb, but the main house was a tatterdemalion that looked as though a stiff breeze would carry it into the ocean a short distance away. It sat in the center of a mass of dense, gray, tangled underbrush that appeared to have devoured everything but the unappetizing morsel at its center. As they walked up some creaking steps to the entrance, Bernard sensed someone observing them from an upstairs window. Christopher murmured, "Kind of scary, Dad?"

Bernard was impressed by the patrician and somewhat imperious manner of the tall, attractive woman who opened the door and invited them inside. A rather close-fitting summer dress covered her shapely figure and a turban-like babushka was pulled tightly about her head, concealing her hair. (They later would learn that she suffered from alopecia and wore turbans constantly.) This, then, was Edie Beale. She directed her guests toward chairs in the living room, where any semblance of an acceptable ambiance ended. The house reeked of offensive odors. An invitation to tea was politely declined as her guests took note of the fetid surroundings.

Bernard as a lifeguard at the Lake Placid Club.

Bernard's brother, Dan, army officer.

Bernard's son, Christopher, at Albany Academy, 1978.

Bernard awarding diplomas at New York Police graduation.

Kate and Bernard with Governor and Mrs. Carey.

Bernard with Governor and Mrs. Carey, and Mayor Erastus Corning of Albany.

Kate, Matilda Cuomo, and Bernard.

Governor Pataki at the Conners' house in Loudonville.

Governor Mario Cuomo and Bernard.

Bernard with Governor Cuomo and Paul Daly, former top official with the FBI and DEA.

The Conners' camp at Lake Placid. Built in 1898, the camp has been a favorite gathering place for the Conners family and their friends for three decades.

Kate and Bernard in the Whimsy, *one of their boats, which appeared in a documentary involving Bernard's novel* Dancehall.

Kate and Bernard's eight grandchildren.

Left: Sarah and Norman Livingston.

Kendall Kraft and Christopher.

Jane and Tony Loupessis.

Kate and Christopher.

From left, son-in-law Norman, Bernard, Kate, daughters Sarah and Jane, son-in-law Antony, daughter-in-law Kendall, and Christopher.

Left: Kate with daughter-in-law Kendall Kraft Conners. Above: Chris and Bernard golfing.

Son Christopher and daughter Sarah.

Nuremberg *Film*

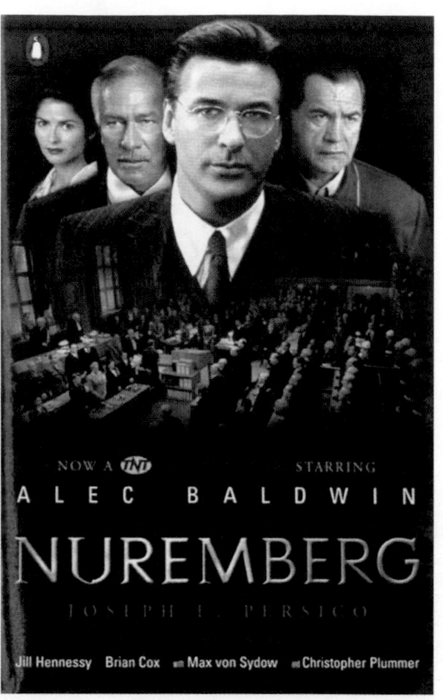

The Nuremberg *book by Joseph Persico was adapted for film starring Alec Baldwin, Christopher Plummer, Max von Sydow, Brian Cox, and Jill Hennessy. The award-winning film was produced by Turner Broadcasting and British American. Below: Joe Persico and Bernard on the* Nuremberg *set.*

Nuremberg *Film*

(From left) Brian Cox, who received an Emmy for his role as Goering; director Yves Simoneau; Joe Persico, author; Tom Leahy, producer and president of CBS Broadcasting; and Bernard.

Bernard at podium prior to Nuremberg *premiere.*

Left: Christopher, Kendall, Jane, Kate, and Tony. Above: Daughter Sarah with husband, Norman Livingston. Christopher and Kendall in the background.

From left: son Christopher, author Joseph Persico, and Tom Leahy, president of CBS Broadcasting.

Bernard with Ann-Margret, one of his favorite actresses.

Bernard with Pulitzer winners William Kennedy and Frank McCourt at literary awards in Saratoga. Photo credit: Maria M. Buccifero.

Bernard and Bill Macci, who drove the Phantom V Rolls-Royce for twenty-eight years. Bill's quiet, dignified manner was the outstanding feature of the Rolls.

AUTHOR AND PUBLISHER Bernie Conners and his wife, Kate, enjoy Marylou Whitney's garden party Sunday at Whitney's Cady Hill House on Geyser Road.

Kate and Bernard with Marylou Whitney at the Governor's Mansion.

Bernard with daughter Sarah and Joseph Lyons, a Gannett and Hearst Newspaper executive, who was a dear friend and helpful with Bernard's writing endeavors.

Kate at Ida Lewis Yacht Club, Newport, Rhode Island.

Bernard and Kate after tennis matches at Forest Hills.

Yes, she was interested in selling the house, but was concerned about what changes would be made. It was important to her that the place be restored to its original condition and its character preserved.

Bernard was wondering how he had managed to find himself in such a situation when suddenly Edie heard people in the other room. Bernard listened, but it seemed the only one who heard the voices was Edie. Although there was no one else in the house, she continued to refer to the people in the adjoining room. Bernard knew it was time to leave. The woman was somewhere else mentally, and any thoughts of completing a real estate transaction disappeared with the wind that rattled the broken shutters. Bernard left the debris of Grey Gardens with ambivalent feelings, struck by the winsome attractiveness of their hostess, and appalled by the conditions under which she was living.

Bernard declined future overtures regarding a sale, and the property was purchased in 1979, by Ben Bradlee, former editor of the *Washington Post*, and his wife, Sally Quinn, who restored Grey Gardens to much of its original grandeur. The Beales would later become the subjects of a heart-rending documentary film, *Grey Gardens,* which described their lives in their East Hampton manor.

The encounter with Edie Beale inspired Bernard to start a novel about the mother and daughter, as well as the East Hampton community. It was heavy on satire, lampooning the East Hampton social establishment and its conservative haunts. The Bayrock Club, a fictitious place that bears a resemblance to the Maidstone Club in East Hampton, is characterized in the opening passage, and gives a preview of the novel's leitmotif:

"A faint breeze nudged the yachting flags atop the Bayrock Club—a curious configuration of steeples, spires and banners outlined against the sky, like a battle line drawn to defend Bayrock against unchristian encroachments. . . ."

George Plimpton, a prominent member of the Maidstone Club and the WASP community that it served, was uncomfortable with the manuscript. He was a close friend of Jackie Kennedy, who often came to their *Paris Review* parties. The book was clearly on sensitive footing, and George offered some critical assessments. "How will you feel when the book comes out and you see Jackie at our parties?" he asked Bernard. "Oh, well, it's all in good fun," Bernard answered. "Everyone knows we're writers. After all, you *were* editor of the *Harvard Lampoon*."

George was not mollified. Eventually, Bernard changed the book from a mother and daughter storyline into *The Hampton Sisters*, deleting some of the satirical passages. But George was never happy with the finished manuscript. The publisher called him several times for a comment for the book. George never returned the calls, and never did give a blurb for *The Hampton Sisters*.

The book was published by Donald Fine, a somewhat prickly but prominent figure on the New York publishing scene. One of the characters in *The Hampton Sisters*—a fictitious portrayal of a mercurial publisher called Richard Fox—bore some resemblance to Donald Fine. For this reason Bernard was hesitant when his agent, Oscar Collier, had first told him he was going to submit the manuscript to Arbor House, Fine's publishing company. Bernard was doubtful if Fine would take the novel, given the description of the publisher, but believed that if Fine took the work he'd address the role, and make Richard Fox more attractive. But Don never did object to the character. The only time he mentioned the similarity between Richard Fox and himself was once in an offhand manner. "John," he said, referring to one of his assistants, "mentioned that there are a few similarities between that Fox character in your novel and me. I don't see it at all." That was the end of it.

Although a diminutive man, Fine had a gargantuan ego and temper.

Legend had it that when he sold Arbor House to the Hearst Corporation in 1978, after signing the sales contract, he said to the Hearst representatives, "Okay, now get out of my office!"

Bernard first met Fine a few years before when Oscar Collier was making submissions for Bernard's second novel, *Dancehall.* Oscar had told Fine back then that Bobbs-Merrill was taking *Dancehall,* but Mr. Fine had requested the meeting, nevertheless. Oscar had been uneasy then about the impending meeting. "He wants *Dancehall,*" Oscar had said, while describing Mr. Fine. "The man's brilliant—a legend in the publishing business. He's edited works by top authors. James Jones's *From Here to Eternity,* Ken Follet, Kurt Vonnegut . . . many of Norman Mailer's and Irwin Shaw's works. . . . But he's impossible. Terrible temper. He has a new secretary every few months. But it's important to know him."

That original meeting with Donald Fine regarding *Dancehall* was memorable. He berated his staff from the moment Bernard and Oscar arrived at his office. It was embarrassing. "Why are you going with Bobbs-Merrill?" he exclaimed. "The book will never get the distribution from them. They're owned by ITT!" He couldn't understand why Bernard and Oscar didn't rescind the agreement with the other publishing company and sign with him. He proceeded to denigrate Bobbs-Merrill and just about everything else, including Oscar. They fairly raced out of his office. "See what I mean?" said Oscar, once they had escaped. "You could never publish with him. He'd drive you crazy!" Oscar would prove to be right in this initial contact with Fine, but it would take some time before Bernard would find out just how painfully accurate was Oscar's prophecy.

43

"Delectation and Delight" with Donald Fine

THE SUCCESS of *Dancehall* and *Don't Embarrass the Bureau* had subsequently prompted Don Fine to express a keen interest in *The Hampton Sisters*. Harriet Pilpel, a noted publishing attorney who had worked with Don Fine on projects in the past, had agreed to represent Bernard. She had not mentioned the acrimony that existed between the two. Harriet, a prominent civil libertarian and women's rights advocate, was a frequent guest on William Buckley's television show, *Firing Line*.

Bernard was reading *Publishers Weekly* at the time, and noticed an article about Fine walking his dog on Park Avenue. The article described his illustrious career and how, after selling his publishing company Arbor House to the Hearst Corporation, he had started his new firm, Donald I. Fine Inc. It was a flattering article that covered the man's outstanding accomplishments in the publishing world, as well as his mercurial temperament. When Bernard read about his dog, he thought rather cynically, "I wonder if he kicks his dog. . . ." He would soon find out.

One day Bernard arrived in Don's office with *The Hampton Sisters* manuscript. A receptionist directed him down a long hallway where a large black dog suddenly came galloping up the corridor toward him. Just then, Don appeared from his office and yelled sharply at the dog. The animal tumbled to a halt, turned, and rushed madly back toward its master, who promptly kneed the animal, sending it crumpling to the floor. The incident did little to endear Fine to Bernard, an ardent dog lover.

Don greeted Bernard cordially, and ushered him into a large office toward a chair in front of his desk. Bernard found himself looking up at Fine, who sat in a chair positioned well above his guest. His dog was at Bernard's feet munching on something while Fine held forth on his throne telling Bernard what a mistake he had made a few years before by not letting him publish *Dumbbell*. There followed a lengthy description of what he had done for a host of famous authors, including Morris West, John D. MacDonald, and Norman Mailer. Eventually he got around to *The Hampton Sisters* and the "outrageous" $50,000 advance Bernard was seeking. The conversation was concluded with an invitation to lunch at the Harvard Club (Don was one of Harvard's esteemed alumni) and a final shot at Bernard's lawyer. "How could you sic Harriet Pilpel on me?" he said, incredulously. "Of all people, Harriet Pilpel! We could have worked out this contract just fine between the two of us. Of all people, Harriet Pilpel," he repeated bitterly. Bernard sensed Don had not done well in his previous dealings with Harriet Pilpel, and experienced a moment of comfort that she was representing him.

Finally, as Bernard rose to leave, he looked for his glasses case. Nowhere to be found. Suddenly Don discovered it at Bernard's feet in the mouth of his dog. After some struggling and a growling, expletive-filled tug of war, Don wrested it from the dog's mouth. With a casual motion he wiped some of the saliva on his trousers and handed Bernard what remained of the case. "Here, it's not bad," he said. "He likes chewing leather things like that." The soft leather case was unrecognizable, one end virtually shredded. Bernard still has it, preserved in his office—a memento of his long, contentious experience with this venerable publisher.

Donald Fine and Harriett Pilpel somehow agreed on a contract for *The Hampton Sisters,* and the editorial phase of Bernard's manuscript began. It was a continuous struggle of raging confrontations. Don and Bernard had two entirely different stories in mind. The back-and-forth culminated in a telephone call during which Bernard said, "Don, I can't take anymore. My daughter Sarah is being married tomorrow morning. I've had all I want with this book. These suggested revisions are just awful. Send me back my manuscript. I'll return your advance this afternoon!" The following letters describe the blistering acerbity that sometimes develops between an author and his editor/publisher:

BRITISH AMERICAN

BERNARD F. CONNERS
CHAIRMAN

(518) 786-6000

February 26, 1987

Mr. Donald I. Fine
DONALD I. FINE INC.
128 East 36th St.
New York, New York 10016

Dear Don:

Perhaps my worries about the publication date for THE HAMPTON SISTERS are unfounded, but I thought I should express my concern to you....

With a July pub date, we should have bound books by the end of May, to achieve good distribution. Since the manuscript has not even gone to the typesetter yet, I cannot see how all this is going to happen. When I look at the enclosed milestones, I can't help but conclude that the summer will be half over before the books will be in the stores.

I agree that the book should do well in the summer. In fact, George Caldwell, who owns the Bookhampton in East Hampton, ~~told me~~ that he had reported DANCEHALL as a bestseller on a regular basis to the New York Times. THE HAMPTON SISTERS should enjoy the residual benefit of this.

and other book stores in the Hamptons

Continued....

BRITISH AMERICAN BOULEVARD • AIRPORT PARK • LATHAM, NEW YORK 12110

Mr. D. I. Fine
February 26, 1987
Page 2

I may be unduly concerned about all this, Don. After all, you are the wizard in such matters - at least everyone says you are. But I have had a great deal of experience myself with distribution, and I am all too familiar with things that can go wrong.

I plan to go to Aspen for a week of skiing on March 10th. I should like to have my revisions completed before I leave. Would it be possible to have lunch with you next Wednesday or Thursday? We could discuss some thoughts I have for promotion and perhaps you could fill me in on things you would like me to do.

These next two books are very important to my reputation as a novelist, and I am ready to assist in whatever way you feel appropriate.

With kindest regards.

Sincerely,

BFC/pm

BRITISH AMERICAN

BRITISH AMERICAN

BERNARD F. CONNERS
CHAIRMAN

(518) 786-6000

April 13, 1987

Mr. Donald Fine, Inc.
DONALD I. FINE, INC.
128 E. 36th Street
New York, NY 10016

Dear Don:

I hope this letter finds you well, and back from Israel. Lord, I hope you are well and back, because my concern is mounting about THE HAMPTON SISTERS. The manuscript should have gone to the copy editor by this time, and I haven't yet had a chance to review the editing. It is imperative, of course, that I see the work before it goes to the typesetter. I should like to add a few lines which I think will improve the personna of Lydia. It is only a paragraph or two, but important.

I was with George Plimpton yesterday. He took me to his club, where we lunched and played tennis. It is called The River Club, and, frankly, reminded me of The Bayrock Club in THE HAMPTON SISTERS. (Everyone spoke with the English "RP"; no Conners or other ethnic names on the club roster.)

George and I talked a lot about the PARIS REVIEW EDITIONS, which is what George thinks we should call our new publishing venture. He wants me to be the publisher of the magazine as well as the books - a prospect I am not that keen about since the magazine loses a ton of money. It is all in the hands of Harriet Pilpel and James Goodale, George's lawyer. I am not sure where this will all end up.

I am glad you 're back. God, I am glad you're back. Please get the edited manuscript to me as soon as possible.

It is probably best if you call so that I can arrange to have the manuscript picked up rather than mailed. I can be finished with it in a day or so.

With warmest regards,

Sincerely,

Bernard

P.S. When are we going to talk about my new novel?

BRITISH AMERICAN BOULEVARD • AIRPORT PARK • LATHAM, NEW YORK 12110

Don responded to Bernard's concerns about the manuscript with several reassuring letters, one of which stated that the manuscript was "altogether tight and wonderful" and that he had shown it to "one of the most important book buyers in America, who believes that we have a potential winner." He sent the final edited manuscript to Bernard with the comment that it was being sent to Bernard for his "delectation, delight and enthusiasm."

Bernard's responding telegram was devoid of delectation and enthusiasm:

MAILGRAM SERVICE CENTER
MIDDLETOWN, VA. 22645
28AM

4-003766S118002 04/28/87 ICS IPMMTZZ CSP ABLA
1 5187866000 MGM TDMT LATHAM NY 04-28 0853A EST

BRITISH AMERICAN DEVELOPMENT CORP BERNARD
CONNERS
3 CORNELL RD
LATHAM NY 12110

THIS IS A CONFIRMATION COPY OF THE FOLLOWING MESSAGE:

5187866000 FRB TDMT LATHAM NY 51 04-28 0853A EST
PMS DONALD I FINE CARE DONALD I FINE INC, DLR
128 EAST 36 ST
NEW YORK NY 10016

DEAR DONALD:
DO NOT, REPEAT, DO NOT SEND HAMPTON SISTERS MANUSCRIPT TO TYPESETTER.
NUMEROUS REVISIONS HAVE BEEN MADE WITHOUT MY KNOWLEDGE. MANUSCRIPT
SERIOUSLY FLAWED IN PRESENT STATE. WILL THROW MY BODY INTO PRESSES TO
STOP ITS PUBLICATION. I SHALL SEND MANUSCRIPT BACK TO YOU FORTHWITH.
I AM DOING SOME "SHADING".
BEST
BERNARD

0851 EST

MGMCOMP MGM

Don responded predictably, stating, “I kept you fully informed repeatedly about what I was doing . . . to which you said you were positive that since you liked me so much you were certain that you would like whatever I did.” Don concluded his letter with a P.S. which said, “Don’t throw yourself into the presses. I don’t want to lose you.”

The matter was concluded amicably as reflected in the following letter regarding a party at the 21 Club:

BRITISH AMERICAN

BERNARD F. CONNERS
CHAIRMAN

(518) 786-6000

June 9, 1987

Mr. Donald I. Fine
Donald I. Fine, Inc.
128 East 36th Street
New York, NY 10016

Dear Don:

I should like to host a PUB party at "21" for a couple of hundred luminaries, in the style of our PARIS REVIEW parties. McMillan is having one for George Plimpton's new novel, next week. (see enclosed) I shall ask him for his ideas. As I mentioned during our call, I may also use the party to start the word about the new Paris Review Publishing Company.

Before I forget, please don't let the writer of the flap copy for THE HAMPTON SISTERS give away the storyline. (see enclosed)

It was nice to talk to you today - well, most of the call, anyway. Why is it you become angry over silly things? I have been so good to you, and I know that most publishers are not blessed with such good-natured authors. I wish you'd be more appreciative.

I shall try to improve your luncheon habits by taking you to "21" when you come back from your trip. Incidentally, how do you have so <u>much</u> free time? Israel...now you're going off to the West somewhere.... I have <u>no</u> free time.

Thanks for everything. With warmest regards

Sincerely,

BRITISH AMERICAN BOULEVARD • AIRPORT PARK • LATHAM, NEW YORK 12110

Don published the book and it did reasonably well in hardback, receiving good reviews—although Donald shared little with Bernard, treating post-publishing matters like unpatented treasures. Dell Publishing purchased the paperback rights and brought out 500,000 copies—a strong first printing. Bernard's royalties amounted to a fraction of that. As for Donald Fine, in spite of their struggles, he and Bernard became good friends. He even sponsored Bernard for the Publishers Lunch Club, a prestigious organization composed of prominent publishers.

DONALD I. FINE, INC. 19 WEST TWENTY-FIRST STREET, NEW YORK, N.Y. 10010
Telephone 212•727•3270
Fax: 212•727•3277

March 19, 1993

Mr. Bruce Harris
Membership Chairman
Publishers Lunch Club
Random House, Inc.
201 East 50 Street
New York, NY 10022

Dear Bruce:

Other letters in behalf of Bernard Conners' candidacy for membership in the Publishers Lunch Club have mentioned his career as a Chairman of British American Publishing. I'm familiar with Bernard for much longer than most, having published two of his novels, and rather successfully, by the way. He is a man of parts, former FBI agent, a gentleman of letters, a book publisher, a marvelously creative business man. I've known Bernard for some ten years, and know that he is a charming man and, rare avis, a gentleman.

Sincerely,

bcc: Bernard Conners

Bernard became quite fond of Don Fine and appreciated his editorial and his business acumen. At one point he considered Don's firm as a distributer for *The Paris Review*, but the arrangement never came to fruition as is explained in the following letter:

BRITISH AMERICAN

BERNARD F. CONNERS
CHAIRMAN

(518) 786-6000

February 2, 1987

Mr. Donald I. Fine
DONALD I. FINE INC.
128 East 36th St.
New York, NY 10016

Dear Don:

Thank you for your note regarding the distribution proposal for the Paris Review press. George Plimpton and I are attempting to determine what the tax status of the magazine should be before we proceed with the publishing company. We shall be meeting with the tax lawyers during ensuing weeks, but until this matter is resolved everything else must be held in abeyance. The problems we are incurring do not indicate any quick solution, and I am certain that it will be at least a year before we can even think of publishing anything. I appreciate your interest very much, and I shall keep you informed of developments.

I hope wherever you have gone there is some decent weather. I last saw you disappearing in a gust of snow, down 42nd Street.

With warmest regards.

Sincerely,

Bernard

BFC/pm

Both Donald and Harriet Pilpel are gone now, remembered as notables in their field. Bernard missed Don, feeling he was a brilliant person and fun to be around—most of the time. He loved Harriet, far and away the best memory he had of the publication of *The Hampton Sisters*.

44

Boldfaced Names

COME WITH ME. People over here want you to join them."

Bernard was dining alone when Elaine appeared at his table with her bidding. He had patronized the restaurant for over forty years, and with Elaine's guidance he had become acquainted with many of the regular patrons. It was not unusual for her to surface at his table with instructions to go with her. Bernard rose quickly and followed her to a nearby table where he suddenly found himself dining with A.E. Hotchner and Arthur Miller. It was a treat for Bernard, but he was somewhat uncomfortable with Hotchner, who, although gracious, seemed exceedingly somber. Bernard had the impression he may have been intruding. Arthur Miller on the other hand was fun to be with, although he did seem elderly. Bernard was perplexed by his marriage to Marilyn Monroe because of the age difference. As he was leaving, Bernard asked Elaine if perhaps he had intruded on their dinner; she replied, "Hell, no. They saw you and told me to get you."

It was not unusual for Bernard to dine with such celebrities at Elaine's. One of his most memorable evenings was spent dining with the delightful actor Leslie Nielsen. On another occasion Bernard was having a drink with Leonard Bernstein at George's apartment, and Bernstein asked him to Elaine's for dinner. Bernard, surprised, said "sure," and away they went in the old limo. They were having dinner when Leonard suddenly leaned over and gave him a big kiss on the cheek. "Gotta go!" he said. His kiss and abrupt departure were somewhat puzzling.

It was unpredictable at Elaine's, always exciting. Mostly good experiences, but there were times. . . . Once he was sitting alone when James Brady, the editor of *Parade* magazine, came to his table. Bernard had first met him at the Beverly Hills Country Club swimming pool. They seemed to get along well at the time, and it had led to a few days of tennis together. Bernard was mindful of Brady's position with *Parade,* and the potential for what he could do for Bernard's books. This led to some generous line calls on the tennis court—something for which Bernard was not particularly noted. "Are you sure?" from James. "Yes, of course," from Bernard. "Caught the line!" They left Beverly Hills with a budding friendship, at least from a tennis standpoint.

At Elaine's this particular night he greeted Bernard warmly. "Bernard, I'm here with my daughters. I was telling them about you and we thought maybe you'd join us for a drink." Bernard was delighted, particularly when he saw his daughters—two beauties who looked as though they had just stepped onto the red carpet. Bernard sat down with them and ordered a drink, flattered indeed that James had invited him to his table. It seemed they had barely begun to converse when James rose, extended his hand, and said, "Bernard, so nice of you to stop by!" And that was it!

But that's New York. If one plays in the big leagues, one must become accustomed to striking out. Rejection is part of the game. Bernard did receive very nice treatment from James Brady. They later saw a good deal of each other in the city and in East Hampton, where James lived. He gave excellent blurbs for Bernard's books. If one's an author it helps to give generous calls on the court.

But this was not the case with Andy Rooney. The journalist first received recognition during World War II as a reporter for *Stars and Stripes*, the army newspaper. Later he became a popular commentator on *60 Minutes* with Mike Wallace, dispensing folksy, somewhat whimsical observations, on a variety of worldly matters. He also wrote a syndicated newspaper column, which offered entertaining, sometimes droll, comments about everyday subjects. Although an engaging personality, he was regarded as a curmudgeon by some who knew him well. Bernard had a cordial relationship with Andy. Kate and he dined with Andy and his wife Margie on several occasions, sometimes at the houses of mutual friends. Bernard thought him to be unusually direct, leaving little question regarding his feelings on issues, and never regarded him as the genial personality seen on television. Once Bernard sent him a note asking for a blurb for one of his novels. The response was all Andy: honest, direct, actually admirable. He wrote that he had declined to give blurbs to twenty-five different friends in just the past six months because he felt it was not anything a writer should do. His letter further stated that if the publisher wished to send him the galleys he'd be pleased to read them but with no comment. He closed his gracious letter with best wishes for the success of the book.

A similar kind and complimentary note was sent by Norman Mailer, who said he found Bernard's *Dancehall* novel to be "interesting and well written" and Bernard's performance "skillful and professional" but that it was not his kind of book. He concluded his rejection stating, "So let's leave it that I wish you all kinds of luck which you richly deserve and I look forward to having a drink with you one of these days."

Bernard socialized with Norman on occasion, once for a few hours at the Lotus Club in Manhattan where they finished off a fifth of Jack Daniels at three in the morning. Bernard always found him pleasant, notwithstanding his reputation for combative behavior, both verbal and physical. Bernard did his best to nurture his friendship with Norman. His efforts to ingratiate himself with the boldfaced names were boundless.

Bernard's aspirations both socially and otherwise had always been high. Few sixteen-year-old boys would have read Emily Post cover to cover to enhance their social skills, or expressed a keen interest in his mother's or elder sisters' endless rules of etiquette. There was protocol governing introductions, treatment of women, and (particularly challenging) conduct during formal dining, which consisted of a bewildering array of procedures from seating a woman at the table, to the continental use of a fork in one's left hand. It was important to engage the woman seated at one's right—regardless of the fact that the woman on one's right might display no reciprocal interest whatsoever. One had to say "house" rather than "home," "woman" instead of "lady" (since being a "lady" was assumed). Although Bernard sometimes suspected such rules were little more than a mother's or sister's whim, he nevertheless catalogued them for future use.

The one thing he could not affect was the cool urbanity common to the patrician world. Unlike Kate, he was far too eager. Bob Bennett, marketing director of IBM, a close friend, once said to him, "You should try cooling it a bit!" But for Bernard it was difficult. Whether climbing the corporate ladder or social climbing, during such times the Butterflies were restive—and it showed!

Part IX

45

In Xanadu a Parvenu

MOVING from the bucolic, modest quarters in Hillsdale to the estate in Loudonville, New York, in 1969 was a significant step for the Connerses. They now had three children, all bearing the same middle name: Christopher Parker, Sarah Parker, and Jane Parker. Parker was Catherine's mother's maiden name—an important genealogical factor for her mother, who was a member of the Daughters of the American Revolution (DAR). Catherine would later become a DAR Regent, a title which designated her as the official representative of her chapter. It was a splendid institution, which treasured its history promoting God and country. Bernard recalled many gatherings at their house with elderly ladies carrying Bibles and unfurled flags and pledging allegiance to the USA.

But some of the other social gatherings at 60 Old Niskayuna Road were less sedate. Indeed, many of the parties were popular affairs that went from dusk to dawn. One annual event, billed as a "Midsummer Madness" party sometimes attracted over six hundred guests. The 108-acre estate could accommodate such large numbers. The main structure was an English manor house, which had been constructed in 1930.

Much of the interior had been imported from Europe: large leaded windows with colorful intaglios, substantial amounts of woodwork including paneled disappearing doorways, and large stone fireplaces. The house had been built for Anthony Brady Farrell, "the Broadway angel," described by *Time* magazine as "an angel with the largest wingspread ever seen on Broadway." Farrell was a producer of shows such as *My Fair Lady*, *The Sound of Music*, and *Pal Joey*. He was the owner of the Mark Hellinger Theatre where many of his plays were produced. Farrell died in the late sixties and his widow, a gracious philanthropist named Dorothy Donovan Farrell, sold the estate to Bernard.

"Xanadu."

It was a challenge at the time. Mrs. Farrell's price was reasonable, but the cost of maintaining the property was significant. On the grounds were three houses, gardens, and a polo field on which Mr. Farrell landed his plane on occasion. In 1974, Bernard constructed a drive-through gatehouse with nearby garages and overhead apartments, which served as a courtyard at the entrance to the property. It all conformed to the European style of the main house, but provoked considerable interest from the ultra-conservative community, as evidenced in the following article:

By ROBERT BASLER

G-man to millionaire

Workmen put finishing touches on gatehouse at Loudonville mansion of Bernard F. Conners. (Staff photo by Bob Richey)

Everything along the winding road is his, from the gatehouse at the beginning to the Rolls Royce at the end.

He is Bernard F. Conners, a comfortable blend of Jay Gatsby and Jack Armstrong, dandy millionaire and all-American boy.

Dressed entirely in tennis court white, Conners is lounging just outside his Loudonville mansion. He looks out over his 86-acre estate, and after some reflection admits he has been "very fortunate."

That is rather an understatement, considering that only a few years ago he was a Federal Bureau of Investigation agent, tracking down criminals in Albuquerque, N.M.

Now he owns and/or operates a variety of soft drink facilities, real estate and construction concerns and an antique shop. Conners has written one best-selling novel about his G-man days, and he is working on another book. From all outward appearances his biggest worry right now is whether he would like to be publisher of Paris Review, the prestigious literary magazine of which he is already executive manager.

Conners has spent much of his life doing a variety of things and doing most of them well. "Everything he touches becomes a success," says Conners' old friend George Plimpton, the Paris Review editor.

Which is pretty much the way it has been since Conners' Albany boyhood, when he attended Albany Academy and participated in every sport from football to boxing.

The same thing happened in college at St. Lawrence University, where "Bernie" Conners made a big football name for himself, and in the Army, where boxing took up much of his time.

Conners' friend Plimpton, author of "Paper Lion" and himself known for a varied career, says he is constantly amazed at the things the ex G-man is willing to try.

"I first met him in Italy, when we were in the Army—he was training for our divisional boxing championship, and I was his sparring partner," Plimpton recalls.

"After that I lost track of him for a long time, but I kept hearing rumors that he was making a fortune." The two met again a few years ago to discuss Conners' book, and Plimpton says he happened to mention the Paris Review's financial problems.

"The next day there was a check in the mail—he saved the Paris Review," Plimpton says. Conners' association with the magazine continued, and last month the two met again in New York City. "He never ceases to amaze me," Plimpton says. "It was a really hot day in the city, but there was Bernie wearing a white suit, picking me up in his Rolls Royce."

Now, at 49, Conners continues to branch out and try new things. Like most rich people, he insists that money isn't all that important to him, but he is realistic enough not to expect the non-wealthy to believe him.

Bernard Connors

It was by chance that Bernard heard that Mrs. O'Donahue, a Woolworth Department Store heiress from Long Island, was interested in selling her Phantom V Rolls-Royce limousine. It was a magnificent seven-passenger vehicle, garnet and black, with large classic headlamps custom carved on the fenders. Bernard bought the limousine and retained William Macci, a dignified, white-haired gentleman, who would be their chauffeur for the next twenty-eight years. With his gray English livery and soft, respectful manner, he and the Rolls were a perfect complement to the estate.

Of course, it was all quintessentially nouveau and, in a provincial community such as Loudonville where a parvenu inevitably would be the object of derision, there were moments. . . . Although Bernard was sensitive to an undercurrent of ridicule by some, it did not bother Kate one iota. Settling in the back of the Rolls and tooling out of her Xanadu, she was the chatelaine, always comfortable in her role. Her acceptance of the prominence to which she was subjected surprised Bernard. Kate was the antithesis of pomposity. Her hobby was flowers. She remarked once, "I could live in a nursing home. I wouldn't care. If they gave me a window box I'd be fine."

But for Bernard, with his middle-class rearing, reappearing in his hometown on an opulent Loudonville estate was not without its social challenges. An older friend who had achieved prominence in the legal field told him, "Never practice law in your hometown. You'll always be known as 'Joe Fisheye.'" Bernard understood. He would always be "Bernie the boxer"!

Bernard rarely worried about the social stigma of his boxing career, notwithstanding the opinion of his mother and sisters, who regarded it as an inelegant pursuit and were not reluctant to say so. And there were times when these skills proved beneficial. One night, when he was still an FBI agent, home on leave, he took his niece and his younger sister to a pub on River Street in Troy, New York. It was a rough part of town, a dangerous place to be at that late hour. But his niece and sister, attractive young women, wanted to see some pictures of themselves taken at a nearby college and displayed in the pub. They stayed only a few minutes and walked back to their car parked directly across the street. As they started to leave, a vehicle with three men drew alongside, preventing them from pulling out. The men attempted to talk to the girls whereupon Bernard left the car and ordered the men to let them out. The man on the passenger side, who obviously had been drinking, became aggressive and jumped from his vehicle. He was a large man, well over six feet. Bernard would later learn from a subsequent FBI investigation that he was a marine on leave, though not in uniform. He became bellicose and shoved Bernard. By this time, the other two men had left their car. It was obvious from their aggressive manner that something bad was going to happen—most likely to Bernard.

By now, the white horse Bernard had been riding in defense of the girls had galloped off to safer pastures, and the Butterflies swarmed. Faced with such dire potential consequences, Bernard reached for the last refuge of a coward: his FBI credentials. The marine was unimpressed. Bernard had barely displayed them when the man struck him with a solid blow. Bernard felt his lower front teeth being driven back in his mouth. At that moment he thought he'd lost his teeth, but somehow they returned to normal. He threw several quick punches and landed what may have been one of the more fortunate punches of his career. It must have been a left hook because later he found a deep gash on his left knuckles. The marine dropped in his tracks. One of the other men, a slender person flailing away at him, posed no problem at all. Bernard knocked him down so quickly it was almost as though the man wanted to go down. Although witnesses said the third person was part of the assault, Bernard didn't remember hitting him. It seemed to Bernard that the man ran toward his car.

There were many witnesses to the scene, including patrons of the bar who had been attracted by the spectacle. It was fortunate for Bernard that there were many onlookers, since rules of engagement were rigid in the Bureau. The consequences could be severe if it were deemed an agent had become involved in a brawl. Questions would be asked. Why was he in such a bad neighborhood at that time of night? Had he been drinking? Had he provoked the assault? Bernard got the assailants' license number as their vehicle sped away. The police arrived shortly and conducted an investigation including interviews with spectators who had witnessed the attack.

During the ensuing FBI investigation, the encounter was described in glowing terms by witnesses who portrayed Bernard as a heroic FBI agent who had thwarted the thugs on River Street. Because of the vivid description provided by witnesses, the special agent in charge of the Upstate New York division recommended Bernard for a letter of commendation from Hoover. It was never forthcoming. When asked for his comments, Bernard's SAC in Chicago, where he was assigned at the time, wrote to the Director stating that while Bernard had acquitted himself well, he did not feel the circumstances warranted a formal citation from Mr. Hoover. Bernard concluded that he was probably right. Bad neighborhood . . . why was he there. . . ?

The day following the assault, Bernard and his brother-in-law Everett Dibble went to the scene on River Street where the attack had taken place. They found considerable blood in the street and felt that not all of it could have come from the wound on Bernard's left hand. They suspected the assailants must have received significant injury. This was later borne out by the FBI's summary investigation, which included interviews with the subjects, and concluded that the attackers had sustained injury and no further action was required. It was typical of the Bureau's response to such incidents, not wanting the publicity of an agent becoming involved in a brawl after leaving a bar late at night . . . in a rough section of town . . . had there been drinking. . . ?

Bernard was ambivalent about the decision. If he had had more time to reflect, he would have insisted that the assailants be charged. It was a totally unprovoked assault. He could have sustained serious injury had he not landed a few punches. Bernard knew from experience in law enforcement that three on one is not a good ratio for victims. In retrospect, it could have been far more tragic. While in the FBI in New York, Bernard had a friend named Joe Yablonski, an agent who was attacked by four thugs in Harlem. During the melee he was compelled to shoot one of them. In Bernard's case, it was not that bad. No knives . . . he was not wearing his pistol. . . .

46

Fireworks with Plimpton

PARTIES AT the Connerses' estate in Loudonville were extravaganzas that attracted friends as well as prominent people. Although not always the stars that one would see at High Winds or Elaine's in Manhattan, there were usually notables who would turn heads. Since they were held in the Capital District, prominent politicians were among the guests, including the state's governors: George Pataki, Mario Cuomo, and Hugh Carey.

Often the guests were of different ages and dissimilar interests. But whatever their station—rich or poor, beautiful or plain, old or young—each possessed some quality perceived by Kate as an asset to her party. It was always planned with the meticulous Kate Conners style. Guests received a warm personal reception from Kate, who had an inimitable ability to convey to each arrival the feeling that the affair had been conceived with that person in mind; as if now that he or she had arrived, the party could begin in earnest.

George Plimpton, of course, was a frequent guest, usually accompanied by renowned *Paris Review* supporters. George had great drawing power. If it were a *Paris Review* Revel, which was often, he would insist on fireworks. Bernard never did fully understand his fascination with pyrotechnics. George would show up at Bernard's house with a dozen or so canisters resembling small cannons that had to be buried in the ground. Fueling these would be a truckload of fireworks that posed all kinds of liability in a residential community.

As one might expect, things did not always go as planned. On one occasion a missile landed on the roof of a house some distance away. Unfortunately the owner had not been invited to the party. This, combined with a hot air balloon and a noisy helicopter carrying guests over the party, resulted in the arrival of the police. "Where were the fireworks?" . . . "Had a permit been obtained?" . . . "Where was Mr. Conners?" . . . "Who set them off?" . . . "The fireworks commissioner from where???" Bernard had flashbacks to their Hamptons revel, only this time it was not George being led away in handcuffs.

Somehow they got through it. With assurances from George that the fireworks inventory was burnt out (which was only half true), the police pushed their way through a gaggle of curious guests and were soon gone—mumbling, "The fireworks commissioner from *where*???"

No one enjoyed the galas more than George, as evidenced by an excerpt from his letter following one of the soirees at the Connerses' estate in Loudonville:

THE PARIS REVIEW
541 East 72nd Street
NEW YORK, N. Y. 10021
UN. 1 - 0016

7 Juin '77

Dear Bernie --

This is a belated note (it should really be an extended panegyric!) to thank you for that extraordinary blast. It may not have made any money, but it will certainly go down in literary history as one of the more interesting evenings -- I mean will anyone ever believe that six parachutists dropped in on us, or that a balloon stood at the ready to go up, or that bottles of fine champagne stood in galvanized tubs, or that fireworks were shot off, or that a battalion of limousines offered a ferrying service, or that speeches were delivered from battlements . . . no, certainly in the great tradition of Paris Review if not international galas! I will treasure the memory.

I very much want to get you involved in plans for the 25th Anniversary year -- really an astounding plateau for us to have reached, and which is going to get a lot of public attention. . . .

Can we get the two of you to come to Easthampton for the 4th? Fireworks!

As ever,

George

Aside from his idiosyncratic preoccupation with fireworks, George was a wonderful host at parties. His speeches, with his marvelous delivery and entertaining stories, captivated the crowd. Bernard felt uneasy following him on the podium. While George spoke, the audience would be rapt in silence, whereas when Bernard took the microphone, attention would soon begin to wander. It was understandable, since Bernard's remarks usually were a plea for money to help the struggling magazine. At one of the *Paris Review* parties in Loudonville, George was the featured speaker. It was a lovely, moonlit night with a large crowd gathered on an expanse of lawn in front of the main residence. George turned admiringly toward the house, which had a marvelous gothic look in the moonlight, and praised its beauty, adding, "When I first met Bernard he was living in a tent!" It was an obvious reference to their army days and drew a burst of laughter from his audience.

Yes, Bernard felt colorless following George.

47

Self-Publishing versus the Orphanage

SIMON & SCHUSTER, the book distributor for British American Publishing and its imprint *The Paris Review* Editions, was a respected publishing house. Although British American enjoyed a mutually rewarding relationship with this firm and its chairman, Richard Snyder, and president, Charles Hayward, for a number of years, this changed when Charles departed and accepted the presidency at Little, Brown. His replacement, Jack Romanos, had a different perspective on book publishing from his predecessor, and changes were swift and profound. With deference to Mr. Romanos, it must be said that permutations he implemented were consistent with much taking place in the industry at the time as large conglomerates took over publishing houses. Publishing was considered a gentleman's profession. Often the purpose of the takeovers was little more than offering cachet to the acquiring firms that were undergoing criticism for their exploitive measures. Although such acquisitions were invariably accompanied by assurances that the publishing houses would continue to be run as they had been in the past, this was rarely what happened. Inevitably, the new company fell prey to the soulless bottom-line philosophy that afflicts all conglomerates. The proverbial "handshake" that was the cornerstone of the industry and had sealed transactions for years was replaced by lawyers, litigation, dismissals, mergers, and great emphasis on commercial books that would enhance revenue. Obviously, British American and its *Paris Review* Editions, which concentrated on literary prose and poetry, faced a daunting future in such a milieu.

Bernard found the new management dismissive of their books, particularly after working with Charles Hayward, who had approved of their efforts to publish literary works of lasting interest. *The Paris Review* Editions hardly conformed to the conglomerate's formula for profit. It was inevitable that such books would be displaced by commercial projects. George Plimpton was particularly offended by the new management, and on one occasion Jack Romanos was the target of an enraged tirade by George that bounced off the walls of the small *Paris Review* offices at the Plimpton apartment on Seventy-Second Street. Despite his great civility, George was never intimidated by corporate types, and held his own with the most abusive ones.

Soon, British American and its *Paris Review* Editions, as well as other Simon & Schuster imprints, were without a distributor. British American Publishing managed to survive, however, with another distributor, the National Book Network—a firm that conducted its business in a traditional manner of publishing.

Fortunately for aspiring writers, some aspects of publishing have changed dramatically in recent years. Virtually anyone with perseverance can see his or her work published as a result of innovative printing methods such as "on demand" printing that does not require a large print run to be economical. (It has also enabled publishers to keep backlist titles technically in print by printing a small number of copies when they run low on stock.) Self-publishing no longer has the "vanity" label the industry found it convenient to use. Authors do not need to rely on large publishing houses to see their works in print. Bernard commented on the self-publishing process in the following letter to George Plimpton after George recommended a publisher for one of Bernard's books:

BRITISH AMERICAN

BERNARD F. CONNERS
CHAIRMAN

(518) 786-6000
(518) 786-6001 FAX

November 18, 1999

Mr. George A. Plimpton
541 East 72nd Street
New York, NY 10021

Dear George:

Herewith is the unedited manuscript about Major Call. As I mentioned, I loathe the thought of it being shunted about with hundreds of books at some other publishing house. I know too much about the process now. I continue to feel it's like sending your baby off to an orphanage. Why do that, when I run my own orphanage? Nevertheless, I look forward to your wise counsel.

Many thanks, dear friend

Sincerely,

B.C.

DICTATED BUT NOT READ

48

Slighted in Southampton

LIVING IN the capital of the Empire State, Bernard inevitably became involved with politicians. Through mutual friends such as Harry Albright and Joseph Persico, prominent members of Nelson Rockefeller's staff, and other highly placed officials, he established cordial relationships with governors. He found the company of distinguished persons stimulating. He would later become friends with Governor Hugh Carey, socializing with the governor in New York at places such as Elaine's and the 21 Club, as well as the governor's mansion in Albany. On one occasion Bernard hosted a small dinner party at his Loudonville estate for Governor Carey, Lieutenant Governor Mario Cuomo, and a few of their friends to raise funds for the governor's reelection campaign. The dinner received considerable attention from the media, including a picture on the front page of the Metropolitan section of the *New York Times* showing Bernard emerging from his Rolls.

The New York Times

Metropolitan News

The New York Times/D. Gorton

Bernard F. Conners, host at the $5,000-a-couple dinner for Governor Carey, emerging from Rolls-Royce in Loudonville

$5,000-a-Couple Party Benefits Governor

By E. J. DIONNE Jr.
Special to The New York Times

LOUDONVILLE, N.Y., Jan. 3 — "I can squeeze you in for dinner if you've got $5,000," Bernard F. Conners said jovially. Mr. Conners is a former agent of the Federal Bureau of Investigation and a wealthy author who gave a small dinner party this evening for Governor Carey.

The Governor joined with about 1,000 other revelers at the Empire State Convention Hall at the Mall later tonight. But at the Conners party, the Governor supped on roast filet of beef bouquetiére and strawberries sabayon with 10 couples in a Tudor-style mansion here, just outside of Albany.

For the privilege of breaking bread with the Governor, the couples contributed $5,000 each to Mr. Carey's debt-ridden campaign committee. For just a bit more — $125 a person — they were able to join the folks over at Convention Hall for some music, dancing and partisan speeches by Mr. Carey, Lieut. Gov. Mario M. Cuomo and the Democratic state chairman, Dominick Baranello.

Host Mentions His 'Very Small Part'

As for Mr. Conners, whose book, "Don't Embarrass the Bureau," has sold formidably, he spoke humbly about his role. "While I'm hosting a dinner, it's only a very small part of the whole effort," he said of his dinner party.

And of his mansion, he said: "It's the usual — you know, a swimming pool, a tennis court, a gatehouse."

The mansion is actually something more than Mr. Conners's idea of "the usual." Built in the 1930's, the stone edifice was modeled after a Tudor castle. Its leaded windows were made in Europe, and there are elaborate wood carvings in many of the rooms.

It is situated on an estate of "not quite" 100 acres, Mr. Conners said, and there are four other houses on the property, built for the children of the main house's original owners.

"Some of them are quite nice," Mr. Conners said.

Mr. Conners was distressed by the interest that surrounded his little gathering.

"I can see why they would be very interested in the ball, but certainly not in me," he said. "I'm just the host at a dinner party."

Armed Guards at Gate

Anne Ford Uzielli, Mr. Carey's friend, did not attend the party. Instead, the Governor went with his daughter Nancy. Lieutenant Governor Cuomo and his wife also came to the dinner as did Mr. Carey's top aide, Robert J. Morgado, and his wife.

As they arrived at the mansion, guests were greeted by armed guards who opened the heavy iron gate to let them in.

When cars that the guards did not immediately recognize appeared at the gatehouse, their license plate numbers were radioed to the Loudonville police for a check.

The guest list for the smaller party, said to be dominated by New Yorkers, was held in confidence, and Mr. Conners politely declined to divulge it.

"Good taste would dictate on this particular occasion that any particulars concerning the party go through the Governor's office," he said. The public-relations firm handling the affair was equally guarded.

But an incomplete guest list, one that did not give first names or any other identification, was obtained. It bore these names:

Mr. and Mrs. McGowan, Mrs. Bercule with Mr. Picotte, Mr. and Mrs. Grossinger, Mr. and Mrs. Kutscher, Mr. and Mrs. Jacobs, Mr. and Mrs. Parker, Dr. and Mrs. Marcelle, Mr. and Mrs. Gerrity, Mr. and Mrs. Abrams.

On another occasion, he mentioned to Governor Carey that he was going to East Hampton for the day to look at some real estate. "I'm going to Long Island," said the governor. "You can ride down with me. We just got a new Sikorsky helicopter. Beautiful. Wait 'til you see it. We'll drop you off at the East Hampton airport." Bernard had made an appointment with a Southampton realtor to look at beachfront property, and agreed to meet him at his Southampton country club. The governor dropped Bernard at the East Hampton airport and told the pilot to pick him up on his way back that evening.

Bernard arrived by cab at the country club to find the realtor, a tall, dignified gentleman, waiting for him on the veranda. Following a few welcoming remarks, delivered with a pronounced British accent, his host motioned toward the interior, asking if Bernard would care for something to drink. Bernard declined, and suspected that the gentleman was relieved that one of his social protocols had been handled without an acceptance. "Very well, my car's over here," he said, moving swiftly toward the parking lot, it seemed lest Bernard change his mind about his invitation for tea. "This shouldn't take long. The property's not far."

Bernard had the distinct impression that his host was less than impressed with his visitor, and anxious to complete his real estate obligations quickly. Intimidated by the man's condescending manner, Bernard made no effort to engage the man in conversation on the way to the site. The property was not what Bernard had expected from the promotional material. Although a lengthy stretch of Long Island shorefront, it adjoined a public beach, and the price was exorbitant. Bernard attempted to conceal his disappointment, but he sensed the man knew he did not have a buyer. "May I give you a ride back to the airport?" asked his host. It was apparent that he did not want to become entangled with Bernard back at his club. "No, no, that's all right. I can take a cab," said Bernard.

Possibly aware that he'd been a trifle cavalier with his client, the man was now in recovery mode. He insisted on the trip to the airport. Indeed, he became more approachable, talking at length about his real estate activities and how he was involved with commercial property abutting the MacArthur Airport on Long Island. In relaying some zoning issues that involved both local and state governments, he allowed as to how he was acquainted with people in the governor's office, letting Bernard know he was well connected.

It took some restraint for Bernard not to mention his friendship with the governor, but he resolved to be quiet. They arrived at the airport around dusk. The East Hampton airport at this stage was like something from Amelia Earhart's period, so small that vehicles would drive right up to the runway, where old logs were placed end to end to keep cars off the tarmac. Quaint might be a suitable adjective. "What time does your plane leave?" asked his host. "I'm not sure," Bernard answered. "It should be here pretty soon. You don't have to wait."

They pulled up to the runway and then Bernard saw it. The shiny new Sikorsky helicopter, even more beautiful in the twilight. Displayed on its side over crisp lettering was the New York State emblem. "Say, look at that," the man said, looking at the helicopter. "Must be the governor's here." Bernard said nothing, preparing to leave the car. Suddenly, from the helicopter, the pilot appeared. "Hi, Mr. Conners. We're all set, whenever you're ready." Bernard thanked his host profusely. The man said little, for a moment the British accent stuck solidly in his throat.

For Bernard, having spent an entire afternoon with an individual who had made him feel inferior, it was total redemption. As Bernard walked toward the helicopter with the pilot, he glanced back toward the wide eyes in the car and offered a friendly wave.

Part X

49

Social Climbing

Evenings at Elaine's were fun. There was always anticipation . . . chance meetings and the challenge and mystery surrounding new relationships . . . a sort of romance that permeated the place, promising exciting encounters. Elaine's was the perfect spot to meet some luminary, some star. On one occasion this happened and Bernard was unaware of it. It was shortly after George Plimpton's death in 2003, and Bernard had gone to the restaurant anticipating dining alone. Elaine greeted him at the door with a hug and guided him to a table in the rear. He had become accustomed to sitting in the back even though it appeared the excitement was up front near the entrance. He had learned that it was far more chic to be in the rear where notables dined. Indeed, it was the table at which Jackie Kennedy usually sat to which Elaine escorted him. The table was close to where two women were seated. Bernard thought it odd that Elaine would put him so close since there were vacant tables nearby. He smiled and murmured an apology as he squeezed past them. At first, he was uncomfortable virtually sitting with them. They started talking to him and soon one of the women suggested that he join them. Bernard responded that it seemed he was already doing just that. It was like three astronauts dining in a space capsule.

As the evening wore on, he found the women quite engaging, although it seemed awkward since he didn't want to intrude. They were reasonably attractive, but not dressed that well. In fact, they may have been wearing jeans. Because of the low lights he could not be certain, but he suspected they may have been without makeup. Uncomfortable sitting so close, trying to make conversation, he ate hurriedly. Finishing dinner, he rose, and after offering to buy them a drink, which they declined, he squeezed past them and left. Elaine was at a table near the door as he was leaving. "Did you like who I sat you with?" she asked.

"Oh, yes. They were very nice," Bernard replied. "We had a nice dinner."

"You didn't know who that was?" she asked, surprised. "That was Kim Basinger!" In retrospect, Bernard still had difficulty reconciling the pleasant and unpretentious blonde with the glamorous movie star whom he adored.

Bernard had a similar experience not long after. He was seated by himself when an attractive, dark-haired woman sat down with him. "Hi," she said. "Elaine suggested I join you. I'm Cindy Adams." Cindy Adams was a popular journalist whose column covered much of the entertainment field in Manhattan. The Butterflies were immediately alerted. Why would the famous Cindy Adams bother to sit with him? As it turned out, Bernard's picture had been prominently displayed on the front page of the *New York Times* metropolitan section that week in connection with his efforts to buy the Albany Municipal Airport. Perhaps the article had attracted her attention.

The New York Times

Metropolitan News

NEW YORK, NEW JERSEY, CONNECTICUT / MONDAY, OCTOBER 9, 1989 B1

Albany Gets Private Offer To Purchase Its Airport

By CARL H. LAVIN
Special to The New York Times

ALBANY, Oct. 6 — While virtually every American airport served by scheduled airliners is publicly owned, Albany County is considering an unusual offer by a private group to buy its 61-year-old airport.

If the deal goes through, other airports may follow suit.

The Albany County Legislature is considering a proposal from a private group that wants to buy or lease the airfield, the gateway to the capital region and the Adirondacks. Aviation experts said that the investors would be the first to gain control of a large public airport and that public agencies in other states would probably jump at the chance to do the same thing, thereby bolstering budgets while escaping the headaches of managing a complicated transportation resource.

The New York Times/David Jennings

Bernard F. Conners, chairman of British American, at the Albany County airport, which his company has offered to buy or lease. "The natural solution is the privatization of airports," he said.

Cindy talked with Bernard for a while and then, rather abruptly, said, "Give me something for my column." All Bernard could think of was that she was prettier than her picture that accompanied her column. The thought seemed an inappropriate response to her question, and he answered with some banal comment, probably about weather in Albany. She soon left.

Not all of Bernard's social life was confined to Elaine's. After moving from the Wallace estate in Westchester to upstate New York, Bernard found the need for a Manhattan residence to handle his publishing and entertainment interests. George Plimpton suggested an apartment adjoining his on Seventy-Second Street, a building that also housed the sparse offices of *The Paris Review*. At first, it sounded like a good idea. By knocking down a few walls, they could expand the offices of the magazine and still provide quarters for Bernard. After reflecting on the bevy of interns working at the

Review, and their constant need for quarters, Bernard had second thoughts. He opted instead for a small apartment on Park Avenue. (George, however, saw an opportunity for expansion of his own apartment and went ahead with the plan.) After several years on Park Avenue, Bernard moved to a larger place at 825 Fifth Avenue. It was a lovely two-bedroom with two baths on the ninth floor with marvelous views overlooking Central Park. Thanks to Catherine and her friend Mary Tracy, a talented interior decorator, the apartment was very attractive. George Plimpton, who was not given to hyperbole, exclaimed upon first seeing the apartment, "This is perfect . . . just perfect!"

The building at 825 Fifth Avenue was a comparatively small structure as Fifth Avenue buildings go, next to the renowned Pierre Hotel on the Upper East Side. Its residents included some of the prominent families in America: Du Ponts, Whitneys, Auchinclosses, Wainwrights, Firestones. It was from the Firestones that Bernard purchased his apartment, and only after scrutiny by the 825 Fifth Avenue board of directors. Final approval came following interviews with Bernard and Catherine, as well as reviews of personal financial statements. References were important, but when Bernard listed individuals such as Governor Carey, George Plimpton, and other prominent people, he was advised by the woman preparing his credentials that he should reconsider such names. The board was adverse to high-profile personages, preferring people who were "under the radar" and less likely to disturb the tranquility of the residents. Marylou Whitney, with whom Bernard had socialized in Saratoga, was particularly helpful with introductions to board members and others living there. It was like a small exclusive club. To be admitted one had to undergo what seemed tantamount to an FBI full-field investigation. The building had its own dining room, which was splendid for entertaining. Cocktail and dinner parties were common, and the dining room staff relieved the burden of preparations.

Bernard was the beneficiary of Marylou Whitney's considerable charm and presence in Manhattan. It occasionally afforded him entrée to social circles he would not ordinarily have had. Marylou was single at the time and Bernard sometimes escorted her to places such as the 21 Club, the Four Seasons, or Elaine's for dinner. As a bon vivant, she made a marvelous dinner companion. Although theirs was no more than a platonic relationship, there were a few passing moments when Bernard sensed more familiar emotions. This was doubtless a result of Marylou's infectious, endearing style, and Bernard's overly active imagination. Indeed, on one occasion while they were dining with Elaine, Bernard placed his hand over Marylou's in a seemingly intimate gesture, whereupon Marylou gently withdrew her hand as if concerned that their relationship be regarded as more than a friendship.

Although at first intimidated by the inhabitants at 825 Fifth Avenue, Bernard gained more confidence with time and developed a friendly, if casual, relationship with many occupants. The design and general ambiance of the building contributed to spontaneous and friendly interaction with other residents, sometimes on the elevator. At one point he started a humorous, satirical novel entitled *The Elevator*, which dealt with his social elevation in the building. But after discussions with George Plimpton regarding personal relationships that had led to *The Hampton Sisters* and, upon reflecting on Truman Capote's "La Côte Basque" chapter in his unfinished novel *Answered Prayers* (containing thinly disguised, satirical portrayals of women from lofty social circles that caused him the loss of friends), Bernard put the book aside.

Beyond the doormen at the front entrance of the building was a large room decorated with oil paintings, flowers, and Jacobean furniture. An alcove on the side housed a large desk where two mature, attractive women were seated. In addition to greeting visitors, they acted as rather sniffish concierges for the occupants. Beyond the foyer were elevators and the entrance to the dining room. It was an imposing entranceway.

The manager of the building was Mr. Curtin, a gracious man who had held the position for a number of years. Bernard sensed the manager thought well of him. Perhaps it was because the manager was less intimidated by his new resident than by some of the old guard. Whatever the reason, Bernard felt that Mr. Curtin went out of his way to be friendly and helpful. Bernard was a trifle surprised at times by his candor. Once while they were going up in the elevator together he turned to Bernard and said, "You know, Mr. Conners, you're the first Irishman we've ever had in the building!" For Bernard it was a surprising comment. The manager's revelation, less so.

Notwithstanding his anomalous heritage, Bernard would later be elected to the building's eight-member board of directors, a surprise exceeded a few years later when he was invited to succeed its chairman of many years, Carroll Wainwright. Mr. Wainwright was a charming, handsome gentleman who was a partner at Milbank, Tweed, one of New York's most prestigious law firms. Despite his social aspirations, the rarefied air of the WASP establishment was too much for the Irish Butterflies, and Bernard respectfully declined.

50

British American Entertainment

IT WAS THROUGH Donald Trump's brother-in-law, James Grau, that Bernard met Tom Leahy. Tom was a member of Trump's board of directors and had spent his entire career with CBS, eventually becoming president of CBS Broadcasting. A personable man who knew many prominent figures in the entertainment world on a first-name basis, he was the catalyst for Bernard's involvement in film. The result of their friendship was British American Entertainment, which produced movies such as *Our Mother's Murder*, the story of Anne Scripps, publishing heiress to the Scripps publishing dynasty; *The Joe Torre Story*, the life of the New York Yankees manager, starring Paul Sorvino, Isaiah Washington, and Robert Loggia; and *Nuremberg*, which featured Alec Baldwin, Christopher Plummer, Max von Sydow, Brian Cox, and Jill Hennessy.

Joe Torre:
CURVEBALLS ALONG THE WAY

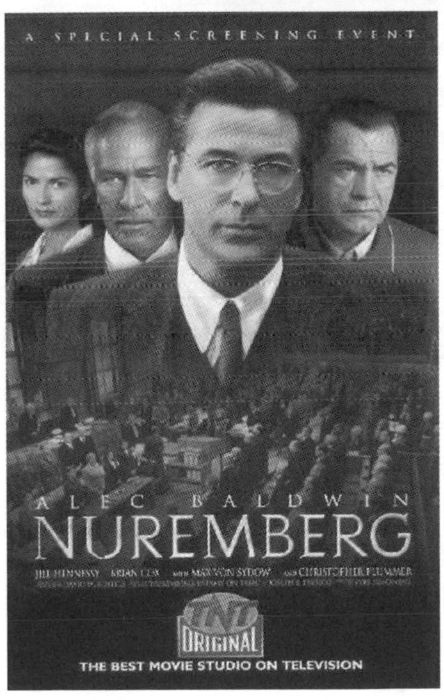
A SPECIAL SCREENING EVENT
ALEC BALDWIN
NUREMBERG
TNT ORIGINAL
THE BEST MOVIE STUDIO ON TELEVISION

OUR MOTHER'S MURDER
Loving him was her first mistake. Trusting him was her last.
UNIVERSAL

The *Nuremberg* miniseries received a number of awards, including two Emmys, and during its first year had the highest Neilsen rating in the country for a cable TV audience. Its success prompted the following letter from Plimpton:

THE PARIS REVIEW

541 EAST 72 STREET
NEW YORK, N.Y. 10021

TEL. (212) 861-0016 FAX (212) 861-4504

Dear Bernie— July 17, 00

I have not seen as much of *Nuremberg* as I should have—evenings haven't permitted—but I have seen enough to be enormously proud of you and what you have done with your life. How odd to think that two of Ryan's cadre have had their lives intertwined in the way that they have. This last, on your record, is truly wonderful!

Your comrade in arms...

George

Another film with which British American was involved, although not as producer, was *Stroke of Genius*, the life of the golfing great Bobby Jones. Jim Caviezel, who played the part of Christ in *The Passion*, had the role of Bobby Jones. Jim, who was personable and well liked by the crew, told Bernard that playing Jesus was easier than Bobby Jones. *Stroke of Genius* was a beautifully crafted film but was a disappointment at the box office. The box office was not the problem with Jim's other film, *The Passion*. Unfortunately, that film was subjected to strong criticism from the Hollywood Jewish community, which felt that the film depicted Jews in an unfavorable light. One of the producers of *Stroke of Genius* said that some technical people shooting the *Passion* film had requested a bonus, feeling that the criticism from Jewish filmmakers could affect future employment opportunities. British American published books in connection with the film, including the film book *Bobby Jones: Stroke of Genius*, as well as republishing *Down the Fairway*, which was written by Jones and O.B. Keeler.

Of the films produced in association with British American Entertainment, *Nuremberg* was the one in which Bernard was most involved. He secured the movie rights for the book by Joseph Persico, and guided the work through the complex labyrinth of Hollywood auteurs to its shooting completion in Montreal. It was frustrating, like being on the firearms range at the FBI Academy in Quantico, a course called "Hogan's Alley," in which agents lined up their targets, had them in their sights, only to have them disappear. Prior to the selection of *Nuremberg*'s final cast, actors such as Marlon Brando and Anthony Hopkins had expressed keen interest, but had vanished before the trigger was pulled. Sidney Lumet was the original director, but after several rewrites of the script by David Rintels he withdrew, stating he was too old. As frequently happens in Hollywood, he was soon directing another, less rigorous production. When the work was finally filmed in Montreal, Bernard found himself generally in the way, confining himself mostly to one of the trailers, reviewing daily shots. When on the set, he was sometimes taken by the shoulders and moved out of the way with a friendly, "You really don't want to be in this picture, do you, Mr. Conners?"

It was during the making of this film that he learned how important credits were. Bernard's contract designated him as the executive producer, but it seemed everyone connected with the film was an executive producer. Although he had optioned the original book and shepherded it through the arduous maze of preproduction and production to its completion, he became one of several producers, which seemed little more than a credit accorded someone carrying a prop.

Ghost Story, a film with which Bernard became involved personally, although not as a producer, brought him into contact with a number of movie legends who starred in the picture: Fred Astaire, Melvyn Douglas, Douglas Fairbanks Jr., John Houseman. Parts of the movie, directed by John Irvin, were filmed in Bernard's house in Loudonville, and served to intensify his interest in the genre.

Though immersed in film, Bernard continued his writing. After his novel *The Hampton Sisters,* he tried his hand at nonfiction. The result was *Tailspin: The Strange Case of Major Call. Tailspin* was an arduous undertaking, which began with a major in the US Air Force named George Warburton, who was convinced that another USAF major, James Arlon Call, had killed Marilyn Sheppard, wife of a Cleveland physician. Major Warburton, whose nickname was Mickey, became obsessed with the notorious case and conducted research about it for some thirty years. After reading one of Bernard's novels and learning that the author was a former FBI agent, he asked him to investigate the murder and to write a book.

At first, Bernard had no interest whatsoever. After reading material sent by Warburton, however, he agreed to author the book. The work was well received by critics—described by the American Library Association as "downright mesmerizing" and others as "the crime book of the year."

Although the book received extensive publicity, sales were disappointing. After spending some four years on the project, which included many newspaper, radio, and television interviews, Bernard concluded that it just wasn't worth the effort—particularly the media exposure. Although some writers appear comfortable with promotional tours, most authors deplore the process. Despite considerable time on TV promoting his own books, George Plimpton shared this antipathy, as reflected in the following letter:

THE PARIS REVIEW
541 East 72nd Street
NEW YORK, N. Y. 10021
UN. 1 - 0016

Mar 30 '83

Dear Bernie --

I agree about the lunch for Williams, who won your prize. Perhaps our respective offices should confer about a date. Also, Hallie-Gay and the staff have some ideas about judging the prize which would be of interest to you.

I've just come off the promotion trail (for EDIE) and never want to see the inside of a studio again. I often heard word of you passing through in front of me. It's an odd procession, isn't it? The last show I was on was Kupcinet's round-table session in Chicago -- on which I was settled in with three sex therapists, one of whom (on camera!) swallowed two pills he said would give him near instant potency — a statement which caused some concern (or perhaps anticipation) on the coutenance of one Dr. Ruth, the sex therapost sitting opposite.

As ever. George

Ultimately, Bernard declined to appear on a number of prominent shows. In one instance, Dianne Henk, a talented colleague of Bernard's who managed their publishing operation, arranged an appearance for Bernard on *The View*, a popular television program hosted by Barbara Walters and three other women. Thoughts of appearing on the show with four women grilling him about his book was too much for the Butterflies. About a week before his scheduled appearance, Bernard called Barbara Walters's producer and allowed as how he didn't feel the book would be suitable for their program. The call was not well received. Later, at the conclusion of a strident, conversation with Henk, the producer stated flatly, "One just didn't do that to Barbara Walters!"

Bernard probably should not have canceled the appearance. *The View* had a large national audience. Still, even after hundreds of shows of this type, the Butterflies never adjusted. They had already appeared on the *Today Show* with Barbara Walters, and that seemed sufficient. Bernard missed many opportunities that may have made a difference in his career because of a lack of self-confidence. Even relatively benign things, his alter ego found daunting. Notwithstanding the daring he displayed on occasion, in his own mind such bravado covered for the heart of a sissy. Yet in spite of such pusillanimous moments the machismo of his other self was ever watchful, threatening to be uncaged. For Bernard, these conflicting emotions remained a lifelong conundrum.

To some, however, Bernard may have been less of an enigma. Joseph Persico, a close friend and prominent author, described Bernard in a narrative as "an incurably insecure personality with no reason to be insecure, ironically wrapped around a core of inner self-regard."

Despite his timorous nature, Bernard had his own super stud whimsy. "We're all basically male animals," he was fond of saying. "Most of us have our macho fantasies. One of mine is a Harley Davidson bike complete with goggles, leather jacket, and a blonde chick riding on the back, arms wrapped around me, all the way to Lake Placid!"

Unlikely. Given the Butterflies, a more realistic scenario might have him on the Harley, but on the jump seat hugging Kate.

51

The Honeymooners

THE HONEYMOONERS! It was a sobriquet sometimes used by fellow members when referring to Bernard and Catherine at their country club in Loudonville. Schuyler Meadows was a small club with the usual amenities: golf, tennis, swimming, bridge, parties, and a waiting list of applicants. Founded in 1926, it had survived its earlier reputation for discriminatory practices, its membership having consisted mostly of prominent WASP families. Although it had overcome much of its earlier bias, it still clung to many of its older social values, and was referred to in the community as "Stuffy Meadows."

Located near the Connerses' estate, it provided Catherine and Bernard with convenient access to social engagements. They were members of other clubs in Manhattan, Long Island, and Bermuda, and, with residences in Lake Placid and Palm Beach, their use of the Schuyler Meadows Club was sporadic. Although they enjoyed the club, when they dined there it was usually by themselves. Some may have thought them withdrawn, which may have led to some criticism. Hence, "The Honeymooners!"

Having worked at places such as the Lake Placid Club, where the management was very considerate of its staff, Bernard was sensitive to employees' feelings and supportive of their efforts. Some of the Schuyler Meadows staff became valued employees of British American. Bernard's association with employees may have been frowned upon by some in the club hierarchy, and perhaps rightly so. Established protocols govern interaction between members and staff to ensure efficiency and avoid misunderstanding. On one occasion the membership chairman became aggrieved when Bernard proposed a former employee for membership. "Next thing," the chairman said bitterly, "we'll be putting up the cook for membership!" It probably didn't help matters when he heard Bernard's riposte to the effect that the staff was probably a cut above the membership.

As chairman of British American, Bernard frequently hired children of the membership at their parents' request for summer jobs, or as interns for his publishing firm. Some would move on to prominent roles in the British American companies. So prolific was the employment practice that one colleague referred to Schuyler Meadows as "Bernard's Personnel Agency." It was his son Christopher who managed to incorporate these new arrivals seamlessly. From the time he was sixteen and working in the soft drink companies, Christopher devoted his life to the firm with great success. Working with one's father can be challenging. (As Gertrude Stein once said, "There is too much fathering going on and there is no doubt about it, fathers are depressing.") But Christopher handled it, as he did everything, with great reserve, accomplishing major tasks while protecting his desire to remain behind the scenes. This modest, low-key approach he derived from his mother—a trait that served the British American companies well.

Because of the efforts of Christopher and his fellow managers, Bernard was able to avoid much of the tedium of commercial affairs, and to devote time to other pursuits, such as film and publishing. His interests inevitably led to serving on a number of boards, where his candid views did not always comport with fellow board members. This was the case one memorable Monday morning when Bernard stood uncomfortably before a distinguished gentleman in the boardroom of a large commercial bank:

"I understand you're the director who objects to personal guarantees!"

The speaker was chairman of the bank. Bernard, who was a director of the bank's New York Capital Region, had just been introduced to the chairman prior to a meeting of the board. Bernard's opinion regarding personal guarantees was well known by other directors. Personal guarantees were documents often signed by applicants seeking commercial loans. They sometimes empowered a bank to seize all of the borrower's assets, including his home, should the bank foreclose on the loan. Bernard felt that in many instances it was a dispiteous process—indeed, an unconscionable act—which should have legal restraints when it came to commercial lending on businesses. Bank clients who gave personal guarantees on commercial loans were frequently desperate for money, and were prepared to sign over everything, including the wife and kids. Bernard thought it shameless to take a man's home and furniture, which was sometimes the case when a business failed. It was an opinion not widely shared by hard-nosed veteran bankers.

The chairman's comments took Bernard by surprise, causing a mild fluttering in the abdominal region. After all, Bernard was a lowly regional director, in awe of the top executive of the bank who was now calling him to account barely seconds after their introduction. At first, Bernard stuttered out an apologia to the effect that he was referring to commercial loans rather than personal mortgages; that he believed the decision to loan should be based on the credit-worthiness of the business and not the man's home and furniture. The chairman appeared a trifle annoyed and, as the man expressed the folly of such logic, Bernard sensed the Butterflies being pushed aside by the dark, macho side of his personality.

Their bank was experiencing problems at the time and was negotiating a buyout by a large international firm. When the gentleman concluded his admonitions on guarantees, Bernard was inclined to remark that he had over a million dollars in their bank and no banking executives had given him personal guarantees. It would have been an inappropriate correlation, and fortunately for Bernard they moved on to less confrontational subjects.

Although recognizing the need for oversight of an institution provided by a board of directors, after considerable experience on a variety of boards Bernard became aware of the system's deficiencies. He believed it was difficult for a group to meet relatively few times a year and to understand the myriad problems confronting an institution's management. A true understanding of an operation comes with the daily grind and stomach-wrenching details that confront those on the firing line. Boards often are composed of remote individuals acting for self-serving reasons, sometimes the prestige or monetary rewards. It seemed to Bernard there were few directors on the boards on which he served who had the time or dedication to immerse themselves in a way that could achieve substantive results.

Bernard thought the State University of New York's board of trustees on which he served was unusual, however, in their strong level of involvement. The board oversaw sixty-four colleges, 465,000 students, and 88,000 faculty members. The annual budget exceeded $10 billion—from Bernard's point of view, a surprising amount when he considered the budget for the FBI is only $8 billion. Efforts to effect remedial changes within the system were sometimes met with fierce resistance by political and academic influences. Part of Bernard's frustration as a member of this fourteen-member board, which governed one of the largest higher educational systems in the world, was his ambivalence about tenure. Although understanding the elements that justify its practice, and recognizing the need for protection of academic freedom, he was troubled by the shield it offered unqualified professors, and the impediment it presented to essential change. It was a sensitive subject which was always handled carefully during discussions with the faculty senate. Bernard believed the age-old issue involving the efficacy of tenure required meticulous and continuous scrutiny at all levels of the educational system.

52

The Hermeneutic Principle

ALTHOUGH there is ample justification for author readings, the practice at times seemed wearisome to Bernard. Authors are not necessarily good performers, and this can be painfully obvious when they read from their own text, often in a stilted and unnatural manner. Nowhere is this more evident than readings by poets. Yet, judging from actual poetry sales, Bernard feared much of the reading in this publishing category was probably done by the authors themselves. He realized expressing such a thought might provoke questions such as, "How did this philistine ever become publisher of *The Paris Review*?" Much of the poetry discipline was, indeed, beyond his comprehension. As publisher of a literary magazine, he learned from experience that frequently it took a savant to glean understanding from submissions.

Bernard admitted that his dubiety regarding poetry may in part have derived from his own unsuccessful efforts as a poet. He submitted his most prized work, *The Balloon*, for consideration in *The Paris Review*'s longest poem contest—an award, incidentally, called the "Bernard

F. Conners Prize for Poetry" (which of course, made the submission a bit awkward). The Bernard F. Conners Prize for Poetry had originated a few years previously, and Bernard only reluctantly had permitted his name to be used, given his limited knowledge of the discipline. His attempt to have his name removed from the prize a few years later was met with some resistance. Jonathan Galassi (a gifted writer who later became president of Farrar, Straus and Giroux) and George Plimpton both urged Bernard to reconsider:

RANDOM HOUSE, INC.
201 EAST 50TH STREET, NEW YORK, N.Y. 10022
TELEPHONE 212 572 2176

JONATHAN GALASSI
EDITOR

3.29.84

Mr. Bernard F. Conners
60 Old Niskayuna Road
Loudonville, New York 12211

Dear Mr. Conners,

George Plimpton has told me that you are considering removing your own name from the Bernard F. Conners Poetry Prize that we have been giving for the past few years at the Paris Review and I wanted to write and let you know that I--for what it's worth -- think that this is a TERRIBLE IDEA. I appreciate and respect your wish for anonymity, but I fear that's it's practically too late. The prize has become known by your names, it is winning recognition as an important literary event on the contemporary scene, and changing the name at this point could be a great set-back to the awareness we're trying to create in the reader's mind that long poems of great merit are being written. So I am hoping you will reconsider.

. . . I very much hope that you will be willing to let us continue to use your name. You are intimately connected with the history of the magazine, and it is one small way that we can honor your commitment to it. I hope you won't mind my injecting my own opinion into this, but the prize is important to me as one of the most interesting things we do at the Paris Review. I hope we can get you to change your mind.

Cordially,

Jonathan

GEORGE A. PLIMPTON
541 EAST 72ND STREET
NEW YORK, N. Y. 10021
—
UN 1-0016

March 30, '84

Dear Bernie --

May I echo Galassi's words! Well put they were, and I think he reflects the value of the award as it is considered in the poetry world. . . . Please reconsider. Even if you withdrew your support we would want to continue the prize in your name. That's how strongly we feel about it.

As ever,

George

To Bernard's disappointment, *The Balloon* was summarily rejected by *The Paris Review*. He thought the rejection may have been due to a basic error of judgment on his part. He had confided to the poetry editor what the poem was all about. (Poets never should be too quick to explain their work. Better to follow the hermeneutic principle of the German philosopher Friedrich Schleiermacher, and permit the reader to understand the author better than he has understood himself.) Perhaps Bernard's dubious feelings about the genre were influenced by what *The Paris Review* poetry editor said about his poem. He heard that the editor, in rejecting the work, had referred to *The Balloon* as "a flatulent, overblown, piece of shit!" Even George Plimpton thought it "a rather inelegant rejection for a poetry editor."

53

Kate as Prison Guard

THROUGHOUT his career it was important to Bernard to be well liked. Whether it was a prisoner in a maximum security prison or a competitor in athletics, he treated the person with respect. Although often dissembling, he managed to cultivate a congenial personality. He felt as an FBI agent he never sent a man to jail who didn't think he was fair. Nor was he able to hold a grudge. He once mentioned this to a woman at one of his clubs who was renowned for her strong opinions, and she remarked that it showed a lack of character on his part. Perhaps. He preferred to think it derived largely from his rearing. With eight children growing up in relatively confined quarters, grudges didn't work well. There were always shoot-outs, but passing clashes were soon forgotten. The "guerrilla fighters" had bigger fish to fry, and their baby brother was forgiven quickly.

Bernard recognized early on that he was destined to be a performer. As noted previously, one of his high school teachers observed that Bernard was an introvert pretending to be an extrovert, possibly alluding to a dual personality. In college he was frequently master of ceremonies at school functions, and once had a small role in a college production of *Androcles and the Lion*—a play in which Catherine had the lead and teased Bernard for overplaying his bit part. While in the FBI he was sought after by other agents to do pretext phone calls, in which he acted the part of a fictitious person to elicit information. He was fond of telling bizarre stories about Catherine to tease her. His embellished accounts were sometimes too much for Catherine, who rated truth on a "come to Jesus" scale. She often interrupted his stories with an emphatic "that's not factual" or "he's stretching that, you know."

It was difficult telling tales around Kate. Bernard likened it to being married to a lie detector. She was a wonderful sport, though, and bore the brunt of his kidding, usually passing it off with a good-natured laugh. She had a marvelous laugh, and thought everything was funny. There was a limit, however. When once asked by an acquaintance how he first met Kate, Bernard said she was working as a prison guard at Leavenworth, a maximum security facility where he was interviewing a prisoner. Bernard had intended the comment as a joke, but when the person seemed to believe the story, he continued to improvise. "Actually she was doing a little time," he said. "Nothing too serious. After the fourth or fifth year she finally became a trustee in the prison library." The listener still seemed to swallow this nonsense, so Bernard just kept on. "If it ever comes up when you're with her, she prefers to tell people she was a guard rather than an inmate. Keep it to yourself, though, will you? You know, she gets embarrassed by the whole thing." A look of genuine compassion crossed the listener's face. "But heck, it could happen to anyone," Bernard continued. "A lot of good people are doing time, you know. . . ." "Yes, yes, of course," the man responded. "A lot of good people. . . ." Unfortunately, their conversation was interrupted before Bernard could add that it was inconvenient finding a place to live after her release because she had to register and couldn't reside near schools.

He never did have the chance to tell the man he was joking.

Another time he told someone that Kate had been a mess sergeant in the military. Actually, Kate disliked cooking. When they first talked of marriage she'd say, "Remember, you're not marrying a cook!" Subsequent experience would bear this out. Once Bernard asked her, "What's for dinner?" Kate's answer, always straightforward, "Why do you want to eat? It's no good!"

When he told the mess sergeant story he had no trouble convincing his listener. "Really?" the man marveled, his eyes widening. "That's right," Bernard continued. "She was discharged from Fort Dix, New Jersey. She told me that on her last day she was standing in the chow line helping to serve the food. When she served the last man, she turned around, banged the spoon on her tray and said, 'That's it! That's the last mother I'm ever going to cook for!'"

"My, I never would have guessed," the man said with a combination of surprise and wonder. General Traub, the resolute West Pointer, was thrilled when he heard that she'd served in the military, and was rather angry when Kate told him it was all nonsense.

But for Bernard such nonsense was permissible when you were married to someone with Kate's good nature. Whenever she did remonstrate, it was usually mild. Upon hearing the story about her doing time she simply commented, "Oh, I don't care. I'm sure you told him you were joking." When Bernard didn't answer, she said, her voice rising, "You did tell him you were joking, of course?"

"Yes, yes, of course!" replied Bernard, looking away. "Of course. . . ." Kate regarded him closely for a moment. Then, with realization came an un-ladylike response unusual for Kate—something about a shot that would "drive his mandible up into his ears!"

54

Death of George

AUTHORS respond differently to bad reviews. Some shrug them off as part of the business; others react bitterly. It could be said that Norman Mailer sometimes reacted excessively. Bernard recalled being with Norman at a *Paris Review* function when Norman rebuked a critic in response to a bad review. It was a bracing exchange, but less confrontational than a previous altercation between Norman and Gore Vidal at a social function. Vidal, one of many writers who found their way into the pages of *The Paris Review*, was known for his provocative, acerbic wit. After a heated argument, an enraged Norman punched Vidal in the face. Retaining his composure, the unflappable Vidal responded with what onlookers described as a winning counterpunch when with cool disdain he quipped, "Once again words fail Norman." No stranger to adversarial relationships, when asked for a comment following the death of his arch critic Truman Capote, Vidal responded with customary drollery, "Good career move."

To Bernard, however, it seemed Mailer was more bellicose than Vidal—more inclined to forgo verbal jousting and to resort to fisticuffs. And it did not always involve his reviews. Bernard recalled a *Paris Review* affair on Long Island to which Bernard had brought Governor Hugh Carey, hoping to impress the governor with cultured friends and prominent literati. The evening had gone well at first: George Plimpton graciously mentioned that Bernard had saved *The Paris Review*, and Norman had expressed his appreciation to Bernard personally. Things appeared to be going exceedingly well until Norman began his scheduled readings. In no time everyone, including the governor, was on edge. Some of it was reflected in the following news article:

Page Six™

By RICHARD JOHNSON
With TIMOTHY McDARRAH
and SETH KAUFMAN

Cooler heads

THAT was real animosity which flashed between Norman Mailer and Peter Jennings at the Paris Review party in East Hampton over the weekend for George Plimpton. The urbane anchorman, performing readings from back issues of the magazine, seemed a little testy in the midst of such literary lions as Kurt Vonnegut Jr., Tom Wolfe, E.L. Doctorow, Jay McInerney and Tama Janowitz. Earlier he'd even ranked out on Dick Cavett's casual attire. When Mailer lost his place in the script, Jennings strutted across the stage and showed him where his next line was. The crowd — including Mike Wallace, Lauren Bacall, Alec Baldwin and Liz Tilberis — held its collective breath. But Mailer, wiser with his years, seemed merely amused.

Although Bernard had his own share of poor reviews, occasionally writers spoke kindly of him. But there were times their remarks seemed puzzling. An example appeared in the following article:

> Another plus for Conners is that he is just about universally considered to be a great guy. "I like to be liked, maybe at the risk of being mendacious at times." Conners said he tries not to hold grudges, "and that's hard to do."
>
> "I've always gotten along with people," said Conners, who was voted most popular student at Albany Academy, where he graduated in 1945. "I like people very much. I like to socialize. I'm very gregarious."
>
> * * *
>
> Journalist George Plimpton, a long-time friend, said, "There's a disparity between this courtly, polite man and the obviously successful and powerful businessman that he is.
>
> "There's a curious Great Gatsby quality about him — an air of mystery. He's quite shy and self-deprecatory," said Plimpton, who co-owns the Paris Review, a quarterly literary magazine, with Conners.
>
> Another friend, Pulitzer Prize-winning novelist William Kennedy, met Conners back in the mid-1970s. With a shared interest in literature, they have gotten to know each other well. "He's lively and he's witty and he's great company," Kennedy said.

In speaking to Bernard about the piece after its publication, George Plimpton allowed as to how he had offered a virtual panegyric on Bernard's behalf during the interview. An example of his panegyric appeared in his closing remark for the article:

> **Plimpton observed that when Conners gets into the Rolls, it's as if he doesn't belong there. "It looks like he's hitchhiking a ride."**

Bernard was surprised by the hitchhiking comment. A "panegyric"? Well, perhaps. . . . He had often hitchhiked in early years, although he was never picked up by a Rolls. Indeed, some of the rides were in jalopies where sometimes he found himself warding off sexual predators with the comment that he was a good boxer—a pitiful rebuff from a puny youngster fending off older men.

At times the Rolls could be a valued part of Bernard's business as well as social life. Friends frequently borrowed the limousine for use at charity balls and weddings. During the 1980 Olympics at Lake Placid, the organizing committee used it to transport the King and Queen of Norway to various events. When Bill, the chauffeur, was unable to go to Lake Placid, Bernard's secretary, Deborah Playford, suggested she drive. Dubious at first, Bernard agreed after assurance from his staff that Deborah could handle the Rolls. It was a good decision. Deborah was a star in Lake Placid, a stunning tall blonde in her chauffeur's livery. The Rolls was particularly helpful during summer days at Saratoga, enabling Bernard to rub elbows with the racing gentry. Although he had few credentials entitling him entrée to crowded racing festivals, the Rolls invariably provided the ticket, receiving preferential treatment.

Saratoga was a congregating spot for the literati as well, notably at Yaddo, a writers' retreat that hosted many prominent authors during their formative years. Bernard was not above soliciting a blurb or two at Saratoga (even a review from an idle reporter if the opportunity presented itself). Many aspiring writers harbor thoughts about good reviews, even an award or two. Bernard was no exception. Notable prizes such as the Nobel or Pulitzer bring wide recognition and increased book sales. Bernard's modest awards provided neither, and sometimes involved stressful situations. One summer evening in August 2005, Bernard received a literary award from a distinguished organization before a large audience at the Saratoga Reading Rooms, a private club whose membership consisted largely of racing's elite. Many civic and social luminaries, including prominent authors, were present.

Receiving an award at the same time as Bernard was Rick Pitino, a notable sports figure who coached Louisville to the 2013 NCAA basketball championship. Pitino had achieved fame as a coach as well as an author of several books, including an autobiography. Bernard dined with Pitino and his wife, Joanne, at a small table near the dais as they awaited their awards. He found them to be a charming couple, but was somewhat overawed at being a recipient on the same stage. His uneasiness intensified when Pitino proceeded to the podium and delivered a polished and well-received acceptance of his prize.

Following resounding applause for Pitino, Bernard was given a lengthy introduction by a noted government leader who commented effusively on Bernard's background, exaggerating some of his achievements. Bernard, surprised by the unexpected encomium, became increasingly nervous, pondering what to say. Should he correct some of the embellishments of his career made during his introduction, or just let them stand? Should he acknowledge notables on the dais, or just plunge right in? When finally at the microphone, his stage fright was palpable. Recovering, he struggled through a few disjointed remarks, and concluded by thanking the chairwoman of the event, calling her by the wrong name. Following a sprinkling of tepid applause, he left the podium quickly, lest they change their mind about his award.

Although his literary prizes were modest, Bernard courted the favor of more accomplished authors. It was his friendship with George Plimpton that had the most influence on his writing career. The passing of George in his sleep on September 25, 2003, came as a shock. Although George had confided in him about benign medical problems, nothing seemed life-threatening. During their last dinner at Elaine's only two nights before he died, George was in excellent spirits as they planned for a *Paris Review* Revel. His death tolled the end of *The Paris Review* as Bernard knew it.

To help facilitate the transition of the magazine to a not-for-profit venture shortly thereafter, Bernard exchanged his ownership in *The Paris Review* for George's interests in British American Publishing. The exchange of stock was confirmed in the following document:

DEBEVOISE & PLIMPTON LLP

919 Third Avenue
New York, NY 10022
Tel 212 909 6000
Fax 212 909 6836
www.debevoise.com

October 27, 2004

Bernie Conners
British American Publishing
4 British American Blvd.
Latham, NY 12110

Estate of George Plimtpon

Dear Bernie:

I am enclosing original stock power for transfer of 100 shares of British American Publishing, Ltd., signed by Sarah Plimpton as Executrix for George's Estate, and the original stock Certificate Number 3 for the same.

This will complete the swap of your interest in *The Paris Review* for the Estate's interest in British American.

Thanks for your help.

Best regards,

James C. Goodale

Cc: Naftali Leshkowitz

21821229v1

New York • Washington, D.C. • London • Paris • Frankfurt • Moscow • Hong Kong • Shanghai

Although Bernard would continue to support *The Paris Review* with moderate financial contributions, the death of his friend brought to a close Bernard's active management in the magazine and a chapter in his life he had come to hold dear. Manhattan, the revels, George's parties, the Hamptons, haunts like 21, Elaine's . . . all lost much of their allure. A part of Bernard seemed to have passed with George and his fireworks.

55

Requiem for a Writer

AGING IS NOT for the faint of heart. Leo Tolstoy, who died at eighty-two, said, "Old age is the most unexpected of all things that can happen to a man." Perhaps that was true in Bernard's case. He was active after most people retire. But notwithstanding his energetic lifestyle, and his awareness of the inexorable erosion of time, the later years seemed to catch him without warning. Suddenly, he found himself an aging author struggling to be heard, a requiem of rustling dead leaves in the wasteland of old age.

He believed he should have been better prepared, given his intense interest in the nature of time. From childhood he felt that present time was a measureless phenomenon; that the reality of events seemed diminished by their transitory character. As a youngster he was bewildered when informed there was no Santa Claus; shocked that something so important as Santa was little more than a fable fabricated in childhood. Parents sometimes do not realize the emotional attachment a child may have to Santa. One mother was startled by a comment from her five-year-old: "Mom,

I like Santa better than Jesus." For Bernard, such revelations during the dreamland of childhood provoked an early skepticism about time and reality. Perhaps more than other children, he became concerned with the impermanence of things.

When reflecting on his life, Bernard thought of it as a string of momentary events, both happy and sad, emotions often intermingled. The happiest were those intimate interludes with Kate and her irrepressible good nature, and their children, who provided great pleasure, rarely presenting the serious problems that confronted some parents. There were exciting moments including thrills on the athletic field, producing movies, publishing books, socializing with friends such as the Wallaces, summers in the Hamptons, and, of course, the quixotic evenings at Elaine's, where a sense of intrigue and anticipation was ever present.

Yet for Bernard, happiness was frequently tempered by abstract concepts regarding the nature of time, which he sometimes described during polemic discussions as an incomprehensible force that renders life meaningless. He reasoned that events lacked reality because of their ephemeral character. Such enigmatic thoughts prompted an interest in ontology, a branch of metaphysics that studies the essence of existence. Such forays into this highly theoretical world of philosophy were rarely satisfying and, rather than enlightening, may have heightened his melancholic feelings. Theoretical physicists and philosophers have recognized time to be one of life's most elusive and unfathomable mysteries, the intense study of which has been for some scholars a passage to madness. The tormented lives of prominent philosophers such as Descartes, Camus, Diogenes, Nietzsche, some of whom were afflicted with mental disorders in later life, indicate the dearth of satisfying answers to life's profound questions treated in the study of cosmology, ontology, and epistemology.

For Bernard, even commonplace experiences could evoke feelings about the temporal nature of events. An example was an incident at the Lake Placid Club. He was lunching alone on a terrace that offered a lovely view of the surrounding Adirondack Mountains when he observed an attractive young woman stride confidently across the terrace and join an elderly man at his table. Although always conscious of pretty women, Bernard was particularly taken with her hat. Ladies' hats had interested him since his marriage to Kate, and he sometimes surprised her with ones he found in the trade.

The straw hat covering the girl's blonde hair impressed him so much that he mentioned it to his waitress. When she agreed, Bernard asked for a pencil and paper, so that he could sketch the hat and try to find a simi lar one for his wife. Following lunch he left with his drawing preparing to leave in his car when he noticed the tall man with whom the girl had been dining walking past. It was apparent from the man's gait that he was quite elderly—perhaps in his mid-nineties. Although moving slowly with a cane, the man's carriage and tilt of his jaw projected a certain elegance and distinction. Hesitating, then on impulse, Bernard left his car to address the man.

"I beg your pardon, sir. Forgive me for intruding, but I was admiring the hat on the young lady at your table. In fact, I sketched this picture of it to see if I could find one for my wife."

"Well, now," replied the man genially, taking the picture. "How interesting. That's a good likeness. Here comes my wife now," he said, glancing toward the club. "She'll be delighted to see your picture."

Bernard followed the man's gaze toward the entrance to the club in the distance from which the young woman emerged. "His wife?" thought Bernard. "Impossible!" Bernard focused on the figure as it moved under a grove of trees toward him. And then suddenly, almost surrealistically, the form began to change, seemingly to age with each step as it moved through the rippling shadows of fluttering leaves. Within a few stunning seconds he witnessed the stark transformation of a comely young girl into an elderly woman.

A gracious exchange followed, in which Bernard learned the couple was from Manhattan with additional homes in Lake Placid and Palm Beach. The meeting ended quickly, but memories of the passing experience would remain with Bernard, reminding him of a comment by Marcel Proust, who devoted a lifetime to the study of the mysteries of time. In *Within a Budding Grove*, Proust wrote "The charms of a passing woman are usually in direct relation to the speed of her passing." For Bernard, the woman's "passing" in Lake Placid was a paradigm of the impermanence of life that caused him to reflect on his own wife.

Few handled the aging process with more dignity than Kate. The years brought little change in her emotional poise. Menial household duties, gardening, hosting parties, painting the Lake Placid camp . . . all were handled with her inimitable brio. When others sought relief from the torments of aging, Kate remained sanguine. For the sake of appearance some turned to cosmetic surgery (including Bernard with his ring-battered nose). Not Kate. She rejected the unnatural.

"I'm supposed to look old," she said. "I love my wrinkles. I wouldn't trade one of them. They all turn up when I smile."

It was true. There was nothing downcast about Kate. She was totally genuine, her sunny disposition transforming redeeming wrinkles into an ageless smile.

As for his alter ego and Butterflies, they were a component of Bernard's ongoing concept of time, always there forewarning of the future. He realized that although a disturbing affliction, they were also a restraining presence for what may have been a restive spirit. He had seen less inhibited associates succumb to the ubiquitous temptations of the entertainment world of New York and Los Angeles—sometimes to great regret.

Although the Butterflies were worthy sentinels, they were downright sissies. Unlike a classic alter ego such as Clark Kent, who emerges from the phone booth as Superman the courageous crime fighter, Bernard's alter ego was fearful in the "phone booth," emerging from the FBI Academy a crime fighter with Butterflies. The slightest provocation, a mere smile from a pretty girl, could start them fluttering.

Yet in life's closing moments, awaiting the ferry on the River Styx amid a cargo of ghostly wares, Bernard would have expected a final flurry of gossamer wings. But it was strangely still. No Butterflies.

— End —

Afterword

Comments by Joseph E. Persico

Acclaimed historian and biographer Joseph Persico had planned to write an introduction to this book, but passed away shortly before its publication. A close friend who had written introductory passages for the author's previous books, Mr. Persico submitted the following two memos before his death, offering comments about the manuscript during its development. In them, he refers to "Butterflies"; that was the working title of *Cruising with Kate*. Since he did not get a chance to write an introduction, his complete remarks, including both praise and criticism, are presented here.

Bernard Conners

From: Joseph Persico
Sent: Monday, December 19, 2011 9:56 AM
To: Bernard Conners
Subject: Butterflies

Hi Bern,

I've just finished *Butterflies*. You did it. You have taken a many faceted life and made it come alive. The reader is there, walking with you all the way.

What I found refreshing and so rare in memoirs is your frankness:

__On dodging Korea

__On your lows, along with your highs. (Setting pins? The most degrading work I ever performed.)

__Sensitivity to social rejection as laid out in the story of 825 5th Ave.

__Worry over JEH and *Don't Embarrass the Bureau*, and the guts to go on anyway.

__Laying it out how shamefully and opportunistically the fate of the Rosenbergs was handled.

__For me the most fascinating parts of the book were the chapters dealing with real life for an FBI agent in the field, hours of tedium broken by moments of sheer drama.

__I particularly liked your insider expose of the myths about the so - called cunning, savvy colorful denizens of the mob, "Disorganized crime:" a great phrase that blows a hole through the myth.

__There are passages where the Conners humor shows through delightfully.

:The visit with Agent Kelly to the cat house

:Teasing Kate in front of people as a Leavenworth inmate and Army cook.

__ Everybody likes to read about the bold face names, and I liked the combination of little boy wonder and ground eye view of the celebs you encountered along the way, Plimpton, Elaine, the Wallaces and so many more.

__Finally, you handled your lifelong love affair with Kate touchingly even humorously, without getting mushy.

Now, I am sure you won't mind some constructively intended suggestions.

12/19/2011

__I am so relieved that you say you are going to drop the present structure of a narrator and the principal telling the same life. I found it continuously irritating. Good riddance!

__All the guys are tall, handsome and charming, the women gorgeous. When the reader spots such patterns, it is not good.

__Sometimes you pull your punches. You paint a vivid, hard edged portrait of your mother-in-law, for example. And then smudge it saying she was a wonderful woman. Readers will divine that themselves from everything else you say about her.

__Give a little more on the subject of women you dated, knew, etc. hinting even with use of a low key word like "intimacy." Otherwise you come across as the 40-year old virgin.

So where do I come away on the life of my friend? I get a picture of an incurably insecure personality with no reason to be insecure, ironically wrapped around a core of inner self regard.

I thank you for letting me read your story. I count it an honor that you sought out my judgment of *Butterflies.*

12/19/2011

Bernard Conners

From: Joseph Persico
Sent: Thursday, September 19, 2013 9:43 AM
To: Bernard Conners
Subject: Conners autobiography

Hello Bernie,

I have read your manuscript carefully and here are my reactions. Accept the positive points that I make at face value. They are my best judgment. Take any negative points I make with a large grain of salt. They are only one reader's fallible views.

OK, Here we go.

- My first impression: this version is a vast, vast, improvement over the earlier draft you asked me to read. The take away message is that this guy, Conners, has led a helluva life!. And he has written of it honestly. The writing is seamless, highly readable, with surprising self introspection – no punches pulled. The author has also written with humor, especially becoming when aimed at himself.

- I told you in my earlier critique that your FBI experiences should be the core of your story. Now, you've done so, and a lively story it is. Further, I now realize more clearly the courage it took to write *Don't Embarrass the Bureau*, far more than what I gleaned from anecdotes over lunch.

- Your eventual success story comes across much more dramatically when told against your necessity to take on working stiff jobs early in your life -- steeple jacking at dizzying heights, setting pins in a bowling alley, waiting on tables.

- I liked both the humor and the frankness in your telling of personal disasters – at least what you perceived as disasters -- for example the story of Valerie Jennings and the TV interview.

- Some of your heroics, the fight in the alley with the thug, the rescue of the drowning life guard, are told with a becoming modesty, but nevertheless register your physical courage.

- The bold face name episodes are an attractive feature. People are always fascinated by the doings of the high and mighty and the book makes clear that you have moved among a flock of them.

- I must confess that I was stunned by the self-awareness exhibited on page 301 where you write, "Although often dissembling, he managed to cultivate a congenial personality." Right on and admirably truthful. I am also honored that my reading of the Conners persona is quoted.

Criticisms?

- I know it is pointless to try to persuade you to abandon the use of the third person to which you are wed. It still seems awkward and dulls the sense of intimacy that makes an autobiography come alive. I'll say no more.

- You make a theme of the "butterflies." The continuous use of this metaphor seems like an attempt to stretch something special out of the everyday anxieties that we all feel in similar stressful situations. Maybe one descriptive "butterlies" paragraph early on would put across what you mean without all the repetitions.

- If you are inclined to cut anything, I suggest reducing the full text of so many letters, memos at al, what I call scrap book stuff. You could still capture their point with a well chosen excerpt from the document.

As I reread these critical observations, I fear that they may distort my overall pleasurable reaction to a fine piece of work. The most positive thing that I can say about the book is that it hooked me early on and I read it straight through almost nonstop.

Congratulations . You have captured your life; no small feat.

Good luck!

JEP

9/19/2013

Acknowledgments

The author would like to thank his colleagues Cori Corvino and Kate Cohen for their immeasurable help in the preparation of this book. James O'Shea Wade, former Executive Editor and Vice President of Random House, who provided editorial assistance with the author's previous work, offered invaluable assistance with this book as well.

About the Author

Bernard F. Conners, former publisher of *The Paris Review*, has had a distinguished career in government, business, publishing, and film. He is the best-selling author of *Dancehall*, *Tailspin*, *The Hampton Sisters*, and *Don't Embarrass the Bureau*. Mr. Conners lives in Loudonville, New York.

Index

—T—

—U—

—V—

—W—

—X—

—Y—

Page design and typesetting by Toelke Associates, Chatham, New York
www.toelkeassociates.com

Text composed in Adobe Garamond; chapter heads in Bodoni MT Ultra Bold; chapter numbers and folios in News Gothic Bold

Printed on 50# Glatfelter Natural
Bound in Rainbow Brillianta

Printed and bound by Versa Press, East Peoria, IL
www.versapress.com